AS
GOOD
AS
GOLD

AS GOOD AS GOLD

1 WOMAN, 9 SPORTS, 10 COUNTRIES, AND A 2-YEAR QUEST TO MAKE THE SUMMER OLYMPICS

BY
KATHRYN BERTINE

Published in the United States by ESPN Books and distributed by
Random House, Inc.

ISBN-10: 1-933060-53-0
ISBN-13: 978-1-933060-53-8

 Printed in the United States of America on acid-free paper

www.espnbooks.com
www.randomhouse.com

9 8 7 6 5 4 3 2 1

First Edition

Book design by Patrick Borelli

ESPN
BOOKS
a division of
ESPN publishing

DEDICATION

This book is dedicated to the people who let me sleep on their floor/couch/futon while I lived and wrote its contents. Thank you for being my home when I didn't have one of my own:

Robin and Dan Bratone, Natalie and Tom Siano, Beth and Alan Hall, Natalia Schultz, Pete Bertine, Jr., Beth Avery, Meg Forbes, Amory Rowe, Courtney Bennigson, Lara Kroepsch, Katie Blackett and Matt Schneider, Diane Dedek, Teri Albertazzi, Libby Ford, Alison Meadow and Dan Ferguson, Sarah and Charlie Hatfield, Tara and Todd Williams.

And to my parents, who surrendered sleep, weekends, and normalcy to take me to the rinks, fields, and races of my earliest athletic adventures. The roots of this quest grow deep. Thank you.

That road racing of mine ... five thousand miles of training and three hundred and nine races, just to play the cyclist. It was wonderful, though, that having started at the age of thirty I was still able to get a body that could really do something, that came in a solid twelfth in races amid a hundred hungry twenty-one-year-olds, that won occasionally in lesser races ... It was wonderful enough to have taught any number of these glory boys a lesson in strength, in courage, in character.

Tim Krabbé, *The Rider*

CONTENTS

FOREWORD

BY *KATHRINE SWITZER*

Opportunity is everything.

Somewhere near the top of Heartbreak Hill in the then all-male 1967 Boston Marathon, when twenty-one miles of running into an icy headwind had erased all fear and anger, those words popped into my head with a clarity that changed my life.

Up to that point, I thought other women didn't "get it" when it came to sports. I exulted in the feeling of limitlessness that running gave me and felt sorry for the women who believed in their own powerless status. Despite being attacked earlier in this race by an event official who tried to throw me out of the competition simply because I was female, I prevailed and went on, determined to finish. And then, right at crunch point in my first big marathon, it struck me: I was just plain *lucky*. I was not physically talented, I was not a freak, I was not a firebrand feminist—all things people later called me. I was just a kid who wanted to run. And lucky for me, I was given an opportunity to try by a few men in my life who didn't care whether I was male or female. *If I can just get this same opportunity out to other women, everything will change*, I thought.

And it did. In just the few years since, there are now more women runners in the United States than men, we have near-parity in Olympic sports, and, thanks to Title IX, there should not be a single girl in this country who is denied a sports opportunity or who grows up with a sense of physical limitation. This is more than change; this is a revolution.

Kathryn Bertine was lucky, too. She was born into this current era of opportunity and knew it. Feeling both thrilled and obligated by the opportunities, she chased them down, first as a figure skater, then a rower, then a cyclist in search of the Holy Grail of sports—to make an Olympic team.

But she was also unlucky: Bertine is that particular kind of athlete who is very good at many things, but not great at anything . . . and greatness is an Olympic requirement. This only fueled her, as athletic brilliance almost always is more than talent—it is the product of many years of hard work, something she loved doing.

And then, at thirty, her drama begins. With time running out on the Learn-A-Sport body meter, Bertine is offered the athlete's Greatest Dream: a salary and support to train and travel to make an Olympic team, any team, and write about it. For Bertine, who (like many of us) had forsaken love, possessions, security, and even her health in her drive to be a great athlete, to be given such an opportunity is priceless.

She takes it, and her story is unique in all of sports. Relentlessly, she takes us around the world, to sports training camps where we learn what it takes to be an Olympian in even the most obscure sport, to inside the arcane and murky political and administrative world of sports federations. Then, breathlessly we plummet with her down icy luge runs and pedal up volcanoes. We experience the bruises, scrapes, and chronic soreness that can be inflicted by nine different Olympic sports and the desperately hunting heart of a woman who is willing to give everything she has for a dream.

This is a story about hope, belief, and God knows, *persistence*. It is also a story of the future. Never before have there been so many opportunities in so many sports for women, never before has sport so opened its arms for global and transnational acceptance, and never before have so many women realized that they can excel beyond their wildest dreams.

Opportunity is everything.

KATHRINE SWITZER was the first woman to officially register and run in the Boston Marathon. She ran thirty-five marathons, won the New York City Marathon, and led the drive to make the women's marathon an Olympic event. She is now an Emmy-award-winning broadcaster of marathons and is the author of *Marathon Woman: Running the Race to Revolutionize Women's Sports* and *Running and Walking for Women Over 40,* and is co-author of *26.2: Marathon Stories.*

HOW IT ALL BEGAN

While the idea for this book was conceived by ESPN, the first chapter was born in the lobby of a fertility clinic.

In the summer of 2005, I was living in a small town just west of Boulder, Colorado, doing my best to make it as a professional triathlete. For three years, I lived something of an atypical athletic lifestyle that involved training twenty to thirty hours a week in a sport consisting of three disciplines: swimming, biking, and running. The training was physically grueling, mentally draining, and financially debilitating. My annual salary was in the high four figures. I worked as a substitute teacher, a pet-sitter, a waitress, and a plethora of other jobs for which my master's degree was entirely irrelevant.

But I loved my chosen life of poverty, pride, and pasta. I was doing something that repeatedly taught me the greatest lesson—how to live in the moment. At thirty, most of my friends' lives were on a different track. They had husbands, savings accounts, and in some cases multiple children. I had a troubled relationship, credit card debt, and three bicycles. But I also had a dream: to go as far as I could in triathlon. To compete against the best and see where it got me. The Olympics? Ironman World Championship? Nowhere? But journeys always lead somewhere, and that was good enough for me.

In the autumn of 2005, the journey got bumpy. I was engaged to the wrong man. He carried the burden of alcoholism on his shoulders, and when the engagement became impossible, I left. The problem with leaving, however, is that it usually means you have to leave. House, job, bed, dog—everything. Leaving is hard. Harder still when you're not sure where to go. On a chilly October morning, I gathered up what was left of my confidence, courage, and energy. My few clothes and cheap furniture went into storage. I put my ring on his table, my bags and road bike in my truck, and drove to what would be the first of twenty-two places up and down the East Coast where I would sleep over the next ten months, broken down as follows:

- 11 beds
- 4 futons
- 3 couches
- 2 car backseats
- 1 floor
- 1 tent

My hosts were thirteen friends, three strangers, two lovers, and five hotels.

I had no job, no plan, and a little over two hundred dollars in my checking account. Not enough to go back to Colorado, not enough to start over. I found work as a lunch-shift waitress in a suburb outside New York City, near my hometown, and spent the first leg of my new life as a third-wheel tenant at my brother's girlfriend's house. They were nothing short of saintly to take me in and tolerate my mental and emotional turmoil. It was there that I canceled my wedding, cried over the What Ifs, and watched more reality television than the human eyeball should ever endure.

My triathlon career and dreams withered away. There was no way I could race again. My mind was too cluttered, my funds too depleted, and my body—which once marched forth with certainty—became too saddled with doubt and confusion. Over and over, one question ran through my cluttered mind: *Have I done the right thing?* Worse, I wasn't even sure what area of my life the question referred to. Relationships? Sports? Career? Daily choice of socks? Doubt is contagious. It spread from one emotional area to another until it destroyed its host—and my confidence.

I didn't *completely* lose my perspective. I knew my personal problems carried little weight in the great scheme of things. I was in good health. I'd get over my confusion and sadness. The only thing that was dying was my athleticism and the dreams that went with it. *Bury them,* I thought. *Move on. Grow up.*

The months, the couches, the lunch shifts went by. My body grew restless in the dreary East Coast winter. I began to work out at the local YMCA, shamefully sneaking in the back door because the daily five-dollar guest fee was beyond my means. Weights, treadmills, and swimming began to resurrect me. I realized how much I missed adrenaline. I missed lactic acid build-up. I even missed chlorine. Mostly, I missed myself.

My body began to feel better. So did my head. They both seemed to want me to be an athlete again. *Okay,* I agreed, *okay, I'll try.* There was even an edible reason for me to keep trying: I was offered a sponsorship to compete as a triathlete for Team Sport Beans/NTTC, which would give me stipends based on my race performances *and* eighty pounds of free Jelly Belly beans each year. The small packets of Sport Beans became everything from meals to currency to thank-you gifts, often astonishing me how far one can get in life by handing out free candy.

But the reality of my financial situation was daunting. Weekday lunch tips were not fast-tracking me to affluence. I needed something more to get me started. I needed to find an apartment and stop living off the generosity of friends, strangers, and sibling's girlfriends. In February, a single mother with three children (whom I'd met through a local triathlon club) took me in and charged me no rent on the condition that I adhere to the pay-it-forward creed. I assured Natalie that someday I'd buy an entire house for transient athletes and pay for all their memberships at the Y. For months, I hoarded my tips in an old Hello Kitty purse and ate the leftovers of wasteful lunch customers, just like Maggie Fitzgerald in *Million Dollar Baby*. Only I hadn't seen the movie yet.

There are few respectable options open to women in need of quick cash, but online I found one I could handle: egg donation. I liked the idea of helping someone's fertility dream come true and being reimbursed for it. I had no hang-ups about passing on my DNA to anyone who thought it worthy enough of nurturing. I made an appointment. A doctor fished around inside me.

"Congratulations," he announced. "You have two functioning ovaries."

This was easily the best news I'd heard all year.

Sitting in the lobby, filling out donor paperwork and going over the list of drugs and hormones about to enter my body, my 200-monthly-minutes cell phone rang. It was Chris Raymond, an editor I'd worked with when I did some freelance assignments for *ESPN The Magazine* a few years ago.

"Hi Kathryn," he said. "Hey, we've got an assignment we'd like to offer you."

🚲   🚲   🚲

As I was stealing doggy bags and breaking into YMCAs, a bunch of ESPN editors had been sitting around their offices, watching the sport of luge on TV.

"*I* could do that," one of them said offhandedly.

A lively discussion ensued. Were there any "easy" sports in this day and age? Sure, winning an Olympic medal might be kind of difficult, but just how hard is it to qualify for the Olympics these days? The editors cracked some jokes about how easy luge appeared and questioned the validity of some "interesting" Olympians. One them cited Eddie the Eagle, a chunky forty-six-year-old British ski jumper from the

1994 Lillehammer games, wondering how he got into the Olympics. Another mentioned Eric Moussambani, the swimmer from Equatorial Guinea who swam the 100-meter event in the 2004 Athens Games nearly twice as slowly as his competitors. How did these guys even get to Olympic trials, let alone the games themselves? Have the Olympics become a joke? Or were Americans just totally ignorant of the various sports, the talent they required, and the qualification procedures for Olympic athletes today?

Then someone said, "Let's find out." He suggested they find a writer/athlete to see if he or she could make it to the 2008 Beijing Summer Olympic Games, which was coming up in two years. But who?

"What about that freelance writer we had write for the magazine about trying out for Cirque du Soleil a few years ago?"

"Kathryn Bersomething?"

"Yeah. Find her."

"Is she *in* Cirque du Soleil?"

"No, she didn't make the cut as a circus acrobat. I think she's a triathlete now."

Actually, I was busy canceling my wedding, selling my eggs, sleeping on couches, and asking my boss at the restaurant if I could come in thirty minutes late to my lunch shift because I needed to get in a long bike ride that morning. Triathlon season was approaching, as was my thirty-first birthday. But all that was about to change. Except the part about my birthday. I was getting older (apparently, I didn't make the cut in my audition for time travel, either). The mix of my athleticism and journalism was exactly what ESPN was looking for, so they hired me to be their Olympics guinea pig. And they did it knowing nothing of my actual aspirations to be an Olympian.

What you hold now is the outcome of that cell phone call in the fertility clinic's waiting room. To you, it's a book. To me, it was a life preserver. From 2006 to 2008, I was given an opportunity to mesh my two life passions—writing and athletics—in a quest to make it to the 2008 Olympic Games. The journey would bring me the things that most quests bring: the expected, the unexpected, the highs, the lows, the triumphs, the shortcomings, the life lessons. A good quest will do much more than take you from point A to B. A good quest unlocks the myth of failure, the truth about success, and the reality of the What Ifs. A good quest will confirm that yes, you did the right thing simply by attempting. A good quest will provide inner peace and mental harmony.

But first you have to hunt down Doubt and kick it square in the balls. From the bottom of my ovaries, thank you ESPN.

AS GOOD AS GOLD

1

ON YOUR MARK,
GET SET ...

June 2006

I grew up in the tiny, rather sheltered suburb of Bronxville, New York, just outside New York City in Westchester County. Please don't hold it against me. I would have preferred being born in a log cabin in upstate New York, or perhaps a rural Western state with lots of bike paths, but my preferences were difficult to communicate while in utero. Westchester it was.

While I navigated my way through the bizarre social structures of childhood/adolescence in Bronxville (for example, going to school for thirteen years with the same class of seventy kids), I spent most of my time in the humble city of Yonkers, at Murray's Skating Rink, where I began figure skating in 1986 at age eleven. By twelve, I was putting in close to four hours a day, beginning at 4:45 A.M.—an ordeal from which my chauffeur, who doubled as my father, has yet to recover.

As far as I know, I never made a conscious decision to be an athlete. Athletics was hardwired in my DNA. On a warm September morning in 1983, I was picked last for kickball during a third-grade recess scrimmage. Something snapped. Wiping my sweaty palms on my Wrangler jeans and Pac Man T-shirt, I went Incredible Hulk on that red rubber ball and got my first taste of adrenaline off a grand slam kick. The dream took flight immediately; I was going to play kickball in the Olympics and no one was going to stop me. Except the International Olympic Committee, which still refuses to acknowledge kickball's Olympic potential.

When my kickball dreams were put on hold, I fell in love with figure skating. I fell in love with the physical effort. I fell in love with the coldness. I fell a lot, in general. At fourteen, I actually had a dream one night that I was at the Olympic Games. There were a lot of lights and screaming fans and a really nifty USA warmup suit. But I couldn't see my feet. I didn't know if I was wearing skates or not. The dream felt so real it woke me up. There were no screaming fans next to my bed, just the *chhk chhk* of the second hand on my Hello Kitty alarm clock. I never had that dream again, but I never forgot it.

Despite my dedication to skating, I soon realized there was not enough talent in my limbs to get to the Olympics as a figure skater. I made it to the highest level of competitive skating, Senior Ladies, and competed with the best nationally throughout high school and college. But my talent and placings were never impressive enough for me to be considered the next American ice queen. Wanting to stay involved with the world of skating, I was left with two choices: coach the next generation or join a professional ice show. After graduating from college, I chose the latter, signing contracts with the Ice Capades (which quickly went bankrupt), Holiday on Ice (which made me wear an elephant costume), and Hollywood on Ice (which toured South America and paid us in IOUs handwritten on Post-its). What a damn fool mistake that was! Now that I'm older, of course, I subscribe to the If-I-hadn't-done-that-then-I-wouldn't-have-gotten-here view of life's journey. One of the great perks of being a writer is that it turns out there are no mistakes in life, just a lot of long paragraphs greatly in need of editing.

In 1997 and 1998, I toured with these skating shows, learning the hard way that athletic ability took a back seat to physical appearance and corrupt management. Professional skating was about as athletic as professional pinball. There was no need for strong muscles and diligent training. We were simply required to look as Barbie-ish as possible. Lots of the women starved themselves, drank, and did drugs. I got out after a year. I needed to be an athlete again—the only lifestyle that made sense to me.

I didn't want to go back to amateur skating; a fresh start seemed better. I considered a return to rowing, a sport I had competed in at Colgate University. Unfortunately, there was not a lot of open water in Tucson, Arizona, where I started graduate school in creative writing. What *is* in southern Arizona are lots of cyclists, runners, and swimmers. I joined a local triathlon club. I was hooked. Being a triathlete was a hell of a lot better than wearing makeup and sequins and worrying about how many calories were in a cup of coffee. I decided to make a real push to become an elite triathlete. I moved to Boulder, Colorado, in 2003 and trained with world champion Siri Lindley. I improved. After six years as an amateur, I was good enough to turn professional and compete for money. I met the qualifications to race as a pro—placing in the top three at three amateur races in one season, within 10 percent of the winner's time, and in races with no fewer than five hundred women.

At about the same time, my writing life took flight when Little, Brown offered me a book contract to write about my life as a professional skater. *All the Sundays Yet to Come* hit the shelves in 2003. While my memoir was well received (*Entertainment Weekly* gave me an A- the same month John Grisham got a D+ and Toni Morrison got a B! Not that I'm competitive or anything. Noooo.), it didn't launch me into literary stardom or pay a lot of the bills. I returned to substitute teaching and relied on that and my meager triathlon winnings to finance my chosen life of what could best be described as athletic slumming.

Life was good, but not perfect. Because my triathlon skills were better suited for long-distance races—like the 140.6 mile Ironman—rather than the thirty-two-mile Olympic distance event, my

Olympic dream seemed a little too dreamy. I just wasn't fast enough to be one of the top three females at the Olympic trials. There was also the issue of my personal life falling apart. I was choreographing the closing ceremonies of my Engagement Games. Relationships—mine anyway—tended to become an emotional triathlon of jump in, give all, cry lots. I have multiple gold medals in this event. I was learning the hard way that my drive and motivation were great attributes as an athlete, but terrible faults in the I-can-fix-my-alcoholic-fiancé competition. I simply couldn't understand how I could fix crooked derailleurs, dropped chains, stripped screws, locked pedals, broken laces, and leaking goggles but could not properly rewire another human being's happy button. It took me years to realize the password to that control panel is strictly owner-operated.

In the spring of 2006, I met with my two editors at the ESPN compound in Bristol, Connecticut, to discuss the intricate details of my assignment/Olympic quest. Surely, attempting to get to the Olympics in two short years necessitated intricate details. The conversation went something like this.

"So, Kathryn, you have two years to try to make the 2008 Beijing Summer Olympics in any sport. What sport are you going to try?"

"Well, I'm going to see which U.S. sports are lesser known and start there," I said, knowing I wasn't exactly a shoe-in for becoming a 'four-foot-eleven, eighty-eight-pound gymnast. Nor did I have the skill set required for popular sports such as soccer and basketball. My only (naive) hope was that the off-the-beaten-path, media-starved sports might be underpopulated and undertalented.

"Okay. Try some sports and write about it for the magazine and web site. We'll cover your travel and training expenses. You'll get a monthly stipend for your articles," ESPN said.

"Okay!" I said.

"Okay!" ESPN said. "Any questions?"

Yeah, I've got questions. How the hell do I get to the Olympics in two years? Aren't you going to help me with this? Do you have any buddies at the IOC? Is ESPN giving me this Olympic quest because you want to see me succeed or do you want some back page comedy sportswriting schtick that no one takes seriously? Because if it's the latter, you've got the wrong girl, misters. Just because you're ESPN doesn't mean I'm going to let you edit or undermine my Olympic efforts as an athlete or a writer. Do you think you intimidate me? Do you think I'm gonna get all starry-eyed by your media magnitude? Can I meet Lance Armstrong?

"No," I lied. "No questions."

"Excellent! Keep in touch. Go get 'em."

Before I could figure out how to go get 'em, I had to go get myself a place where I could live and train and write and, most important, be happy again. My heart wasn't ready to go back to Boulder, where my relationship ended. My mind couldn't handle training for any summer sport in the climate and confines of New York City. The idea of moving somewhere new and unfamiliar was unsettling. I only had two years to attempt to get to the Olympics—and in new surroundings, given my capacity to get lost, I would lose some of that time just getting ac-climated. I have the sense of direction of a gnat. So where could I base myself that felt familiar, comforting, and conducive to summer sports? Tucson, Arizona. Having graduated from the University of Arizona with an MFA in creative writing in 2000, I knew the city, liked the people, and loved the climate (with the exception of June and July). And unlike NYC or Boulder, I could afford to live in Tucson without eating other people's leftovers. I packed up my truck and headed west for good.

In Beijing, there would be thirty-two sports and 302 events: ar-chery, badminton, baseball, basketball, beach volleyball, boxing, cycling, diving, equestrian, fencing, field hockey, gymnastics, handball, judo, modern pentathlon, mountain biking, race walking, rowing, sailing, shooting, soccer, softball, swimming, synchronized swimming, table tennis, tennis, team handball, track and field, volleyball, water polo, weightlifting, and wrestling. The idea that ESPN wanted me to "choose" one bordered on the absurd. Maybe if I was five years old, there would be time to experiment with every sport on the Olympic roster. But at thirty-one, the sport would more or less have to choose me.

As an endurance athlete, I had certain skills. Like endurance. That ruled out attempting events like the 50-meter butterfly and the 100-

yard dash. Also, I am most talented at being upright. That ruled out diving, trampoline, and synchronized swimming.

Obviously, it made sense to look closely at any sport/event that crossed over well from my triathlon training or my high school and collegiate sports experiences of running and rowing. Everything else on the list was likely out of reach, due to skill sets, body type, and the fact that most of these sports require training schedules to begin shortly after exiting the womb. Sailing ended up being the only sport I would have liked to try but did not get around to. As soon as there is a sailing center in the desert of Tucson, I'll look into it. But in the meantime, this was the list I came up with.

TRIATHLON: This is my current sport, though I tend to do it at longer, non-Olympic distances, and therefore at a pace too slow to qualify for the Olympic team. I'd have to beat out seasoned Olympians and world champions who, up till now, have been consistently handing me my ass on a platter. On the plus side, maybe I can speed up.

MODERN PENTATHLON: This consists of cross-country running, swimming, fencing, horseback riding, and pistol shooting—all in one day. On the plus side, no one in the United States has ever heard of it and it's obviously crazy hard, two factors which ought to discourage top-level competition. On the other hand, I'd never fenced in my life, hadn't been on horseback in twenty years, and the only gun I'd ever fired shot water … with a very weak stream.

TEAM HANDBALL: No, not the kind of handball with taped palms, a concrete wall, and a hyper little blue bouncy ball. Team handball is a hybrid of basketball, soccer, water polo, and dodgeball, a sport that is all the rage in Europe and South America. On the plus side, not much doing on that front in this country since our unexpected fourth-place finish in the 1984 Olympics. Also, I'm a good team player. I like people and whatnot. The disadvantages: The last time I played a court sport was, um, never. In addition, my hand-eye coordination consists solely of knowing the difference between my hand and my eye.

TRACK CYCLING: On the minus side, brakeless bikes scare the crap out of me, especially brakeless bikes being pedaled by packs of riders zooming around at forty miles per hour on an embanked track made of cement or hardwood. On the plus side, thanks to my experience as a pro triathlete I'm a decent road cyclist, so this seemed to offer a glimmer of hope.

ROWING: On the plus side, I rowed in college. On the other hand, I'm too big to be a good lightweight and too light to be a good heavyweight. But perhaps with a lot of lettuce or a lot of ice cream, there's that glimmer-of-hope thing.

OPEN WATER SWIMMING: While pool swimming has been around (and very popular) for decades, open water swimming makes its debut as an Olympic sport in China. The event is a doozy: a ten-kilometer (6.2-mile) swim across any sort of open water—lake, river, ocean—for roughly two marathonish hours. Whoever gets to the finish buoy first, wins! Simple! Except for annoying things like sharks, jellyfish, parasites, kicking limbs, hypothermia, dehydration, exhaustion, cramping, and, potentially, drowning.

RACE WALKING: All I knew of race walking is that it's the unsung underdog of track and field events. This seemingly bizarre sport merges running and walking into a most interesting middle ground of human motion. Supposedly, there are technique, tactics, and discipline in race walking, but how hard could it be? It's just walking, right?

As for the order of attempting these sports, that was in the hands of fate, luck, and the individual governing bodies of each sport. Did these sports hold open tryouts? Offer development camps? Send talent scouts? Give private evaluations? There was a lot to figure out.

And so, early in the summer of 2006, I put in a call to the U.S. Olympic Training Center in Colorado Springs to enquire about the first sport on my list, modern pentathlon. I told the head coach I was a pro triathlete looking to make the switch to modern pentathlon, if the sport suited me. I told him I had the ability to train full time, to relocate if necessary, and to give it everything I had for two years (and more) if it looked like getting to the 2008 Beijing Games was possible. I told him about my work ethic, my drive, my dedication.

I did not tell him I worked for ESPN. I did not want to be treated like a journalist looking for a story when the reality is that I'm an athlete looking for a chance. I am an athlete first, a writer second. While I have no qualms about proving myself in a sport, I have experienced the let's-humor-the-journalist-but-not-take-her-seriously mentality often enough to know I did not need it interfering with this quest.

The idea that I could be an athlete *and* a journalist seems to confuse people. An athlete who works in a coffee shop while trying to get to the Olympics is rarely considered to be a barista first, an athlete second. She's merely doing what it takes to support her dream. A writer, on the other hand, still evokes the stereotype in which writers write and do nothing else. I would tell coaches and officials all about ESPN after I tried my various sports, but not before. Not if I wanted to be given a fighting chance as an athlete. There was no other way to go about chasing this dream. I didn't lie to anyone. I just let the truth surface in my own time.

"Come to Colorado Springs," said the head coach of USA modern pentathlon. "We'll evaluate your talent level."

2

PENTATHLON IS HARD

August 2006

The U.S. Olympic Training Center in Colorado Springs has a nice pool. It would be nicer, however, if I didn't have a thirty-pound weight belt cinched around my waist while trying to swim its fifty-meter length—*ten* times. I have a weight belt strapped to my hips because I've been invited to spend a week at the Olympic Training Center and try out for the national team in modern pentathlon, a sport comprising swimming, shooting, horseback riding, running, and fencing. This is my third workout of the day. I'm tired and cranky and semi-drowning, yet I can't think of any other place I'd rather be. So I decide to suck it up. But not literally, because chlorine stings.

At the wall, the swim coach of the women's modern pentathlon team stops me.

"Your hips look like this," he declares in a thick Polish accent, slaloming his hand through the air with quick, angular movements. He looks like he's breakdancing. This is not good, because I should be swimming a straight line.

"Oh," I say, making a mental note. *Spazzing hips, bad.*

"Keep going," he says, "with the weights."

I look at the swimmer next to me for sympathy, at least, if not pity. She smiles. "He usually he puts the weights around our necks."

I arrived at the Olympic Training Center at 6 P.M. on Wednesday, August 2, 2006, for national team testing in modern pentathlon. This means that if I meet their swim and run qualification times, they'll accept me for training and give me a chance to make the national team. Best-case scenario, I wind up living and eating at the OTC for free and receiving a $500 monthly stipend. Worst-case scenario, I impale myself while fencing and leave the OTC dejected and full of holes.

I am issued a meal pass and a room key, which necessitate fingerprint scans and microchip cards. They don't fool around here. My room is in the Oslo Dormitory, a rectangular white brick building that brings back memories of high school hallways and uninspired, bunker-like college dorms. An iron fence runs along the perimeter of the OTC property, rendering the training center a private compound in the heart of Colorado Springs. The grounds are clean and well manicured, though the public streets on the other side of the fence show a slightly dingier side of Colorado Springs. The Rockies glisten in the distance, while 7-Elevens and Circle Ks glow grimly in the foreground.

It has been twelve years since my last dorm living experience—my sophomore year at Colgate University. Room 121 of the Oslo Dorm brings back all the things with which I associate my early twenties. The room is a white painted concrete brick square, twelve feet by twelve feet, with a twin loft bed, wooden desk, metal chair, three-drawer dresser, floor lamp, mini fridge, air conditioner, and sink with mirror vanity. Communal toilets are down the hall. Like many college dorms, the carpet is gray and the curtains are orange, but unlike college dorms, this room comes equipped with TV (with built-in DVD and VHS), free wi-fi, and daily housekeeping. Instead of hallway trashcans overflowing with empty beer cans, here foil PowerBar wrappers and empty Fig Newton packages gleam from the tidy receptacles.

My view from the window is the future outdoor pool, which is currently an outdoor dirt hole. My neighbors across the hall are teenage wrestlers and weightlifters. Our schedules are such that we do not interact, but I hear the bleeps and whirs of PlayStations emanating from their rooms in between training sessions. The video games are a study break, athlete style, from the demanding course load of their lifelong double major: Olympic greatness and physical excellence. Most of them are minoring in philosophy, too, even if they don't know it yet.

I stayed at the OTC twice before my pentathlon experience. In the summers of 1995 and 1996, I spent two weeks here while competing in the collegiate nationals for figure skating. Back then the dining facility was a small, one-room unit much like a public high school cafeteria. Today, it's a swanky event center, with photographs of Olympic medalists and inspirational quotes from Lance Armstrong and Bonnie Blair painted on the walls. Three giant TVs fill the dining hall with soft background chatter. Tonight is Mexican night, served up athlete-style. Lean grilled chicken quesadillas and a toppings bar with lard-free ingredients occupy one side of the cafeteria, while pasta, a salad bar, and desert stations are on the other. Nutrition charts loom above every serving tray. The closest thing I can find to unhealthy is a slim slice of lemon meringue pie, which is probably fat-free and low-sugar. Between the seating area and the cafeteria is a "recovery bar," where athletes can grab bananas, energy bars, nutrient shakes, fruit, cookies, and trail mix on their way out the door.

I sit down alone and observe the tables around me. Teenage mountain bikers with shaved legs and red welts occupy the round table to my left. Three paralympic athletes are in the middle of the room. One blind athlete verbally disciplines his guide dog after, en route to the table, the Golden Retriever paused to snarf a tortilla fragment that had fallen from a table of weightlifters. At 7 P.M. things are quieting down. On my way out, I grab a few energy bars and look over the photos of greatness—smiling, victorious athletes with shiny Olympic medals. There is a plaque that reads "2008 Beijing Olympic Medalist" and underneath there is a mirror. I look into it. I am so excited. My chin is going to the Olympics!

DAY TWO, MORNING

I'm having a light breakfast of cereal and toast in the dining hall with Dragomir Cioroslan and Janusz Peciak, the director and the head coach of USA Pentathlon. As the governing director of USA Pentathlon, Dragomir believes in his product and he believes in the people he tries to sell it to. From the beginning, Dragomir, a one-time Olympic gold-medal weightlifter, has made me feel like I'm capable of becoming part of their pentathlon program. Janusz, the 1976 Olympic pentathlon gold medalist from Poland, prefers scare tactics.

Janusz asks me how fast I can swim two hundred meters.

I tell him around 2:40.

He asks how fast I run a five-k.

I tell him about 19:20, hastening to add that I'm currently training for longer distances, like the marathon, but that I can bring my times down dramatically by focusing on the shorter distances.

He looks me in the eye. "Based on the times you told me, I don't think you'll make it," he says.

Ah, directness. So refreshing.

He then adds, totally unnecessarily, "Pentathlon is not easy."

I'm not sure what it is about my nature, my face, or my body language that suggests I think pentathlon—shooting, swimming, fencing, horseback riding, and running, all in one day—is easy. Or that any Olympic sport is easy. Is my eye contact being read as arrogance instead of confidence? Do I throw people off by smiling at the challenge of the sport instead of wrinkling my brow into worry lines? Is it my T-shirt, silk-screened with *I'm Gonna Kick Your Wimpy Ass* that turns people off? Oh, wait, I'm wearing a plain white tank top.

I hold eye contact with Janusz and speak slowly but confidently. "I understand. Penthalon is hard. I'd like the opportunity to try."

To be accepted for national level training, a female pentathlete must complete a two-hundred-meter swim in under two minutes and forty seconds, and finish the three-kilometer run in under 11:20. Both tests are given on the same day, a few hours apart. I will swim at noon, then run at 1:45 P.M., one chance for each discipline. The Colorado Springs training facility sits at an altitude of seven thousand feet. Nothing about today will be easy. Then again, nothing worthwhile is. At any altitude.

DAY TWO, AFTERNOON

It's 11:45. As I finish my warmup for the two-hundred-meter swim test, the stereo at the Olympic Training Center pool is appropriately playing Maroon 5's "Harder to Breathe." Janusz asks if I'm ready. I get onto the starting block and he asks the woman beside me if she'll be my pacer. A high school swimmer and runner, Margaux Isaksen, age fifteen, is here for a summer training camp in modern pentathlon. She is feeling tired and sore from her workouts, but agrees to pace me for the first hundred meters. I'm thrilled. I need pacing. I tend to go out too fast and then slooooow waaay dooooown. On the block I feel good, but the Nervous Willies are throwing a midday rave in my gut. I'm quite familiar with their dance.

Janusz does his thing: "Take your mark ... Go!"

And go we do. Margaux cranks out a 1:12 pace for the first hundred meters and I stay with her. Then comes the second hundred and I'm alone, living out Maroon 5's "Harder to Breathe." I feel splashy instead of smooth, my muscles erratic in the altitude-induced oxygen debt, my breathing strained and gulpy. With fifty meters to go, my brain starts its "go!" chant. It has done this since I was a teenager. When the end is in sight, all I can think or hear is *gogogogogogogogogogogogogo* until I'm over the line, through the tape, the music has stopped, or whatever.

Still, I'm certain that my second hundred meters was slower than 1:12 and I'm worried it was not enough to break 2:40.

Janusz looks at me, cocks a half smile, and articulates carefully in his Polish accent, "2:36.7."

Good God! I actually did it. I let go of the side of the pool and exhale myself down to the bottom, exhausted. Four seconds is a solid margin in swimming, though nothing to get arrogant about. Seeing as swimming is only one of the five sports I'd have to master as a pentathlete, I feel great about my time but nervous about what the rest of the week has in store for me. I bubble up from the depths of the pool and look at Janusz. He seems slightly impressed, though hardly blown away—which accurately sums up my general effect on most people. "Good," he says neutrally. "Okay, go get ready for running."

⚲   ⚲   ⚲

Pentathlon was created by the founding father of the Olympic Games, Pierre de Cou*bertin*. (Note the last name. Coincidence? I think not.) The idea for the five unrelated sports that form pentathlon came from a military fable about a soldier in peril. Apparently, there was once an officer who was brought down behind enemy lines as he crossed a field on horseback, on his way to deliver a message to his general. He defended himself with pistol and sword, then swam across a river and finally ran on foot to deliver his message. While it's doubtful the officer's message said, "Hey, my near-death experience would make a great sport!" pentathlon debuted in 1912 in the Fifth Olympiad in Stockholm, Sweden. Representing America was a young lieutenant from the U.S. Army named George Patton. He finished in fifth place, unable to win a medal because, ironically, he was hindered by his lack of shooting expertise.

But before de Coubertin's modern pentathlon, there was *ancient* pentathlon, which incorporated running, jumping, discus, javelin, and wrestling and was said to be the brainchild of Zeus's semi-mortal off-spring, Jason. I'm not so sure it was fair for the all-humans to have to compete with the half-gods in this grueling sport. How does one wrestle with a demi-god? Are they only partially fleshly? And winged feet are a ridiculously unfair advantage. Nonetheless, pentathlon became a crowd favorite and even Aristotle gave the sport two thumbs up, saying that pentathlon athletes are "most beautiful, for they are naturally adapted for bodily exertion and for swiftness of foot."

Since 1912, Europe has controlled the modern pentathlon podium at the Olympic Games, which is partially the reason pentathlon lacks exposure in the United States. But things are changing. The United States has Sheila Taormina, a two-time Olympic swimmer and triathlete ranked second in pentathlon as of 2008. If she makes the Olympic team, she'll go down in history as the only female athlete to make the games in three different sports. And then of course, there is me, with no Olympic credentials, trying to get onto the national team with a decent swim, a sub-par run, and no experience in three of the five sports.

Between the swim and the run, there is some technical business to attend to. Because Lucas Gilman, the photographer ESPN has assigned to me, is with me at pentathlon camp, we make sure to get proper approval for his presence. A few calls to Bob Condron, the head of PR at the OTC, and we are all set. Lucas simply has to ask permission from any athlete before taking their photo. But for the most part, he'll be photographing me. Unfortunately, there is a downside to having a personal paparazzo: I stick out like a sore thumb. There is a flashing sign above my head that blinks *Journalist! Journalist!*, making it even more imperative to show the coaches (and fellow athletes) that I am here as an athlete. That I want to be treated like an athlete. Because, well, I am an athlete. The journalism part? That is my *job*. That is how I am funding this Olympic dream. They would have no opposition if I were here as a waitress trying to be a pentathlete. Seems clear-cut to me. But not to everyone.

One man in the PR department, whom I shall call Brutus, takes a bit of a dislike to my presence at the OTC. On the first day, he sits down with Lucas and me for lunch, all smiles, and asks me to explain my project/attempt/goals to him. I do. Brutus, unaware I've already been given the legal go-ahead, decides he's discovered a mole! That I'm not an athlete, I'm a spy who might sell the USOC's training secrets to the Russians. Brutus smiles and heads out of the dining hall, only to return a little while later with an agreement for me to sign. The agreement says:

Kathryn Bertine will dutifully uphold the following rules:

1. No photography shall be used of athletes in their personal room or while eating in the dining hall. A USOC official will accompany Lucas Gilman at all times while on OTC property.
2. No use of audio recordings or athlete interviews without permission.

3. No use of video recordings of athletes without permission.
4. Kathryn Bertine is here as a journalist. She is not here as an athlete with expectations of being named to a USA development/residency program.

Brutus holds a pen out for me.

"I'm not signing this," I tell him and head to Bob's office with Lucas. Lucas discreetly mumbles to me that he deals with stuff like this all the time, and the best thing to do is "smile, wave, and uh-huh" the people who just don't get it. The four of us have a meeting. Bob reads the list Brutus wrote and looks at me.

"Is number four bothering you, Kathryn?" Bob asks. He is smiling in a way that tells me he gets it, that he was an athlete once, too.

"Yes. I agree to all the other rules, but number four is incorrect. And insulting. Not to mention counterproductive to the USOC's purpose, whose job it is to seek out possible U.S. Olympians. If I'm not good enough, that's fine, but I'm not signing a piece of paper saying I have no expectations, no dreams, and that I can't simultaneously be and an athlete and a journalist."

"I don't blame you," Bob says. "Let's change number four to 'Kathryn Bertine is here as an athlete and a journalist.' Period. Leave it at that. Okay?"

"Thanks, Bob," I say. With every bit of sportsmanship I can muster, I turn to shake Brutus' hand. "See you at track practice," I smile.

"Uh-huh," Lucas says with a smile, giving a quick wave as we walk out the door.

DAY TWO, A LITTLE LATER IN THE AFTERNOON

The Nervous Willies are back in my gut, partying like teenagers in an empty house. We're at the Colorado College running track, just a few miles from the Olympic Training Center. By "we" I mean Janusz, Dragomir, Lucas, Sandu Rebenciuc my run pacer, and a rowdy assembly of acids whooping it up in my lower intestines. I'm thrilled my swim went well and terrified my run won't. Before I started my Olympic quest, I was in training for a marathon, so I'm much more comfortable holding a 7:45 pace for a couple of hours than attempting one sub-six-minute mile. That is a whole different world of hurt. Today, I have to do an all-out three-kilometer run, which is 1.9 miles or 7.5 laps of the track. This is the typical distance of the running portion for women's pentathlon, though it can be done on a cross-country course or a track, depending on the competition. While I favor trail running over the track, I understand it is easier for Janusz and Dragomir to observe my efforts trackside. I am given fifteen minutes to warm up, so I trot around the track and contemplate my digestive system, which rumbles with equal parts curiosity and blueberries.

As if it wasn't hard enough to get meals in as a triathlete, I can't fathom when and how a pentathlete eats. Do they ever have time to fully digest anything before heading to the next sport? Do they live on smoothies and supplements? I had to eat something before swimming and running to keep my energy up, but now I fear my small portion of blueberries wasn't the best idea. Fiber is great, but not before running. I know this, I understand this, and I have dealt with the repercussions of choosing fibrous foods before training. I have gone out for long runs and come home without socks. These things happen. Still, I took the blueberries from the glorious Olympic Training Center dining hall. Why? Because they were *free*. Because I love blueberries, and before ESPN came along with this assignment I couldn't afford to buy fresh produce very often.

As I start the run, my legs feel good. No, they feel great! Yeehaw! The first four laps of the 7.5 lap run are solid and I clock 5:58 at the mile mark, surprising myself. But the last 3.5 laps prove harrowing. The sky above Colorado Springs has opened itself, pouring down a warm summer storm. The rain doesn't bother me—I'll take rain over heat any day—but the wind is blustery. The thick raindrops feel terrific, cooling me immediately, though it probably wasn't smart to wear light pink shorts. At three laps to go, the Yeehaw feeling has been replaced with a Yeeech feeling. My limbs are struggling, my posture is failing, and my coveted blueberries are slowly retaliating. While the oxygen is tough to find and my lungs are searing from not getting enough, my stomach is the main culprit. It does not like to work as hard as the rest of my body, and it will rebel disastrously when given the opportunity.

My pacer, Santu, tells me we're too slow. I need 11:20 to qualify for the resident program in modern pentathlete. I cross the line in 11:47 and keep running all the way to the Porta-John on the side of the track. Twenty-seven seconds. A small margin in a marathon, but too much in a three-kilometer. Janusz and Dragomir head for their cars to escape the rain. There is no chitchat. I have not made the cut-off time and my pentathlon trial is essentially over. I will not be considered for the national team at this point, but there is still a chance that tomorrow I could wow them with my pistol and fencing skills—despite the fact that I've never picked up a gun or a foil. Januz and Dragomir role down the car window and tell me to be at the pool at 7:30 for swimming tomorrow. They take off. Lucas, the ESPN photographer who will become my good buddy over the next two years, drives me back to the OTC.

"How did you do?" he asks.

"Pentathlon is hard," I answer.

DAY THREE, MORNING

This is my last day at the Olympic Training Center, and it begins with a morning swim of 3,200 meters, a quick fiber-free breakfast, then a fencing session. The fencing gym is small, and in a corner there is a rack of polyester equipment that smells worse than an NHL locker room. Three metal runways about the width of bowling alleys are lined up next to one another, equipped with electronic scorers.

Janusz is busy giving a private fencing lesson to a member of the men's team. After my disappointing run, I have the feeling he's not expecting me to bust some Olympic-level fencing moves. Two female pentathletes show me how to slither into the heavy white knickers and white jacket, how to don the enormous white mesh helmet that renders me faceless. I am a cross between Darth Vader's clone troopers and the Ghost of Christmas Future. I put on a right-handed glove and borrow a right-handed blade, which attaches to a cable that plugs into the scoring system. When an opposing blade hits me anywhere on my body, it sets off a sensor and awards my opponent a point, and vice versa. In the 1976 Olympics in Montreal, a Soviet pentathlete named

Boris Onischencko rigged an épée sword to register "extra" touches. That seems complicated. He could have just fenced me.

Pentathletes practice épée fencing, which means they compete round robin and each duel is finished after the first touch. Not a lot of room for error here, and no second chances. The women teach me how to lunge, defend, and flush—fencing lingo for "dance around and don't get skewered." Within five minutes of bouncing about in the on-guard position, my quads are burning, my entire polyestered body is soaked in sweat, and my right arm feels like it's about to fall off.

Before taking on a human opponent, I practice my "technique" by using my blade to poke a tennis ball dangling from a string in the corner of the gym. I do quite nicely, largely due to the fact that the tennis ball is unarmed.

Next, I face Margaux, the fifteen-year-old pentathlete who was lightning fast in the pool the day before. She proves the same in fencing, but she takes it easy on me because she's kind and quickly realizes I have the same skill level as a newborn. For the first time in my life, I notice that there is a very long period of time between telling my brain to do something and waiting for my body to actually do it. For example, as my opponent and I dance on-guard, I think, *Thrust your blade now! NOW!* My brain then takes a few milliseconds to deliver the message to my shoulder, in which time Margaux has riddled me with stab wounds. When I take off my uniform (and pay homage to the plastic chest protector underneath), I see little red spots on my arms, thighs, and shoulders, and upon closer look I notice they spell out "Pentathlon is hard."

After fencing, we grab a recovery snack and head to the shooting gallery. I am met by a gray-haired, ponytailed man named Sill Lyrathe, the shooting coach, who outfits me with a right-handed air pistol and shows me how to load the five-pound gun. The tiny pellets are not round BBs but instead are shaped like ant-size hourglasses. Although everyone else is quiet, focused, and serious, I fight a burning urge to shout, "You'll shoot your eye out!" or "Freeze, sucka!" Shooting ranges are surprisingly like libraries—with athletic, armed librarians. Sill teaches me to look through the plastic sights on the barrel of the gun and line up the front sight with the rear sight. He teaches me to aim just beneath the bull's-eye, which is ten meters (about thirty-three feet) away, and to pull the trigger very slowly—which, of course, I do too fast. He sets up the target range by attaching a paper bull's-eye to a pulley system that whisks the target along a clothesline-like string to the ten-meter mark against the wall. He lets me take a shot. Around me I hear the *bap, bap, bap* of the pentathletes hitting their paper targets. I raise my pistol, align the sights, squeeze the trigger slowly and gently. I hit the wall behind the target. The pellet bounces away, bapless.

Sill encourages me to try again. And again. And again. Then, *bap!* Upper left hand corner! Woohoo, I hit the paper. After a few minutes of successful bapping, I notice that I'm actually getting better. I've nailed six bull's-eyes right in the cornea. My right arm is incredibly fatigued after two hours of holding a blade and a pistol at a ninety-degree angle, and when practice is over I feel terribly lopsided. The left side of my body hasn't done nearly as much work today. I look over at the woman next to me, who is combating this very problem by holding the pistol in her left hand and extending her arm for one-minute intervals. I hand my targets to Sill and he seems genuinely pleased. Immediately, I conjure up a fantasy in which Sill tells Janusz I should be admitted to the national team program because I'm such a good shot and it would be a shame to waste such incredible potential. This fantasy is rudely interrupted by a pentathlete who informs me it is time to go to riding practice. Crap. I almost forgot all about the horse.

DAY THREE, AFTERNOON

The last time I was on a horse was twenty years ago, as a fifth grader. It was 1985, the year before I became smitten with figure skating. That summer I went to a camp where horseback riding was a required activity. It was fun. I learned to trot and canter and clean up poop. I also learned to hold on for dear life to a large animal who would ultimately do as she pleased. A good metaphor for the larger picture of life: Hold on, life will ultimately do as it pleases.

The assistant riding coach for pentathlon is a recent college graduate named Lindsay Gillette. She puts me on a horse named Breezie, which immediately puts me at eazie.

"He's very slow," she promises.

Too bad I can't fence against horses.

Breezie and I head out to the ring. Margaux is there on a horse named Cheezy, and they both look anything but. Lindsay instructs Breezie to trot, and we bounce along the inside rim of the ring. Strangely, my riding instincts come back to me. I remember how to post, how to control the reigns, and how to not fall off. After a while, Lindsay asks if I'd like to go over a jump.

"Um ..."

"A little one, just a foot high."

"Um ... okay. I guess. Do you think that's a good idea?"

"You'll be fine. Hold onto her mane."

Breezie trots around, then takes the jump in a lumbering lurch. One of us screams (probably not Breezie). We both land safely and unharmed. I release my grip on Breezie's mane, relieved that I haven't ripped out all her pretty, well-groomed hair. Margaux is galloping circles around me and flying over jumps three times as high as the knee-high twig I just cleared. In pentathlon, the horseback competition involves riding a jump course in about one minute and fifteen seconds. The athletes are timed and also judged on presentation. Some jumps in competition are four feet high—four times the height I managed today. Besides holding on for dear life, the rider is also responsible for telling the horse where to go. This seems like a tall order, especially since I don't speak a lick of horse. If I'm going to be a pentathlete, I have a lot of work cut out for me. Soon, my riding lesson is over. Lindsay says I did a great job for a beginner, and I thank her and Breezie for their time.

Beginner. The word sticks with me. I shouldn't feel defensive, but I am. Beginner is so unOlympian. *I'm not a beginner, I'm an elite triathlete!* I tell myself. The horse sneezes.

Back at the OTC, Dragomir informs me that the coaches have left for a competition in China and they will call me next week for a summary/critique/evaluation of my testing. Dragomir then tells me that Brutus has been to see him, informing him that if I do not make the pentathlon team, I may, in fact, try to make a different team in a different sport.

"Is this correct?" Dragomir asks. He looks at me intently, and there is a slight hint of reprimand in his eyes. *Brutus, you slimeball.*

"Yes," I tell Dragomir. "If I don't have the skills as a pentathlete, I am going to try a different sport. I want to go to the Olympics. It's my dream. So I'll do what it takes to see if I can get there. But I assure you from the bottom of my heart, if you think I can make it as a pentathlete, I will devote myself to this sport completely."

"If we select you, you would have to move here and train just like this—eight hours a day, four to five sports a day—and be totally committed to pentathlon. Are you willing to do that?" Dragomir asks.

I assure him that I am. Weight belt, sword, saddle, and all. He tells me we will talk next week. I'm not sure what exactly we will talk about, but I have a feeling it will involve working on my run split if I want to make it into the program. So there is still a chance I could make it as a pentathlete, I think. I'd have to try another three-kilometer run time trial, probably. Go through the whole rigamarole again. And quit that happy marathon pace I like so much. My dedication is not a problem. Reality, however, is.

A week comes and goes, during which I head north to Boulder, where I sleep on the couch of my friend and former Colgate rowing teammate, Beth Avery. While I've made the move to Tucson, I still need to gather the remnants of my past life out of a storage locker in Boulder. Emotionally and physically, I've moved on with my life. Unfortunately, furniture pretty much stays where you leave it.

I hear nothing from Dragomir or anyone else in the pentathlon program. I call and leave a message, it goes unreturned, and I understand the silence loud and clear. At thirty-one and with no pentathlon background, trying to make the national team—let alone the Olympics—in two years, in a five-discipline sport, is not something that is going to happen. The coaches of USA Pentathlon would be better served to invest their time and energy in younger prodigies. Or older prodigies who can rock out some fast times and show some incredible skill. I showed good skill, but not good enough. I am, however, grateful that Dragomir and Janusz gave me the opportunity to try.

While living on Beth's couch, I schedule a tryout with the national team of women's team handball in Cortland, New York. I am excited and determined to take on a new sport, but nervous about the fact that I have never even seen a handball. My brain, which suffers from ignorance-is-blissism, assures me that team handball can't possibly be harder than modern pentathlon. My body, which suffers from reality, is about to disagree.

WATER BREAK

LETTERS TO A POTENTIAL SPONSOR

Now that I'm in my thirties, my body feels things differently. I don't have nagging or acute injuries, which is good, but I do have twangs and twitches. I refer to these as passive-suggestive injuries—small naggings that hint at future musculoskeletal issues. This occurs when any given muscle decides to speak up and voice its opinion about my athletic career. *Hey there, Kathryn! Down here! I'm your right iliotibial band, hanging out over here near your knee. Just wanted to say hey, how's it going, hope you're well ... and oh, if you wouldn't mind, BACK THE FUCK OFF, BITCH!*

The upside to being an older athlete is that I understand and respect my body, and truly appreciate all it can do. Some days my body is triumphant and youthful, some days it feels downright old. No matter. Sweat helps me celebrate, mourn, or decipher everything that life throws my way. All writers have their muse and mine is energy and athleticism. Sports have made me love life. They have also made me puke. Sports have seen me victorious and they have seen me passed by runners wearing gorilla suits and bunny outfits. Sports have moved me. I have passed men. They have passed me. I have been passed by fifty-year-old women and fifteen-year-old girls. I have been passed by athletes with fewer limbs than I have. Long live sport! It is wonderful and glorious.

But trying to make sports the epicenter of life is anything but easy. More often, it's harder on the brain than the body. Unlike teenage or child athlete phenoms, athletes in their twenties (and beyond) usually have to work extremely hard for sponsorship. Sponsors, in turn, prefer to go with sure bets, big-time winners, those who have already proven their worth. So up-and-coming athletes must do what they can to catch the eyes of a sponsor. Letters are usually the best way to open the door. Here is the perfect way to do it.

LETTER NUMBER ONE

Famous Cycling Company
1 Famous Cycling Company Drive
Sportyplace, CO 87654-3210

October 1, 2006

Dear Famous Cycling Company,
I am writing in regard to a potential sponsorship with
your company. As an eight-year veteran of triathlon, I
am switching gears en route to becoming a professional
cyclist this year. I have used your incredible line of Famous
Cycling Company products since I began racing as a
triathlete, and I now hope to represent your company in
my professional cycling career. Enclosed with this letter
are my race resume, my personal resume, and a list of
references. Please do not hesitate to contact me should you
have any further questions or conc—
    Aw, crap. This is the fifth letter I've written to you,
FCC. I was hoping to hear from you by now. I know, I know.
You want to go with the Big Guns—the wringers who
you know will get the coverage and show off your logos. I
understand. That makes sense. After all, they have earned
it. I'm just a newbie. I've got a few small titles from local
races, but I suppose that doesn't really compare to multiple
Ironman victories or cycling world championships. But
you know what, FCC? There's a lot that I do have going
for me. For example, since I am currently slower than the
other pros, spectators will be able to read your logos better.
Investing in me makes sense. First, let's talk results: I
might be an unknown now, but I'm offering you a free ride
as I climb up the ladder of inevitable success. If you were
to cover my coaching expenses, my travel needs, and my
race entries, I'd have more time to train and therefore
increase the likelihood that I will win all my races.

Also, if you were my sponsor I'd promote your company so much that you'd have to open another branch of business. I'd talk up FCC to all my training partners, competitors, friends, and family. I know lots of people personally, at least ten thousand, all of whom would be willing to purchase your product if I tell them to. Then, after I'm done competing, you could hire me to work at your company. I have it all planed out, FCC. Did I mention I have a web site? I'll give you a screamin' banner with blinking lights and a plethora of hyperactive smiley faces. I'm very devoted to you, FCC.

I'm also a freelance writer, so if you sponsor me I can drop you into all kinds of articles. Check this out: Trisports.com is an amazing triathlon store with a staff of incredible, generous people. Sport Beans makes the tastiest electrolyte-enhanced jelly beans, mmmmm! Rudy Project offers the world's greatest sports sunglasses, and by golly, I never go a day without my Athlete Octane vitamins. See what I mean, FCC? We can help each other out. Just because I haven't ever set foot in an Olympic stadium (yet) doesn't mean I can't promote you like a true winner. I guarantee I'll be your greatest supporter ever. I could use your help in financing my training and racing goals, but gosh, I'd be grateful if you sent me a free T-shirt. I'll wear it every day. If it is made of wicking material, I'll shower with it.

You know what else? I am a really well-rounded person. In addition to competing in cycling races and triathlons, I also enjoy swimming, biking, and running in my spare time. If you send me some decals, I will put them all over my equipment and body.

With your utmost devotion,

Kathryn Bertine

LETTER NUMBER TWO

Famous Cycling Company
1 Famous Cycling Company Drive
Sportyplace, CO 87654-3210

November 1, 2006

Dear Famous Cycling Company,
Thank you for the free T-shirt.

Sincerely,

Kathryn Bertine

Sponsorship, if an athlete is lucky enough to attract any, is usually not enough to cover all living expenses. Athletes usually end up taking whatever job they can find that will allow them to put their training first. Freelance is ideal, except for the fact that it is freelance. One never really knows if and when there will be a next assignment.

When I began my career as a professional triathlete in 2005, I spent five to seven hours a day perfecting my stroke, ride, and stride. Finding work to fit around this schedule was nothing short of harrowing, and I took what I could find. Calling upon the career services department at my college, I found a fellow alumnus who worked in the magazine industry. He was the head of one of our country's most popular tabloids. The bad news? I am not a fan of tabloids, specifically how they represent women. The good news? Writing one juicy tidbit kept me fed for a month. A no-brainer at that point in time. For the three years I lived and trained in Nederland, Colorado, I worked as a stringer for the tabloid, driving to Aspen or Denver to chase whatever stars were in town. To counteract the experience of writing for a tabloid, I decided to write about the tabloid experience for a triathlon magazine. At worst, it would make me sound like a celebrity-chasing idiot. At best, it would shine a little light on how necessary it is to sponsor an athlete.

SUPPORTING THE TRI LIFE
BY KATHRYN BERTINE

If actress Kate Hudson tells me what brand of jeans she is wearing, I will be a better athlete. If Nicolette Sheridan admits there is off-screen rivalry amongst the Desperate Housewives, I may very well set a record in my next race. If any given reality TV couple is pregnant, there is a good chance I'll crack the podium this season. During the day, I am a newbie pro triathlete that no one's ever heard of. At night, I am a celebrity chaser for a tabloid magazine. The juicier or sillier the story, the more I get paid. This is how I afford my coaching. This is how I try to be a better triathlete. This is why I need to know what Paris Hilton gave her Chihuahua for its birthday.

I don't enjoy my job, really. I'm not a huge fan of A-list celebrities. I'd much rather ride my own bike than call up gyms in L.A. to see who's spinning there. If Brad Pitt and Angelina Jolie party at the Ritz in Aspen, I could care less, yet if I ever ran into Lance Armstrong in a bagel shop, I'd probably lose all bodily function. I am honestly ashamed that I know Britney Spears' bridesmaids wore pink track suits to her wedding. I try to redeem myself by reciting Natascha Badmann's Ironman splits over and over in my head. To me, true celebrities are found on Alii Drive, not Rodeo Drive, and A-list stars include anyone who can do a triathlon with less than four limbs. These are my heroes, these are the folks I'd much rather chase. But I want to take a shot at a pro season, and that calls for drastic measures in the Funding My Dreams department. So here I am, abusing my master's degree in fine arts, selling myself to the tabloids. In the name of sport, I have become a literary prostitute.

In order to afford my triathlon dreams, I have worked a vast assortment of odd jobs. Some odder than others. My primary career is writing. (You've heard of singer-songwriters? Well, I am an athlete-author. For me, they go hand in hand. Take away one, watch the other suffer terribly.) Though I had my first book published in 2003, until I crack my own personal DaVinci Code, I get by on the following: celebrity chasing, after-school sports coaching, freelance editing, sports journalism, waitressing, public speaking, substitute teaching, and occasionally assisting a cryogenicist replenish the dry-ice supplies in above-ground crypts where willing dead people are kept. Swear to God. It all pays for triathlon.

Chasing celebrities, however, is something of a personal conundrum. Triathlon has taught me to set high goals and, figuratively and literally, race my own race in life. When I am on celebrity duty, I have to compromise these values. My tabloid boss requires that I ask questions like, *So, what kind of Bentley did you buy? How many carats is your new ring? How 'bout that DUI? What brand of shoes are you wearing? Are you pregnant?* What I'd really love to ask is, *Are you happy deep down inside? If you could be any kind of athlete, what kind would you be? Are you mad at me for hanging around outside your hotel room? Do you feel like sponsoring a hard-working athlete?*

Sometimes, on days where my practice sessions are flat-out deathly and my races are less than lively, I wonder if it is worth it—this lifestyle of unfulfilling jobs and physical pain. Racing at the professional level has been my goal for the past six years, but some days I think to myself: I'm thirty years old, I have two degrees, twice as many part-time jobs, no benefits, no money saved for the future, I live paycheck-to-paycheck, I'm an anonymous triathlete, and I spy on famous people for a living … is this bad? I can only hope that not taking a chance on my dream is a choice even worse. (If I can get a Desperate Housewife to agree with me, I'll be set for another two months of training.)

3

NIGHT OF THE MANGLED CARCASS

August 2006

The most common misconception about getting to the Olympic Games is that there are "tryouts." Nope. The reality is that for nearly every Olympic sport, from curling to shot put to cycling, there is a hierarchy of levels, categories, or competitive ranks that it takes years to climb and decades to achieve. There are no sports that, every four years, hang out a hand-painted sign on a neighborhood soccer field that says, "Olympic Trials Today, Everyone Welcome." In lieu of which I have to call the national governing bodies of every sport in the United States and, like an idiot, enquire a) how to play their sport; b) whether or not they think I could be an Olympian in that given sport; and c) establish that that no, this is not a prank call from a local radio station.

Some team sports, like soccer and softball, do have "normal" tryouts and selection procedures for earning a spot on a national team, though usually one must be invited to try out. Being on a national team is a good start, but it's not an Olympic guarantee in this day and age. First, players can be cut from a national lineup at any time. Second, a national team usually has to compete internationally for a berth to the Olympic Games. Remember the Jamaican bobsled team from 1994? Jamaica did not round up four tropical guys and send them to the Winter Olympics. Those four athletic gentlemen had to qualify for the Olympics on an international level. And they made it, edging out favorites from bobsled-crazed cultures across Europe and Russia. Ya mon! That's how it is done. Jamaica, or any other country, cannot send a national team (in any sport) to the Olympics just because it wants to—not since sports have grown on such a global scale. All countries, large and small, need to establish their sports programs internationally before they can win an Olympic berth. So the first step may be getting on a national team, but it's no ticket to Beijing.

As I'm about to find out, these national team selections and "tryouts" take place at the highest level of competition and there are no second chances. No call-backs. Even in a sport you've never heard of.

I discover team handball on an Internet search. I always thought handball was something my Uncle Larry played with his retired buddies at the Y. But in the little picture on the team handball web site, I see a herd of about ten women on an indoor court, running hither and yon and trying to throw a cantaloupe-size ball into a soccerish goal. It looks like the game my elementary school gym teacher made up for us on rainy days. Intriguing! Why had I never heard of this sport before? Oh yeah, I remember. Because ... *deep breath* ... the American sports media are trapped in a loveless, codependent relationship with multi-million-dollar professional men's sports and television networks and are so sadly fearful of branching out that, instead of exposing the world to lesser-known sports that are just as great as our popular favorites, they are content to recycle stats, photos, videos, and stories of old sports instead of educating people about newer sports that might have a positive global impact on everything from rebuilding wartorn nations through sport to ending childhood obesity through athletics. Where was I? Oh, yes—team handball.

Though it has been more than a decade since I played any sort of ball sport (low-level high school softball), I phone Christian Latulippe, the head coach of the USA women's team handball squad, and within minutes obtain an invitation to open tryouts for the national team. I'm shocked. I thought I'd get a thanks-but-no-thanks and maybe, if I really pushed the envelope, the coach would mail me an informative pamphlet on team handball. Tryouts? For a *national t*eam?

"I don't know how to play team handball. Will that be a problem?" I ask.

"Most of our recruits have never seen a handball," Coach Latulippe says.

"Is there anything I should do to prepare?" I ask.

"Throw a softball around to warm up your arm," Coach Latulippe says, "so you don't get too sore."

"Sure," I say, completely unaware of the galaxy of hurt that awaits me.

I arrive on the campus of SUNY Cortland in upstate New York on Sunday, August 13. The summer sky is clear, blue, and warm, the polar opposite of an upstate New York winter. I have not received word from the good folks at modern pentathlon in the eleven days since I left Colorado Springs. Their silence is clear. I'm not going to get a call from Dragomir at the pentathlon offices, and Brutus is probably doing a little happy dance celebrating the "journalist" who didn't make the cut. That's okay. No time to spare.

Winding through the Cortland campus, which offers a home to the women's national team despite the fact that team handball is otherwise unaffiliated with the school, I see an elephantine Ford 350 van with *USA Team Handball* detailed on the side. With peeling paint and dented panels (probably not from handballs), the faded navy blue van—weathered, tough, determined, and severely under-funded— seems an accurate metaphor for the women's national team.

At the team handball office, I meet the coaches. Christian Latu-lippe is a six-foot French-Canadian and six-time Canadian national team member who has coached the USA women for the past three years. His unshaven face suggests a tired nature. "Hi, Katrin. Welcome to team handball," he says in his Quebecois accent. His assistant coach, Dawn Allinger-Lewis, is a five-foot-eleven knockout of athleticism, a Montana native, and a member of the 1996 Olympic handball team. She gives a firm handshake, and her demeanor immediately conveys a love of the sport and a desire to see team handball thrive. Also in the office is Kathy Darling, one of the team's co-captains. A former NCAA champion in the discus and javelin, as well as a Division I basketball player for Johns Hopkins, Kathy is six feet and two hundred-ish pounds of solid, athletic scariness. (I mean that as a compliment.) She will also be my housemate during the next five days of my national team tryout, and a vital component in my quest to discover what exactly team handball is.

The coaches tell me to get a good night's rest and that practice tomorrow will commence with a 7 A.M. weightlifting session. *Excellent,* I think. *The last time I lifted was six months ago, during the base training phase of my triathlon season. This should be hellish.* Coach Latulippe gives Kathy $120 for our grocery expenses for the week and sends us on our way. $120?! That's usually my monthly grocery budget! Two words zing into my head: *snack aisle.* As far as I'm concerned, team handball is the best sport I've never played.

Kathy takes me to the "Handball House." I'm not sure what I'm expecting, after the Olympic Training Center in Colorado Springs. I guess I'm assuming something dorm-ish, but without all the Olympic rings and bronze statues. Kathy pulls into an apartment complex consisting of ten separate two-story units lined up in a row. *Not bad,* I think, *the whole team lives next door to each other in Olympic-funded housing.* Then I see a few kids on scooters and a smattering of bedraggled-looking older people crisscrossing the complex. Some of them are smoking. Kathy explains this is a public low-cost housing complex where rent is $500 a month, not a private dorm facility for the team. Inside unit 94, the carpets and walls are stained and dirty and there is an impenetrable odor best described as neglectifunky. (I was told to bring my own bedding.)

Everyone on the national team works at least part time, most of them as waitresses, bartenders, or clerks, and they all pay full rent. Four of the women, however, are West Point graduates and members of the World Class Athlete Program, which pays them a stipend to train toward the Olympics. West Point is one of the few schools that has a handball team, and since graduating, Sara, Jenny, Jacqui, and Sunny have all played for the national team between bouts of military service. Three of them drive BMWs.

"I hate my dirt job," Kathy says.

I nod empathetically. I've waitressed, substitute taught, and pet-sat my way through the last eight years of athletic dedication. Dirt jobs. Man, I hear ya.

"So what do you do?" I ask Kathy.

"I measure dirt. For an engineering company."

I eat dinner with Kathy and another teammate, Sunny, who recently returned from a military tour in Afghanistan. Hanging out in the living room, we watch TiVo-ed episodes of *Grey's Anatomy* and *Family Guy*.

"How many people do you expect at tryouts?" I ask, thinking of a number around thirty or so.

"Two," Kathy says, "including you." She goes on to tell me that the team has no money for recruiting, so they do what they can by word of mouth and web site advertising. This explains the $250 fee I forked over to USA Handball. Most prospective players come from basketball or soccer backgrounds, Kathy explains. I figure this is a good time to ask what team handball is and how to play it. While most team captains would laugh at anyone who showed up at national team tryouts not knowing how to play the sport, Kathy calmly begins to explain the rules. She's not the slightest bit shocked at my ignorance.

· Team handball is 30 percent basketball, 30 percent soccer, 20 percent hockey (the team plays on an iceless hockey rink, boards taken down), 10 percent water polo, 5 percent dodgeball, and 5 percent hot potato. There are two teams of seven players (three forwards, three defenders, one goalie), and the indoor court measures sixty-seven by one hundred thirty-one feet—just a bit larger than a basketball court. The object is to get the ball into the goal (six-foot-seven by nine-foot-ten) by throwing it. (Strong, scary women try to score the goals, while other strong, scary women try to stop this from happening, but I'm unaware of this yet). There is one point for each goal, and women's games typically see scores in the twenties. Balls are passed by throwing or bouncing, but they still remain in play when kicked, dropped, or beaned off another player (dodgeball not encouraged). The melon-size ball weighs less than a pound, and while dribbling is allowed, it usually slows the pace of this incredibly fast-moving sport. In fact, players cannot hold onto the ball for more than three seconds (hence, hot potato). The game is played in two thirty-minute halfs, with a single time-out per team per half, and substitutions are permitted. There are free throws and foul shots, red cards and yellow ones. When fouls occur, a whistle blows but play is immediately resumed. Visually, team handball resembles indoor soccer, as the uniform is shorts, T-shirts, and low-cut court shoes that have no air holes and stink to the high heavens. Some players wear knee pads, but much to my deep chagrin, there is no other form of protection.

Kathy tells me she's only been playing for five months. A fellow beginner! This all sounds well and good to me and I am confident I'll pick it up tomorrow. After all, I'm in the best shape of my life as a pro triathlete, so all I'll really need to do is get a handle on the rules and plays and I'll be fine and dandy. What Kathy didn't tell me is that she is the hardest-throwing, strongest, most deadly assassin on the women's national team. This becomes apparent in the morning, when she throws me a ball and my palms sting till next Thursday.

That night, my roommate—the only other woman trying out—arrives. Her name is Anne Coulter, but alas, not *that* Ann Coulter. This Anne's not a raving, right-wing Republican but a twenty-two-year-old graduate from Colby-Sawyer College, where she played volleyball, basketball, and threw the javelin. At five-foot-nine-and-a-half, she's an inch taller and thirty pounds bigger than me, and I'm getting the idea that the ideal team handball body type is not what I possess. Strong mass is a good thing in team handball, and I have the lean mass of a distance athlete. I am reminded that despite all the different kinds of athleticism, there are usually two main groups. Group A are those who can whup you silly with their muscle-bound strength. Group B are those who can swiftly outrun group A. I'm a B about to be thrown onto a court of vicious As.

DAY ONE

Dawn, the assistant coach, drives Anne, Kathy, and me in the handball van to our 7 A.M. practice. Kathy tells a charming story about the time the gas pedal got stuck while driving on the highway en route to a tournament. She laughs as she says this, with an *Oh, you silly old van!* tone. Apparently, no one was hurt, but the dents on the side are no longer a mystery to me. There is a partially deflated, withered, lime-green handball on the floor of the back seat. It looks like a miniature soccer ball with its suede octagonal patchwork. It fits neatly in my hand. I toss it to Anne. If team handball were played in a car, I'd be really good.

We arrive at the weight room, which is a small, concrete cellblock in SUNY Cortland's athletic center. The standard equipment of benches, weights, bars, and mats lies crowded among the twenty women rotating around the room. I shake hands between sets and try to remember names. A two-year-old girl clutching a snack-size baggie of Froot Loops wanders among the weight machines, looking quite at home despite the loud clangs of metal. Kaya is the daughter of Tomuke, the team captain best known as T. T is thirty—the second oldest after Edina, also a captain at thirty-two. The majority of the team has a birth date in the 1980s. Coach Latulippe hands me a strength-training sheet and before I know it, I'm hurling a medicine ball against a wall while I wait for the bench press to become available. For an hour, I push and pull weights I haven't done since college (ten years ago). In the back of my mind, I shut up the little voice that asks, "Should you be doing this the week before your Ironman race?" *Shut up, little voice,* I say. This feels great! I'm feeling pretty strong and downright super duper. After the weights, we form small teams and do running drills outside. This is even better. I love running! I do quite well, holding a faster pace than some of the West Point girls. Yeah! Team handball! Bring it on!

And then, unfortunately, it is brought on.

The afternoon training session is in the handball arena, which is actually Cortland's ice hockey rink with the boards taken down and a hard, three-quarter-inch blue matting laid over the concrete floor (in winter, team handball moves to the indoor track and field house). I'm introduced to team handball by a method the coaches refer to as "baptism by fire." We warm up with some throwing and stretching drills. The team is wearing Nike-provided gray shirts and black shorts. A few players have knee pads. There is no other equipment, except the ball, which is covered with a sticky resin (the consistency of rubber cement) for a better grip. I quickly learn this goop is helpful in catching, not so helpful in throwing. My warmup partner is a former soccer goalie from Notre Dame. Erika doesn't seem to mind teaching me the different stretches, and by the end of the week it becomes clear that all the women on the team are not only fantastic athletes, but terrific, helpful people.

Coach blows a whistle, the team separates into groups of offense and defense, and we begin drills of running, throwing, shooting, and blocking. Anne and I get on one of the lines and join in, where I do what I do best in new situations: I become a deer in the headlights. Before I know it, there are balls whizzing at me from every direction and I constantly have to ask what is going on, what do I do, who am I guarding, where am I going, why won't it stop? My court sense is appalling. While the other women seem to run, catch, and throw all in one smooth movement, it takes me three separate thought processes to break down such a basic play. They look fluid, I look robotic.

I notice Anne is doing very well. She has a natural rhythm going, probably from her background in volleyball and basketball. My interpretive dance from my childhood figure skating background is getting me nowhere on the handball court. At the end of practice, we scrimmage. I am re-introduced to a long-forgotten element of contact sports: contact. Since the age of twelve, I've been a figure skater, runner, softball player, rower, swimmer, and cyclist. The common thread? Sports geared towards staying upright and avoiding other people. For twenty years, I've tried to not crash into things. Now, all of a sudden, it's full frontal collisions, arms clawing at me, floor diving and rolling techniques, and elbows, elbows, everywhere. *Be tough,* I whimper to myself. Kathy's shank of a forearm comes down on my nose. *Tougher!*

I warn, my eyes filling with tears. When the scrimmage is over, I relax and actually enjoy the newness of the experience. In my head, I count up the stupid things I've done over the past two hours in an attempt to remember to not do them tomorrow. Some things on the list:

- Letting the ball bounce off me (three times)
- Charging the goalie's box (once)
- Crossing the center line before the ball is in play (at least five times)
- Throwing the ball to a member of opposite team (twice)
- Letting my guarded person go unattended (countless)

At the end of practice, I'm knackered. Anne, Kathy, and I go to the grocery store to spend the $120 food stipend. Kathy buys fifteen pounds of steak. Anne loads up on organic stuff. I hit the prepared meals freezer. Our bill comes to $236. That was pretty stupid to shop after a workout. We eat, and fall asleep by 9:30 P.M.

DAY TWO

At 7 A.M., Anne and I head out to our test evaluation. We're given a series of fitness tests, which the coaches say is an integral part of our tryout. It's the least worrisome part for me because, well, I have much bigger things to worry about. Before the sit-ups, Coach Latulippe tells us he'll be doing body-fat testing with calipers. As a triathlete, my body fat is on the lower side. We endurance fiends are a wiry lot. I thought this was a good, healthy thing, but after practice last night, it's clear that handball is geared toward more powerful, brick-house, athletic bodies. Coach pinches folds of my skin in a variety of locations: triceps, biceps, pecs, obliques, calves. The fat registers between 4 percent and 13 percent, which is what I'd expect based on my triathlete lifestyle. Then he gets to the quadriceps, which, as a cyclist, is my strongest muscle group. Unable to find a meaty skin fold, coach seems frustrated. He fixes this by grabbing the small protrusion of vastus medialis— a muscle just above the knee that peeps out from most cyclists' legs— and clamps his calipers on that. I flex it, to show it is muscle, not fat. The calipers twitch, freeing their grip. Coach clamps the muscle again and announces that I am 23 percent body fat. I have two choices— speak up and defend my "fat" knee muscle or let it go and stay on the coach's good side. I keep my yapper shut for once. This is insanely difficult for me.

On the sit-up mat, Anne holds down my feet. Coach says "go" and I crank out sit-ups for one minute. When the minute is up he looks at me.

"Well?" he asks.

"That was fun?" I offer.

"How many did you do?"

"*I* was supposed to count?"

"Okay, well, do it again," coach says with a smile. And so goes my day of testing. After my forty spine-slamming sit-ups (twice) and one pull-up (which I considered a personal victory after years as a lower-body-dominant athlete), we do the bench press (where I'm only able to put up thirty pounds one time), a vertical jump test (I don't get far), and a throw test, where I stand on the end line and hurl a handball as far down the court as possible. The ball comes down just before the half-court line. A few more tries, this time with loud grunting noises, renders the same result. Hardly impressive. Finally, my salvation: a running "beep" test. I have to run back and forth across the width of the court, faster and faster, in time with a recorded "beep" on a cassette player. If I get to the line after the beep, I'm done. If I get there before, I keep going as the tape speeds up. Anne bows out at 4.5 beeps. I go up to ten, and thinking it is the last level, I stop. The beep beeps. Damn! Apparently the thing beeps on forever. Bummer. That is the end of my test. Anne and I go home for lunch. I nap happily for one drooly hour (before being woken by a screaming, slurring neighbor in the housing project) and return for individual practice drills a few hours later.

In the afternoon, Dawn teaches Anne and me some new handball skills. For an hour and a half we do drills and learn to shoot on goal. She teaches us fakes and how to throw the ball so hard it forces you into a backward somersault on the mat—which is as soft as the concrete floor it covers. For me, trying to take only three steps with the ball is a most challenging feat. As a triathlete, I'm trained to keep going for hours, so to stop every three steps is much more difficult than it should be. Dawn also teaches us the defensive tactic of stopping the offense by putting one hand on the opponent's hip and using the other hand to circularly smash down the opponent's throwing arm. In motion, it looks like something from the Karate Kid. Wax-on, perhaps. I notice my shoulder is a bit sore from the day before, but not too bad. I feel more confident after learning some new moves and eagerly look forward to evening practice, or what I will forever after remember as *Deer in the Headlights II: Night of the Mangled Carcass.*

DAY TWO, EVENING TEAM PRACTICE (7 TO 9 P.M.)

The players arrive wearing red T-shirts and black shorts. What works as unity for them is pure confusion for me. Too many new faces all dressed the same is not a helpful component of my tryout. We warm up with more stretches and drills and then begin an hour-long scrimmage. Coach puts me at left wing, which seems to be the best spot for a weak player with limited skills. I'm put in the corner, literally. My newfound skills don't last long. I try to wax-on my offensive woman, today played by Erin, and she sees right through it and does some sort of lightning-fast pivot and breaks free. These women are so quick, so powerful, so talented. They move through plays knowing exactly where the other person is going, weaving seamless patterns, braiding themselves into successful plays. Their strength is solid, their athleticism top form. By the end of the game, I see the truth before me.

My chances of making this national team are incredibly slim.

The only chance I have is if the coach wants to keep extra players around as reserves. The fact of the matter is, with no court sense and at the age of thirty-one, I'm probably too far behind to gain the knowledge of handball these women have. But I'm not giving up. There are a couple more days, and I haven't lost my desire to try.

DAY THREE

What I have lost, however, is the ability to move my arms or legs. I wake up so sore that I can barely see straight.

"Anne," I call over to my roommate's bed, "can you lift your arms?"

"Not above parallel to the floor," she answers.

At least I'm not alone. The previous days lifting and the two days of throwing, falling, rolling, and colliding have taken more of a toll on my body than I'd accounted for. I can't remember a time when I was sorer. My shoulder, from doing the tilted somersaulty thing over the hard mat floor, is on fire. My shins, not accustomed to sprinting, are aching. My knees, which prefer forward movement, are unappreciative of the stop-start-herky-jerky movements of team sports. Even my brain is sore from the tension between my desire to make a national team and the reality of attempting to do so. We have an hour till practice, so I try to squeeze in some quick laundry at the Kleen Korner in downtown Kortland. My timing is off, and I go to practice in a cold, wet sports bra, which I will later be too sore to remove.

My new boyfriend, Steve, calls and asks how handball is going. Unable to lift the cell phone to my ear, I shout down to my gimpy palm, "This sport hurts. Bad."

"Do you think you'll make the team?"

"Do you think they need a water girl?" I bellow.

Steve and I have only been dating a couple of months, and he is getting a firsthand education in what it's like to be involved with a chase-the-dream female athlete. Moreover, Steve lives in New York City, so he's getting the cell phone version of my life. I decide this works just fine for me. I've always had a knack for long-distance races, so heck, why not a long-distance relationship? Besides, the situation with my former fiancé left me a little wary of actually dating people in person. I clearly needed a little time and distance to sort myself out and lick my wounds. Steve was showing signs of support, so I took comfort in the notion that my Olympic aspirations were understood and respected. I was sure that was all I needed.

We have only two practices today, and the afternoon session is with Anne and Coach Latulippe. We work on passing the ball from a plethora of positions: seated, kneeling, standing, running. We do jump shots, where Coach places a child-size running hurdle in front of the goal and we have to approach it in a three-step sequence, jump up Air Jordan style, hang in the air, then hurl the ball into the corner of the goal. Left-right-left-haaang-shoot! I am aware that knowing left from right is helpful, but in pressure situations I seem to lose my already impaired knowledge of right and left altogether. My jump sequence ends up looking more Michael Jackson than Michael Jordan.

We then do plyometric jumps up the Cortland Ice Arena bleachers, on one foot. I do well at this, but my confidence doesn't stay long. Soon we're on to more goal-shooting techniques, and coach takes me over to the far side goal. He puts me about five feet away from the left post—not in front of the goal, but off to the side of it. He sits me down with my legs outstretched so I am sitting on the goal line facing the side of the goal. All I can see is the profile of the goal. He then tells me to try to throw the ball *into* the goal, while seated. I consult my memory of high school physics to recall if it is even possible to make a goal from this angle. No, it's not. It is, in fact, impossible. Then I recall that I didn't take high school physics.

Inevitably, I have to fall onto my right side to get any sort of angle into the netting. This would not be difficult for Inspector Gadget, but seeing as I cannot detach my shoulder and move it out a few feet to get a better angle, I'm at a loss as to how to get the ball in the goal. I try, and the results are painful. Especially for the shoulder I keep falling onto. Fifteen non-goals later, handballs are strewn across the gym and bleachers, my arm threatens to fall off and my pleas of *go, go, gadget elbow!* remain unheeded.

The worst part of practice comes at the end. We do multiple sets of throw-and-rolls, where I have to do the dreaded backward half-somersault over my right shoulder. Again, this is a move that should be one fluid motion, but I make it look more like I'm on fire and trying to extinguish myself with the good old stop, drop, and roll. A thought comes to mind that I would make the worst stuntwoman ever. My body tries to send me a message, something along the lines of, *Hey moron, you've spent two decades teaching me not to fall down. You now want me to fling myself onto the concrete floor and enjoy it? Fine, but don't expect a soft landing, you uncoordinated jackass.* I tell my body that it should enjoy the challenge of a new experience and quit complaining. It sends a bolt of fury into my rotator cuff. So much for warming up with a softball to prepare for this tryout. Coach should have told me to juggle cannonballs. Coach comes over, notes the goal devoid of handballs, and walks over to check on Anne. He says "good job" now and then, but mostly then. Anne gets the nows. I sense his disappointment in me. While cordial, coach makes little eye contact and I feel that my presence is merely tolerated. I can sense what he is feeling: that I do not belong here, at the national level of team handball.

It frustrates me not to be picking up this sport quickly. I can race a 140-mile Ironman but I can't get a ball into a goal? *Come on, you wussy twit. This ain't gonna get you to the Olympics.* Coach calls for us to collect (my) handballs strewn all over the gym. I feel a bit dejected, but force it behind me. I know enough about sports to understand there is no use crying over spilled handballs and that dwelling on a bad game/practice/national team tryout will only turn an athlete into a raving head case. All athletes need to form a healthy relationship with repetition. Trying to throw a ball in a goal in an effort to find optimal technique—good! Trying to throw a ball in a goal while attaching your self-worth as a human being to each missed attempt—bad! This is where the "dumb jocks" have it over the smart athletes who think too much. When a play isn't working after numerous failed attempts, the best thing to do is walk away, eat, sleep, then try it again later. Simple in theory, but ridiculously difficult for the overthinking mind. There is another practice tonight, and while I make the decision to stay positive, I am aware my time to impress is running out.

DAY THREE, EVENING

During warmups, I reminisce about a time when I could touch my toes. That was Monday. I'm bruised and purple on my knees, forearms, and shoulders from rolling, sliding, crashing, and burning. I do a not-so-decent job of guarding Erin at left wing, as she gets by me and scores frequently. Coach points out, "That's your man, Kathryn," which reminds me of my teenage years when family members used to point out pimples on my face as if I didn't see them myself. *Yes, thank you for pointing out my very public shortcomings. Much appreciated.*

Coach switches me to "circle" position for a while, which is center forward. I'm assuming he's doing this for a laugh, especially as he does not inform me of how to play the position. Circle has a nice ring to it and doesn't sound like such a dangerous position, but it turns out that the position is similar to playing keep away. Only I'm the ball. I'm shoved back and forth between two of the tallest, biggest girls on the team. They seem to enjoy this. One of their forearms lands across my nose, which I've broken in the past (on another person's skull). Luckily, it's only bruised this time. I go back to left wing, and I overhear the other team directing a play toward me. I know it's nothing personal, though I'm sure it's probably fun to make the new girl look like a retard.

I hear Kathy say about me, "She's not very aggressive." Yay! Mental games! My favorite! The nonaggressive comment makes me mad, my adrenaline goes up, and I push my offensive player a bit harder the next time we connect. I'm supposed to make contact with her upper arm and lower hip, but I have accidentally grabbed other nearby body parts. I mumble "Sorry," which does not help me acquire a badass reputation. *Whatever! I am* aggressive! I love aggression! But as I try to stop the offensive players charging at me, I know Kathy is partially right. I'm used to a much different aggression, the athlete versus swim-bike-run kind of aggression, where I only have to beat up myself and not anyone else. That night, I leave the arena with a new respect for the physicality of sports like team handball. Not that I ever thought it was easy to play in the first place, of course. I just didn't think that such an "unknown" sport would have such world-class athletes.

Team handball made its Olympic debut way back in the 1936 Games in Berlin. There, it was an outdoor sport with eleven players on a side. It disappeared in the 1940s, only to reappear in 1976 as an indoor sport with seven players per team. After the boycott of the Moscow Olympics in 1980, the USA sent their first female handball team to the Los Angeles Olympic Games in 1984. They lost the bronze medal match to China, and the fourth-place result remains the USA's best Olympic finish. In the three Olympics between 1988 and 1996, the women slid to seventh, sixth, and eighth places. Handball was suffering from the classic chicken-and-egg dilemma of all under-funded, lesser-known sports: Which comes first, the funding or the exposure?

With a pitiful budget, USA team handball had to make a tough choice in the mid-nineties—fund a national team of aging players for immediate exposure or promote the sport at a young, grassroots level so that the future will produce better teams. While the money went toward building team handball programs in elementary schools and local clubs, the women of the mid-nineties national team got together each year, often using their own financial means, to compete in the Pan Am Games (which were and still are the USA's only chance to qualify for an Olympic berth). With hardly any money or practice time, the women failed to earn a spot for the 2000 and 2004 Olympics.

But things are changing. The current national handball team is at its strongest, after posting an 8–1 record in the 2005 season. Their chances of qualifying for the 2008 Olympics are better, but not golden. As co-captain Kathy explains, "We'd have to beat Brazil. They are all six feet tall and have over ten thousand screaming fans at all their games." I tell Kathy it sounds like a perfect setting for an underdog team. Besides, I'm already a screaming fan of USA team handball and I will do what I can to recruit 9,999 more.

DAY FOUR, MORNING

Rest! No practice till 3 P.M.! No night practice afterward! My body, which is very happy to spend the day in the fetal position, curses me as I try to unfold it. I need to get the lactic acid moving, so I take my bike for a two-hour spin in the morning, because triathletes do quirky things like this. Twenty minutes in, I actually feel looser, almost pliable. My knees are a little creaky, my back is a little achy, my brain is a little wobbly. In other words, I feel completely normal. But back on the couch at the Handball Slum, the soreness returns as soon as I stop moving.

DAY FOUR, PRACTICE (3 TO 4:30 P.M.)

More stop, drop, and roll. I would rather let the fires of hell consume me before rolling over that damn shoulder again. Coach is watching. I roll. Or, more accurately, unroll. I either get stuck halfway through my somersault and tip over to one side, or get too little momentum and roll back the way I came. Not pretty. Coach calls for us to do wide receiver passes, which entails the goalie hurling the ball the length of the gym while someone runs to intercept it. When the ball is caught, we then slam it into the opposing goal. I watch the players do this with ease, grace, and power. My turn comes. I run, catch, and drop. Three times in a row. I'm so sad, seeing as catching (as opposed to throwing) is my strength. At least it was, back when I could open my arms and fingers.

On the fourth try, I finally get it and make a run at the goal. The freaking ball actually goes in, and I want with all my heart and soul to do a touchdown dance but I refrain because no one else has done that. I settle for a silent *woohoo!* inside my head. At this point, my roommate, Anne, is doing very well. She can catch, throw, and intimidate her opponents like she's been playing team handball for years, not days. Despite her newness to handball, her background in court sports is serving her well. I am sure Anne will make the team. Me, not so sure. I notice my soreness is slowly dissipating, except for my shin, heels, arms, back, shoulders, neck, and groin. When practice is over, coach sets up a time to meet tomorrow, where he will go over the evaluation of my tryout.

That night, Anne and I have a supportive conversation.

"I think you made the team," I say.

"I think you made the team," she says.

"Liar."

"No, really," she counters, "It just takes a while to get the hang of the sport."

That is nice of her, but therein lies the truth. It takes a while to learn any sport. And twice as long to play it well. Unfortunately, I don't have a while. I'm thirty-one. Anne is twenty-two. She has a decade more time to develop. Before we go to sleep, she asks me if I've ever read the *Tao of Pooh*, which she is holding in her hands. I have, long ago. When I was her age. She reads a passage aloud to me:

"Saving time is very simple. You can't save time. You can only spend it. You can spend it wisely or foolishly." Anne says she feels like she spent her time wisely this week.

Anne is right. The musings of Winnie the Pooh, a pot-bellied toy bear who can talk but doesn't wear pants, have suddenly made me feel very good about myself. I'm hoping that the new experiences of team handball fall into the "wise" category of how I am spending my time on this Olympic quest. Whatever happens tomorrow, or for the rest of my athletic journey, at least it feels like I'm giving all I have.

THE LAST DAY

At high noon, I mosey into Coach Latulippe's office. Anne is there, and I wait outside until she is done with her assessment. I hear lighthearted banter and positive words like "excellent" and "start soon." Although I know my team handball skills are sub-par, there is still a sense of longing twitching nervously in my stomach. I want to be on this team, I want to see if we can make it to the Olympics. Maybe they really do need some spare players. When it's my turn to go in, coach and Dawn sit down and hand me some sheets of paper. They are friendly, but their smiles give them away. We go over the sheets. They're a computerized list of my strengths, weaknesses, sit-ups, body fat, and so on. For each section, I'm given a score between one and five. There are seventy points of evaluation. I scan the list. I get a 4.5 on overall fitness. A zero on rolling. In between, I'm given ones and twos on most maneuvers. In the comment box, there are fragmented statements like "missing court sense" and "must anticipate better" and my personal favorite, for the body-checking assessment: "still scared and nervous." Under the psychological section, things improve. I'm given more points for discipline, attitude, motivation, and team cohesion. It is nice to know that I'm exactly the kind of person they'd want on the team, if I had talent. But at the end, I've only scored 30 percent out of 100. I feel a little better when I see that the side chart says 60 percent=Pan Am Level Player and 90 percent=All-Star International Player. Thirty percent simply says Inexperienced Player. Which is a correct evaluation, and a lot nicer than saying 30 percent=You Suck.

At the bottom there is a note: "Kathryn, for your age and for our needs, you lack important tools like court sense and upper body strength to continue in this program. We appreciate your effort, your attitude, and your interest in our sport. Thank you, good luck, and pass on the word of team handball."

Coach and Dawn tell me, in the nicest possible way, that they can't put the time and effort into teaching a thirty-one-year-old beginner the basics of the game, but that they would have taken me right away if I were twelve. I file that away as the best backhanded compliment I've ever received. I'm disappointed, but I understand. I can only be so disappointed about not making a national team in a sport I've been playing for ninety-six hours. But it still makes me pout. I was born with a certain amount of competitive drive that I have no control over. All I know is that this ambition is very large, sometimes scary, and that people with this kind of affliction usually end up as Olympians or serial killers. Somewhere deep inside, I simply disagree with reality, odds, and age when it comes to sport. I really think I can be good—Olympic good—at something. Just not team handball. I thank the coaches for the wonderful experience of playing team handball. I also thank them for the free T-shirt.

I leave Cortland with a deep respect for a sport I'd never heard of and a deeper respect for the women who play it. Every member on the national team was kind and courteous, driven and serious. They respected me as a fellow athlete, and if they laughed at my novice abilities, they did so in private. Even on the last day, when it was clear that I didn't have what it takes to play at their level, they still offered tips and advice. "Hold your arm higher, keep your hands up, stay strong through the torso." No one came late to practice, everyone gave their all. They get little funding from the USOC and even less publicity in the media. They work dirt jobs and live in a small town and go to practice in hopes of making an Olympic team in a sport no one has heard of—on a team that hasn't qualified for Olympic eligibility in over a decade. In a world that pays some athletes millions of dollars to fill themselves with steroids and "break records," here is a professional level team that wholeheartedly represents the long lost ideal of amateur athleticism: the love of sport.

As I head out of the team handball offices, it's never been clearer to me that if I want to go to the Olympics at my age, I'm too old a dog to learn new tricks. That means no more attempting to fence, shoot, ride horses, throw a handball, or try my luck with any newfangled sport. Time to stick to sports I know how to play, like swimming and rowing and running and cycling. I have already begun stalking the governing bodies of those particular sports, and now it is time to get serious. In the meantime, my triathlon training will keep me in shape. Next up on my list: track cycling. The downside? No brakes. The upside? No balls.

But, first, a few words about the, um, underside of almost all female Olympic endeavors.

WATER BREAK

THE YOGAFICATION OF SPORTS BRAS

"When did you have your surgery?" the nurse asks me. She is giving me a standard breast exam, part of my annual medical checkup.

"My *surgery*?"

"They did a good job," the nurse says. She is looking at the skin where the upper area of my breast merges into armpit territory. "The scars are barely noticeable. They should heal well."

"I haven't had surgery," I tell her.

She looks at me, pointing to the pale mauve and tannish stripes crisscrossing between my breasts. "Well, what are these incisions?"

"Those incisions," I inform her, "are from sports bras."

My first sports bra was a violet tanktop-ish garment of spandex and cotton made in 1991 by a company called JogBra. The front had no real cups for the breasts, nor did the back straps align between the shoulder blades; rather, they rode bareback atop each scapula. It fit like a slightly flexible piece of armor and lasted me through two years of high school cross-country and four seasons of collegiate rowing, before disintegrating into purple frizz. I then moved on to the Champion product line, which began making cotton-spandex sports bras with a decent shelf of elastic that ran under the breasts and offered marginal support. It also offered chafing, as sweat caused the cotton to distend, rub, and finally saw through the skin like a merciless lumberjack. In the late nineties, DuPont replaced the brutal cotton with CoolMax and other scientific fabrics that wicked away sweat and kept the sawing to a bare minimum.

Seams, however, were still a problem. Sports bras began to get trendy, and trends brought patterns, and patterns brought seams, and seams brought back my old nemesis, chafing. The effect of Adidas' sports bras, with their logo of three vertical stripes—and their six seams—is still visible on my breast pit. To say nothing of the permanent raspberry mark just beneath the center of my breastbone, either glowing red from a fresh chafe or terminally browned by years of scarring in the same place. Lovely. Such are the war wounds of the female athlete. And there was always uniboob, the attractive visual effect of wearing a sports bra. But the worst was yet to come.

At the turn of our most recent century, the apocalypse of the sports bra was brought on by a silent, powerful, and ruthless enemy: yoga. No sooner did I find a sports bra that fit than I would find out the line had been discontinued, or worse, yogafied. Yoga and Pilates did for the sports bra what steroids did for baseball statistics, which is to say rendered a good thing useless. Any impact-oriented athlete—runners, triathletes, team handballers, for instance—needed her sports bra to be a trustworthy eliminator of "the bounce." Yoga, with all its flowy vinyasas and day-at-the-zoo poses, gave women the option to bend and sway their way to fitness, and so the yoga bras, with their strappy little shoulder strings and loosey-goosey elastic, were okay for downward dog but terrible for upright chick. Unfortunately, the folks at Adidas, Nike, and Champion all jumped on the magic yoga mat and rode it to retail glory. Today, it is actually easier to find a supportive, comfortable, nonchafing, lasting relationship with a man than it is with a sports bra. And so, my female athletes, we must turn a corner.

We have choices. We can wait for full-contact team yoga to gain popularity across the United States. We can wait for pilateboxing to catch on. We can lie to the nurses and tell them yes, the surgery was successful and life as a B is much more fulfilling than it was as a DD. Or we can offer the following plea to the manufacturers of women's athletic undergarments.

Dear Fitness Corporations,

We beg you to remember the runners. Remember the triathletes. Remember the athletes of soccer, lacrosse, hockey, basketball, and mountain biking—so many of whom are women now. Think of our breasts, our various alphabetical cups, our strong latissimus muscles, and our mighty torsos. Save us from the delicate evils of yoga. Create for us the bounceless, chafeless padding we so desire and deserve. Add your logos with a silkscreen, not a sewing machine. Make them in the same mold as the ideal man—sturdy, complementary, dependable, and attractive but not too pretty. Put them both on sale.

Do this soon, we beg you. Do this before the dreaded Sag comes upon us, before the Breastbone Lumberjack hacks again, before Uniboob fuses into the genetics of female athletes or makes the breast gene disappear altogether. Do this now, so that someday when my great-great-great-granddaughter comes across my finish line photos she will not have to ask, "Who is this dude?"

Thank you,

Full-contact female athletes

4

THE BIRTH OF DOABLE

September 2006

Somewhere in the process of getting stabbed by fencers, chafed by horse saddles, and pummeled by handballs, one of the voices inside my head suggested cycling.

You like riding your bike, it pleaded.

Yes, I do, I agreed. *I could try track cycling!*

Is that the one with brakeless bikes and lots of riders going thirty miles an hour around a banked concrete track?

Yes, brain.

Long pause.

How about golf?

So I sent an e-mail to Jim Miller, the head coach of USA Cycling, telling him that I'm a professional triathlete looking to try my hand at track cycling. I suppressed my urge to tell him that I need to be an Olympian or my head will explode. Crazy people tend to get less response, so I faked sanity. Jim forwarded my e-mail to Colby Pearce, the women's track cycling coach, noting that I seemed "fairly legit" as an athlete.

Let's think for a moment about the various ways to describe a person's talent.

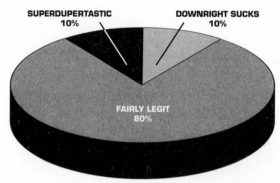

As you'll note, "fairly legit" is the vast purgatory of all human talent. On the other hand, after the feedback from pentathlon and handball coaches, "fairly legit" seemed like a respectable endorsement. I can envision climbing up the track cycling ranks: fairly legit, moderately legit, mostly legit, legit, and then perhaps someday, if I work very, very hard—truly legit. It makes me wonder what it really takes to make it to the Olympics. Luckily, there is a chart for that, too.

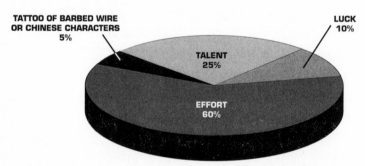

Whether or not track cycling coach Colby Pearce had knowledge of these charts is unknown, but he returned my call and invited me to the velodrome in Colorado Springs to ride the track for an hour and get a feel for the sport. Colby, a self-described "skinny guy who likes bike racing," does not embody the stereotypical/overused Olympic athlete image of a seven-foot-tall chiseled Greek Adonis. At five-foot-eight and maybe 150, Colby, a former U.S. champion and national hour record holder, represented the United States in the track cycling points race at the 2004 Athens Games. He placed a very respectable four-teenth. Now on staff with USA Cycling, Colby is equally talented in coaching, with a gift for explaining things in a clear, concise, and posi-tive manner.

"I don't have a track bike," I told him.

"You can rent one here for five dollars."

In eight years of triathlon training, where top-line bikes carry five-figure price tags, this stands as the best cycling deal I've ever found.

Track cycling has one of the most uncomplicated histories in the kingdom of sports. In the second half of the 1800s, someone invented the bicycle. People liked them very much and rode them all around Great Britain. But the roads in London were rough, so people built velodromes so they didn't have to deal with riding amongst potholes, horses, carriages, and really wide petticoats. Some people wanted to bike fast, so races were set up. Like most things British, cycling ended up in the United States, and in 1897 a velodrome was built in the heart of New York City. They called it Madison Square Garden, and when cy-clists weren't using it, people decided it made a very good event center.

Fast forward a century and a half, and track cycling finds itself at the top of the list of Sports You've Never Tried But Are Harder Than Hell. In the past few years, road cycling has enjoyed a surge of popularity (thanks to Lance and EPO—separately), but track cycling, unfortunately, remains the redheaded stepchild of the sport; ignored by the media and underfunded by the masses. Though there are hundreds of velodromes worldwide, there are only twenty-two in the United States—hardly on every street corner.

The 7-Eleven Velodrome in Colorado Springs is a truly unique architectural structure. The track itself is 333 meters (so that three laps equals one kilometer), and, unlike a regular pancake-flat running track, cycling tracks are banked so that the straightaways are slightly curved but the ends of the track are much steeper and more vertical. Imagine a giant contact lens pinched into an oval, or a giant rubber band pulled flatter along the sides with the ends rounded upward. Now pour concrete on that, paint on a few striped lane lines, and drop in a girl who has no idea how to stop a bike with no brakes. Or start one, for that matter.

Before we step into the velodrome, Colby has me fill out a fifteen-page waiver absolving USA Cycling of responsibility for things like self-inflicted maiming and death by bicycle. Then we go outside to a trailer that is stocked with old track bikes. Some of them have faded race numbers attached to the top tubes. Some of them hang vertically from the ceilings on wheel hooks, others lean clumsily on one another, some are missing wheels or lie in piles of disarray. A few are ensnared head on, handlebar to handlebar, like two-point metal bucks locked in battle. Cyclists are prone to treating their expensive equipment like live beings, so there is something odd about this dark trailer of captive, neglected, orphan bikes. I want to free them. I also want to be perceived as sane, so I decide to keep this thought to myself.

"Here's one," Colby says, guiding me to a generic purple bike. It's light, only about fifteen pounds. He makes some adjustments so the seat and handlebars fit me. To the noncycling eye, track bikes don't look all that different from regular road bikes. They have two wheels, a metal frame, a seat, handlebars, and pedals (with special clips that lock the foot into place so that the rider can not only push down on the pedal, but pull up). But track bikes lack many components of a road bike—derailleurs and double chain rings, for instance. In other words, there are no gears to shift into and no wiry brake cables slithering around the frame. There is a big chain ring in the front and a little bitty chain ring in the back. To brake, you have to reverse pedal like you did on your old Huffy or Schwinn while tearing through the elementary school playground. However, dramatic rear tire skidmarks will definitely not win you any points with track cycling's popular crowd.

Colby and I walk our bikes to the velodrome by way of an underground tunnel that stretches from the velodrome's parking lot to the center of the track. In the metaphorical donut hole of the track, there are a few anemic-looking bleachers, a stumpy and faded wooden three-tier awards podium, a couple of dribble-happy water fountains, and a small scaffolding tower of metal and wood where media cameras get a 360-degree lighthouse view of the velodrome. There are also four Hercules-thighed men in matching Lycra emblazoned with sponsors, spinning away on unstable-looking stationary rollers, warming up for their practice session.

"That's the national team," Colby explains.

"Then they're adept at avoiding collisions?"

"Usually," he replies.

Before we go out onto the banked oval, Colby has me ride around on the inner loop of the track's flat shoulder. I clip into the pedals and push forward, and the track bike feels just like a road bike. I circle along while Colby chats with some other riders. I gain a little more speed and quietly chant to myself, *Don't stop pedaling, don't stop pedaling.* Due to the fixed gearing, every time the wheel moves, the pedal moves. And with it, so does my leg. There is no pedal-free coasting, as in road cycling. Colby tells me I'll probably forget this, and the effect of neglecting to pedal will feel like the bike is trying to buck me off the saddle, rodeo style.

As I come off the warmup lap, it occurs to me that I do not know how to stop. While trying to figure that out, I stop pedaling. Yeehaw! My body responds by sending a ripple of momentum from my feet to my shoulders. It lifts me off my seat for a moment, like I'm riding a mechanical bull or doing some funky new boy-band dance.

"Apply back pressure to the pedals," Colby instructs me.

I do, and the bike slows considerably. I feel the controlled muscle pressure in my thighs, reminiscent of downhill skiing, and understand immediately why track cyclists have quads like tree trunks.

I wait until the bike is at a near stop, then clip out of one pedal by turning my shoe in a quick, horizontal movement. With one leg free and one leg still attached to the bike, I hop along on the free foot as the other foot circles around with the still-turning wheel. Awkwardly, I eventually roll/limp to a stop.

"Ready for the track?" Colby asks.

"Okay," I lie.

"Follow me, stay right on my wheel." That's cyclese for one rider riding directly behind the other to get a good draft or to watch and learn.

Colby leads me onto the track's straightaway, into the lowest lane where there is a black line painted "uptrack" of the shoulder. The embankment is very slight and hardly noticeable. A few laps there, then we go up another lane, in between the black and red lines, and I feel the gravity a bit more. This area is called the pole, as in "pole position." This is where people race and where the men's national team will be practicing, so we can't stay in the pole for long. Up we go. Three meters above the pole is the blue line, where riders warm up or do pace lines and try to stay out of the way of the faster people. Colby takes us higher up the embankment. Immediately, I feel the need to get control of my vision. I'm not sure whether to focus on the blue line of the track or to look straight ahead into the curve of the oval, and there is an odd feeling of dizziness as my eyes try to figure it out. They settle on the blue line and let the rest of the details blur.

Due to the slope of the track, it becomes apparent that my right foot is very close to the concrete and the entire left side of my body is very far away from the ground. It feels like hiking along a steep switchback, where there is a wall of uphill on one side and a sheer drop-off on the other. My heart rate has gone anaerobic, my knuckles are white against the handlebars, and I ask Colby if we can go faster because I notice immediately that speed makes the gravity feel less scary. Other than that I don't say much, because fear shuts me up quick.

"You've got a really low freak-out factor," Colby says.

"Thanks," I say, thrilled that Colby can't see my inner terror. Finally, my college theater minor has come in handy.

I ask Colby what I need to do to really get started track cycling.

"There's a women's development camp in September," he says.

"How do I get into that?"

"I'd have to get you on the list."

"Can you do that?"

"Yes. You're on the list."

🚲   🚲   🚲

On September 18, I arrive at the Olympic Training Center in Colorado Springs for the Women's Track Cycling Development Camp. I am assigned to room 317 of the Innsbruck dormitory, which is right behind the Oslo dorm, where I stayed for pentathlon camp. I'm worried about running into the pentathletes, who'll now think I'm stalking the OTC. I am also eager to avoid Brutus, who will no doubt chase me down with waivers and make me wear a scarlet J (*Journalist!* She's a *journalist!*) on my cycling jersey.

This time around, I have two other roommates in the twelve-by-fifteen-foot dorm room. There will be twelve women here for the week-long intensive camp, which will consist of four-hour morning practices at the track, two-hour road rides in the afternoon, and a lecture in the evening. I assume from this schedule there will also be a lot of eating and sleeping.

To my great surprise, I know one of my two roommates. Lara Kroepsch is a friend of mine from Boulder, where I lived for three years while training under renowned triathlon coach Siri Lindley. Lara lived in a house with my triathlon friends, and I saw her almost every day. I have napped in her bed, slept on her couch, and shared her energy bars. I am thrilled she is here, but also wondering why she is here. After all, she rides for Team Lipton, one of the best women's road cycling teams in the country. She's a Category One rider, which is the cycling equivalent of a black belt, and I'm not sure why she's coming to a development camp for new track cyclists. Within the hour, my other roommate arrives. Sima Trapp is a striking Iranian-American who unpacks her bag to reveal the team-issued clothing of Colavita-Cooking Light. Another one of America's best women's pro cycling teams. As the other cyclists arrive, Sima and Lara call hellos to them as they pass by our dorm room.

"Do you know all these girls?" I ask.

"Yeah," Sima says. "We all ride together on the pro circuit."

The pro circuit? I thought this was a development camp, as in first-timers, fledglings, and neophytes only.

"Why are you here?" I ask, probably sounding both frightened and rude.

"Most of us are contracted to ride at Track Nationals next week, so we do this camp as a warmup," Lara explains.

Nationals!? You're all going to nationals? "So you've ridden the track before?" I ask.

"We do it at least a couple of times every year."

Wonderful. Among twelve professional, seasoned, Category One riders, I'm the only one here who is a noncategory, nonprofessional, amateur road rider who has been on the track once, perhaps amassing forty-five minutes of lifetime experience. Development camp, my ass.

DAY ONE

After unpacking our road bikes (the camp lends us specialized track bikes to use for the week), we all go on a one-and-a-half-hour ride on some local bike paths. The pace is relaxed, but I'm not. I want to make friends with these professional cyclists, not end their careers by causing a massive pile-up because I can't navigate around some pothole I've seen too late. I keep my eyes wide and unblinking and talk in monosyllabic grunts to the other women, especially a cyclist named Kele Murdin, who I hope will impart all of her track cycling wisdom to me as we wind through the roads of Colorado Springs.

"You'll catch on quick," she says. Déjà vu—where have I heard that before? Oh, yeah—just before getting beaned by a handball and stabbed by a fencer. I've learned the truth behind these baptism-by-fire elite athlete camps. I've also learned that Finland has more than 159,000 islands, because Colby has taken to giving us a new noncycling fact each day.

That night at dinner the conversation among the elite female cyclists concerns three topics: boys, parties, and injuries.

"Are you still dating that guy on Health Net?"

"Dude, I got so wasted after the Tour of Philly."

"Liza, how's your road rash healing?"

We're in the ever-glorious OTC dining hall, which is an all-you-can-eat cafeteria (complete with a rotating dessert carousel!), all of it free for athletes staying on campus. Lara refers to our week-long stint of track cycling as "fat camp." Our daily doses of road and track cycling spike our appetites through the roof, and it becomes absolutely normal to consume upward of 3,500 calories a day. I steer clear of the blueberries. Did I mention the dessert carousel? Yes? Okay, well, they have one and it makes me very happy.

DAY TWO

At 8:45 A.M. we convene at the USA Cycling offices and ride six blocks south of the OTC to the 7-Eleven Velodrome. That is its actual name. Much to my chagrin, they do not sell Slurpees. The only snack is the lukewarm water fountain. We can't carry water bottles on track bikes, because dropped or spilled bottles on the slick concrete track would have nasty repercussions. Colby has us warm up by circling the track in a single-file pace line for twenty minutes, each of us taking half-lap leads at the front then pulling off and falling back to the end of the line. He has us do this twice, for a total of forty minutes, then dismisses us from morning practice. No race tactics, no sprint drills. *That's it? I can do this!* I think. Then my brain sends me a photo memory of Handball Camp, where the first day was easy, I got extremely cocky, and the next day I was pelted unmercifully.

By the time Colby explains that "today is just a warmup, it will get harder and harder each day, culminating in a race simulation," it no longer comes as news that I'm in for a week of personal ass-kicking.

That afternoon, we hop on our road bikes for a ride up to Manitou Springs, winding into a neighborhood housing development. Housing developments are typically not synonymous with difficult road rides, so I assume we won't be expending too much energy. As usual, I'm wrong. I forget we're in the Rocky Mountain State. Before I know it, we're riding up an enormous peak of pavement at seven thousand feet and I'm sucking down whatever is left of the oxygen in panting, wheezing breaths. I feel the need to be in the front of the pack to prove myself worthy of being at the "development" camp. Unlike pentathlon and handball, cycling is probably the only sport where I've got an itty bitty legitty shot of impressing anyone. I stay in front near Colby for the whole ride. Feeling good, looking strong. I later find out the other women are fresh off a road race from two days ago and probably have not recovered at all. My ego, which on a good day resembles a partially inflated air mattress, springs a depressing new leak.

DAY THREE

In mid-September, the Colorado mornings grow cold. This one happens to be forty degrees, which is not a happy cycling temperature. Fingers are numb, hats are worn subhelmet. We warm up with two twenty-minute pace lines and then work on two-kilometer (six-lap) sprints. We do this in groups of three, and I'm paired with Sara Caravella of Team Lipton and Sarah Uhl, the world junior track cycling champion, who is twenty-four and regularly passes half the cyclists in the men's development camp. Fun! I manage to stay with them for five of the six laps, but drop quite far back on the last one when they crank up the speed. I seem to have two speeds: slow and fast. The rest of the girls have at least four: slow, fast, faster than me, and much faster than me.

We then do what are known as "flying one-ks" or three laps of the track from a rolling start, as opposed to starting from a dead stop. This involves circling around the very top of the velodrome, then sprinting down into the pole lane and hanging on for dear life as you try to follow the rider in front of you and hope that no one crashes or passes out from exertion. I immediately understand that sprinting will be a challenge to my steady-state aerobic pace, developed during years of long-distance triathlons. When we're done with the flying one-ks, the agitation of near-freezing air on our already-taxed lungs causes all the girls to cough intermittently and speak in raspy voices for the rest of the day, as if we all had a pack-a-day smoking habit.

During practice, speed skating Olympic gold medalist Apolo Anton Ohno shows up at the velodrome to visit his buddies on the track cycling team. I bet Ohno, who's pretty talented at going around circles, would be good at track cycling. Later, when I see him in the cafeteria (near the dessert carousel!) and ask for a photo, I do my best not to gush awkwardly at his accomplishments, as he does not seem like the kind of guy who appreciates gushers. He's very humble, but he obliges, and I disappear before I say something stupid.

After dinner, we shuffle off to our lecture. Last night we learned about proper nutrition and tonight Colby has arranged for Chad Weikel from the United States Anti-Doping Agency (USADA) office to talk to us about drug use and steroids. Most athletes are captivated by the topic. Lately it seems that USADA's mission statement, "Fight for the clean athletes," is getting harder and harder to achieve. After the Floyd Landis debacle at the 2006 Tour de France and the already-rampant steroid use in pro cycling, everyone is interested in the latest doping developments, though it is highly unlikely that anyone at this development camp has ever touched the stuff. Chad shows us before and after slides of athletes on steroids, which include hairy, beefy, alto-voiced women and men with imploded arm muscles. We see dissected hearts of EPO users and pictures of Korey Stringer, the Minnesota Vikings lineman who died of heatstroke in 2001 after using ephedra as a stimulant. We talk about the conundrum of Zach Lund, the U.S. athlete who had to turn in his 2006 Winter Olympics medal in skeleton (the head-first version of luge) because he regularly and openly used Propecia, an anti-balding medication, not knowing it had ingredients found on the banned substance list. Since 1972, asthma medication, cold pills, nasal spray, and caffeine have all cost unsuspecting Olympic athletes their medals.

The first athlete to *test* positive for "drugs" was Swedish pentathlete Hans-Gunnar Liljenwall in 1968. The guy drank two beers to calm himself before the shooting event. While alcohol is no longer a banned substance, it probably should be in rifle and archery events. But in cycling, doping has been around a while. One of the first known case was at the 1960 Olympics, when Danish time-trial champion Knud Jensen fell off his bike midrace and died. An autopsy later proved he took stimulants to "help" his blood circulate.

Chad gives us a pamphlet listing allowed and disallowed medications, vitamins, and supplements. Among the prohibited substances are ma huang (a traditional Chinese medicine), nontherapeutic use of genes, Ritalin, ephedra, cocaine, marijuana, hashish, heroin, ethanol (mmmm!), and just about anything ending in −terol, −terone, and −olone. Among the permitted items are Tums, Prozac, Monistat, Tinactin, NyQuil,

DayQuil, (the nondrowsy version of NyQuil), Ortho-Cyclen (birth control), Ex-Lax, Bengay, aspirin, and Valium.

I'm free and clear, seeing as the closest I come to an ingestible vice is drinking instant hot cocoa. Let me just say that if sugar were a banned substance, I'd be screwed and my readers would have to settle for my latest column on CompetitiveKnittingWeekly.com.

Chad's lecture reaches a high point when, telling us about the ways in which athletes have tried to fake out doping control agents, he flashes a PowerPoint slide of a prosthetic penis and rubber bladder combination called "The Whizzinator" that, when worn undercover, delivers "clean urine" right before the eyes of any lucky USADA witness. While the lecture has humorous points (I can't help but wonder how the first Whizzinator got busted), the message is sad yet clear: cheating happens. A lot. "We don't know how many cyclists do it," Chad admits. "But we're doing everything we can to find them." One of USADA's tactics is to keep track of all prize-money-winning athletes to see if there is a significant spike in their results. Another is watching along with the rest of the world as a televised athlete goes from superbonk to superman within a twenty-four-hour period.

"Those people raise immediate red flags," Chad says. "Sometimes their results are from hard work and smart training. Sometimes they're not." When Chad finishes, we all shuffle out of the lecture. Some of us continue to talk about drugs. I ask some of the girls if they know women who do this stuff. Some of them have suspicions, but nothing they can (or want) to confirm. Personally, I don't get dopers. Not at all. If you're good enough to have to pee in a cup, why would you piss it all away? Some people argue that in professional sports, there should be no limit to what it takes to be the best—drugs included. "Hey, man, it's only human to try to get the edge!" I'm not sure when "edge" became synonymous with "cheating," but when it does, then we need to redefine "best." In my sports dictionary, "best" is defined as, "S/he who wins without putting needles, creams, pills, and other sketchy crap into their body." Duh.

DAYS FOUR AND FIVE

Rain. Some cycling tracks are enclosed, but the 7-Eleven Velodrome is not one of them. Rain causes the slick concrete track to become even slicker, so there is no riding in inclement weather. Until some genius invents the Dryboni, outdoor track cycling will remain subject to delays and cancellations and thus inspire our coach with creative alternative workouts. Coach Colby tells us that we will have two individual watt output tests; one will be a ten-second test, one a thirty-second test. This means we will ride on a stationary trainer connected to computers that measure how much power we put out. Great. Short bursts of power—just what every *endurance* athlete loves! The total time of this workout tops out at forty seconds. Normally, this would be about one-one thousandth of a triathlon workout. My muscles are not at all happy with the demand that they churn out a thirty-plus mile per hour pace even for thirty seconds.

My quads respond, *Hi. Yeah. We don't do that.*

I plead, *Look, just this once. This one week, anyhow. Two years, at the most.*

What's in it for us?

I'll go easy on the dessert carousel.

Deal.

In addition to these tests, I face another one. We are supposed to warm up on rollers, which I've never used and consider quite frightening. Rollers are a sort of stationary bike trainer, but unlike the kind that locks the back wheel of a bicycle into a secure hold, bikes on rollers sit on top of three rolling pin-ish structures that resemble the bottom half of Fred Flintstone's Flintmobile and threaten to throw off any unbalanced rider. With one hand on my track bike's handlebars and the other on a nearby wall or in a death grip on Colby's shoulder, I attempt to ride the rollers. After about twenty minutes, I'm only able to ride for about five seconds without falling over. I consider this an enormous accomplishment and wish I could say the same about my watt tests. I put out 7.7 watts per kilogram in the first test and 10.76 in the second, which is okay but not great. Perhaps it would be greater if I were in an actual "development camp" not otherwise disguised as a bunch of Category One national team professional cyclists. Not that I'm bitter. Just a little overwhelmed is all.

DAY SIX

There has been only one staunch opponent of my desire to be an Olympic track cyclist: my crotch. It ain't feeling the love of this project at all. In an effort to tell you about a tender reality of cycling, I have written a haiku titled "Down Below" to capture the essence of my situation of spending six hours a day in the saddle.

Down Below
Ow. Ow. Ow. Ow. Ow.
Oww. Oooooowww. Oww.
Ow. Pain. Ow. Ow. Ow.

For those who prefer a more clinical description: My vagina is bleeding from the chafing of the incredibly unforgiving saddle against my new bike shorts. The skin is raw and the little open wounds leave blood on the chamois (the fabric that lines the crotch of bike shorts). The wounds heal a bit overnight, only to be reopened the next morning. This hurts. Despite years on the bike as a triathlete, my position on a track-specific bike is much different. I sit much farther forward on the saddle of a triathlon bike, so my hard-earned calluses are misplaced and useless for my position on a track bike. Although many bike companies make saddles specifically designed to accommodate women's anatomy, my loaner track bike doesn't have one. Fortunately, there is a product called Chamois Butt'r that one puts Down Below before cycling workouts to ease the pain of the saddle. Unfortunately, today, bleary-eyed at 7 A.M., I accidentally apply Bengay in my bike shorts instead of the intended cream. I don't remember the morning workout.

DAY SEVEN

For our final day at the track, our main workout is a forty-kilometer time trial (120 laps) where we ride behind a motorcycle. This is fun. We go fast around the big circle for an hour. However, my main concern of the day is my meeting with Colby. I've asked him to sit down with me and explain the Olympic qualification process for track cycling, and, most important, to tell me if he thinks I might have what it takes to make it as a cyclist. On the way to our meeting, I grab a free copy of *Olympic Beat*, the news publication put out by the Olympic Training Center. Maybe it's got an Olympic-sport-committee-seeking-thirty-one-year-old-brunette-Olympic-hopeful-athlete classified ad.

Colby and I hunker down in big comfy chairs in the dining hall. He knows about my ESPN project, but doesn't treat me like a journalist. He treats me like an athlete. This puts me at ease, knowing I don't have to defend the position—for the millionth time—that a person can actually be both. He knows my goal is to get to the Olympic trials and that I'll do whatever it takes to get there. Colby explains that USA Cycling chooses their Olympians from a talent pool, and that getting into the talent pool requires being at a certain level of competence and having already achieved stellar results. Also, he explains that only two women track cyclists are allowed to represent the United States in the Olympics (in the individual pursuit and the scratch race) and only one woman per event is chosen. He tells me the reigning national champions are not retiring, and thus my chances of making it to the trials in 2008 are slim. And on the talent front, he acknowledges that I'm not a natural sprinter.

This is not news to either of us. I've been expecting this.

So I hit him with my Plan B: "Do you think I should give road cycling a try?"

The thought had occurred to me during the week, as I struggled to keep up with the sprinters yet held my own on the afternoon distance rides. What are the qualifications to make Olympic trials in road cycling? What are the events? Could this be a better match for my body type and athletic abilities? Could I meet Lance?

Colby agrees I'm better suited to distance/endurance events. He tells me the Olympic cycling events for women are a twenty-five-mile time trial and a road race usually in the eighty-mile range. He tells me that for each of these distances there will be an Olympic trials race event for 2008. Colby explains that I'd have to move from the Category Four beginner level to the Category One professional level in the next year. He doesn't explain just how this process works, but from my experience in other sports with ranks and levels, I understand they exist for a reason. Greatness and experience can't be hurried. In addition to climbing through the levels, I'd have to get a coach, find a team, and win or place high in a lot of races.

"This could be very difficult," Colby warns, "but it is doable."

Doable. There it is. The most beautiful and harmonious word in the English language. I let it linger in my ears for a moment. There was no doable in pentathlon, no doable in handball, at least not for 2008. But cycling—a sport I've been doing for eight years as part of my triathlon career—actually offers a glimmer of hope. A pale, thin, fragile glimmer, but a glimmer nonetheless. All right then, it's decided. More than that, it feels right. I'm going to dedicate the next two years of my life to road cycling. I have absolutely no delusions about how difficult this will be. I will simply take my fairly legit self, find a truly legit coach and mostly legit team, and we will pedal off into the doable Olympic sunset together while little birdies tweet happy songs and everything works out perfectly.

But before I jump into cycling, there is some unfinished business to take care of with my triathlon career … and my nose.

WATER BREAK

NASAL RECONSTRUCTION

For the love of sport and oxygen, I went under the knife. I had a surgical procedure called nasal septal reconstruction and the removal of enlarged turbinates. Otherwise known as no-it's-not-a-nose-job-but-rather-an-internal-procedure-to-help-me-breathe-better-but-thanks-for-assuming-I-had-rhinoplasty. Since birth, my nose has been the gimp of my five allotted senses. Although my septum was straight, the two internal fleshy sacs on either side of it—the turbinates—were enormously large. Since I was able to receive only 30 percent of my air through my narrowed nostrils, the rest of my oxygen supply came through my mouth. Loudly. Constantly. As a "mouth breather," I rhythmically gulped air, which made me sound as if I was dying, thirsty, stupid, and annoying all at once. As most mouth breathers can relate, I politely answered "no" to the following four questions asked almost daily for thirty years:

"Do you have a cold?"

"Are you about to pass out?"

"Did someone leave the kitchen fan on?"

"Will you make a crank call for me?"

The decision to surgically clear out my bulky nose scaffolding in 2005 was simple. I wanted to breathe better. *Not* because it would benefit my endurance sports fetish (though that was a mighty plus)—I only wanted to go about my day without my mouth hanging open. I wanted to smell things like flowers without shoving them up my nose. I wanted to taste food better. Even energy bars. So I went under the knife. Should any fellow mouth breather athlete decide to do the same, here is a brief rundown of what to expect.

After finding a health insurance company that will pay for the operation (a doctor must verify that the surgery is not cosmetic), you set up an appointment for The Knife. Your doctor will explain the entire procedure and convalescence to you: "mild swelling, sensitivity, and three weeks of post-operation physical rest." Is that all? That's nothing! A small price to pay for experiencing the lifelong glory of oxygen. Your dad will fly out for your operation, since you'll be under the effects of anesthesia and painkillers. You're sure you don't need him to babysit. After all, you're an aspiring Olympian and Ironman athlete. Pain is relative.

Before you drift off under the happy blanket of anesthesia, your doctor explains that when you wake up, your nose will be plugged and bandaged. You will have to come back in twenty-four hours to remove what he calls "the packing." You say okay, no prob—zzzzzzz.

When you wake up, you feel a little groggy. You ask for a mirror. Your nose is wide and achy. A sling that hooks onto your ears and runs beneath your nostrils catches all escaping blood. You are ghoulishly entertained. Your dad drives you back to your apartment. You immediately call your coach to say that you will be ready for tomorrow's workout. You feel fantastic. Better than ever. Then the Vicodin wears off. Then the anesthesia wears off. Then you do your best to hold down Saltines and Jell-O. You are thrilled that your dad is here.

For the rest of the night, your nose gets wider and thicker as the packing expands with gory nasal stuff. You are sure your head will explode like the packet-of-Pop-Rocks myth. The next day, the doctor instructs you to blow gently as he extracts the packing. You are instantly amazed at the vast capacity of the human nose as he pulls a bathmat out of each nostril. "Don't pick at the scabs," he warns. For the next two months, you constantly have your finger up your nose.

The doctor promises that soon the scabs and swelling will disappear. You will be a nose-breathing, air-loving machine.

Your body and mind get extremely fidgety during the three-week period of physical inactivity (higher heart rate will slow the healing process, Doc says—no exercise!). You try to pacify your athletic urges by seeing how fast you can unload the dishwasher. After three weeks, the doctor gives you the okay to start swimming, because swimming will be safer to the healing nose than possibly crashing on a bike. After three weeks, you are very excited to get in the pool. Swimming blissfully along, you don't see the other swimmer get into your lane. With her head, she breaks your brand new nose.

5

PICKING UP THE NIGHT SHIFT

October 2006

Given that I have been an elite triathlete for the past two years, one might wonder, "Why don't you pursue *that* sport toward the Olympics, dumb ass?"

Here's the problem: The Olympic distance in triathlon incorporates a .9-mile swim, a 24.8-mile draft-legal bike ride, and a 6.2-mile run. The distances I'm accustomed to and am most proficient in are the Half Ironman and Ironman events, which are *double* and *quadruple* the Olympic distances, respectively. Sadly, neither the Half Ironman nor Ironman distances are Olympic events. While I was good enough to turn professional and win a few small titles in Olympic distance triathlon, I was simply not fast enough to be one of the top three Americans in this event. For example, my 2005 professional earnings in triathlon were $380.00. Yes, that decimal point is in the correct place. And yet I loved this job. However, just before I began my quest for ESPN, I qualified to race the Ironman World Championship in Hawaii. I had been trying to get to Kona for years, so I did not want to give up the opportunity if it didn't interfere with my Olympic quest. With no development camps or tryouts scheduled for mid-October, off I went to Hawaii.

Many athletes don't like to talk about bad races, games, or events. For some, there is a fear that admitting to a few subpar performances renders an athlete forever incompetent. Hogwash. When I have a great race, I have a great race. When I have a bad race, man, I have a bad race—the kind of race that is so bad it makes me look like I've never played sports in my life. In triathlon, most pros race fewer than ten to fifteen times a year, so if you have three or four not-so-hot performances, there is not a lot of wiggle room left to produce a winning record. So, with that perspective, let me tell the tale of one of the triathlons that kicked my ass. It was in October 2006. Pour yourself some cocoa; it's story time.

Most people associate Hawaii with vacations, honeymoons, and surfing. These people are normal. I, on the other hand, have come to Kailua-Kona to race in the Ironman World Championship. Consisting of a 2.4-mile swim, 112-mile bike, and 26.2-mile run, this race began twenty-seven years ago when two whackos in California sat around arguing which was harder, a long-distance swim, a century bike ride, or a marathon. One of these fellows, likely inebriated and with far too much free time on his hands, suggested stringing all three sports together to see if such an event were humanly possible to complete. Thus the Whacko Trumpet sounded and type-A whackletes everywhere began crawling out of the endurance woodwork. Over the past thirty years, triathlon has multiplied like a mutant gene within the sport's governing body. Now there are four triathlon distances (one of which is an Olympic sport), two kinds to choose from (road and off-road disciplines), and competitors ranging from younger than ten to older than dirt. To this day, the Hawaii Ironman is the holy grail of long-distance racing. To be part of the 1,500-person field, one must first qualify at a highly competitive Ironman race or win one of the fifty coveted lottery spots. Either way, getting to Hawaii is difficult. I should know. I barely made it myself.

Background info: In 1998, I was on tour with a figure skating company in South America. (Yes, seriously. I couldn't make that up if I tried). I was walking through Mar del Plata, Argentina, one day and a herd of cyclists wearing bathing suits flew past me. I was intrigued. When I got back to the states and started grad school in Tucson, I joined the University of Arizona triathlon team. I was hooked. Oddly enough, my figure skating background made me a decent cyclist. The leg muscles used for jumping and landing on the ice are the same muscles used to push down and pull up on the pedals. And the spandex is pretty much the same, minus the sequins. I trained and raced and improved and turned pro in triathlon. Fast forward eight years.

Before embarking on my ESPN Olympic quest, I did ten triathlons in 2006. One of them qualified me for the Hawaii Ironman. This was both a blessing and a curse, because it would be my second Ironman in six weeks and the human body usually does not tolerate such behavior. I "qualified" at Ironman Canada, where I actually had the worst race of my career. Yet I managed to snag a roll-down spot from one of the elite racers who decided to pass on Hawaii. After trying to qualify for six years, I happily accepted the slot.

While I love the Ironman distance, my body rebels in any race where the temperature goes over eighty-five degrees. Perhaps this is a symptom of growing up in ice rinks, but extreme heat simply melts my innards. The tricky part of long-distance triathlons is that one has to eat on the bike to fuel up for the run. My body loves to eat, just not *during* my workout. Most races go just fine, but when the heat is literally on, things don't go so smoothly for me. High temperatures shut down my digestive system, blimp my intestines into distress, and often force me to walk during the run. Or in fact, the entire run, as they did in Canada. This is bad, especially if you race professionally. For starters, you don't win any money when you come in last. Nor do you feel like a rock star when you're staggering across the finish line four hours after your fellow competitors. Also, it doesn't do wonders for the self-esteem when a grandmother sprints by you on the marathon. But I've learned that dropping out hurts twice as much as finishing last in the pro field. In the great big worldly scheme of things, it is a freaking privilege to be able to do these races. Dropping out because you have a "'bad day" is not very karmalicious. But not wanting suffer through another Ironwalk, I sought out three nutritionists and physiologists to help me settle my gut warfare before Hawaii.

In one nutrition session, I did a sweat test to find out how much fluid and calories I need per hour of my race. I was hooked up to a machine that spat out some data as I ran on a treadmill. Turns out I burn twelve calories per aerobic minute and that I'd need about one thousand calories on the Ironman bike and about two hundred per hour on the run. The nutritionist told me I should be drinking ten to twelve bottles of fluid during the bike portion of the race.

"I've been drinking four or five in past races," I tell her.

"That's a problem," she said.

Great. It's taken me eight years of triathlons and probably five thousand dollars worth of bad races to find out all I needed to do was drink more water. At least I had it all figured out in time for the Ironman World Championship in Hawaii. I left the nutritionist feeling very prepared and confident, thus sealing my fate with Murphy's Law.

I arrived in Hawaii on October 15, 2006, the day of the 6.7 Richter scale earthquake. I tried desperately to ignore its omen-like qualities. It was a mere fifteen days since my track cycling career ended, and I needed all the optimism I could muster. My bike, which travels in a very large, cumbersome box, often likes to fly on its own schedule. This time, my other baggage has decided to accompany my bike. Seems that traveling United is anything but. The next day, an airline employee calls to tell me that my duffel bag and "surfboard" have arrived safely.

"Any chance that surfboard has wheels?" I ask.

I put together my Trek Madone bike and ride for an hour along the Queen Kamehameha Highway, where the bike leg of the Ironman will take place. Barely pedaling, I cruise along at twenty-six miles per hour. Amazing. When I turn around, however, my tailwind becomes a headwind and my speedometer reads nine miles per hour. Back in the pedestrian district on Alii Drive, tan and glistening triathletes run around in their Speedos and heart rate monitors at a crazy fast pace, which I refer to as the Speed of Narcissus, meant to impress the spectators. I spend the rest of the day resting with my feet up watching bad daytime soap op—I mean ESPN. I watch ESPN. All day.

The next day, I get up early to swim. Triathletes flood the Kona Pier, swimming willy nilly across the racecourse, completely ignoring the signs directing traffic flow. This frightens me, as I once had my nose broken by another swimmer's oncoming forehead. I've also been stung by jellyfish, cut by barnacles, and kicked in the noggin on countless occasions. I'm sure that explains a lot.

In the afternoon, I go on a recon mission of driving the bike course—fifty-six miles out to Hawaii, fifty-six miles back—to check out the conditions. There is a bit of damage on the road shoulders from the earthquake. The broken lava rocks are dark and crumbly, and the clustered pebbles look like the crunchy cookie layer inside Carvel ice cream cakes. Along the Queen K, windswept trees with permanently slanted branches reveal how windy this island can get. In past years, the wind has been so bad it has blown riders off their bikes. Any weather-related wrath on the island is attributed to the legend of Madame Pele, a rather emotional Hawaiian goddess who has local control over earth, wind, rain, and lava. Superstitious triathletes have been known to leave trinkets of goodwill for Madame Pele at the Church of St. Peter. This sounds like a good idea. People have left leis and flowers and even photographs of themselves. I leave Madame Pele a packet of fruit punch flavored Jelly Belly Sport Beans from the electrolyte-enhanced jelly bean company that sponsors me. I imagine that even spirits need to top off their glycogen stores during a busy day of prayer-answering, and who doesn't like red jelly beans?

That evening my father, also a St. Peter—my official cheering squad—arrives at the Kona airport. I'm quite psyched. My dad is a tri-athlete too, having picked up the sport a few years ago at the youthful age of sixty-six. We go out to dinner on Alii Drive, and as the appetizer arrives, so does a fantastic surprise. My super-duper boyfriend Steve, who was supposed to be on a business trip, has flown from New York City to Hawaii to see me race. Now that's a good man! He also kicks my butt on the bike. I'm learning to cope with that.

The Hawaii Ironman starts in deep water off the Kona Pier. The pros line up at 6:45 A.M., treading water while waiting for the send-off cannon. This day, the undercurrents are cha-cha-ing all over the place and my usual sub-hour swim time is in jeopardy. The 2.4-mile swim seems to drag on longer than usual and at the halfway point, I think I see Japan in the distance. I finish twelve minutes slower than normal. This is not a happy omen. I weave through the transition area and onto the bike. Slowly over the next few hours, the heat sets in. Worse, my legs feel heavier than whatever really heavy thing hasn't been used in a metaphor for a while. I'm thigh-fried, calf-knackered, and my toenails are turning black and falling off. Probably due to my recent Ironman Canada walkathon. Or possibly from eight continuous years of racing. Don't even mention my pentathlon, handball, or track cycling bouts of cross-training. I try to think cheery, uplifting thoughts, like, *Hey, mile marker ten! Only 102 to go! And then a marathon! Sweeeet!* I stick to my customized nutrition plan, but at mile seventy, my system rejects all food and fluids. The words of my friend, Diane, come to mind. Her amateur assessment of my stomach rebellion is, "You might just be messed up inside, Kathryn." I'm in for a long day.

I finally roll in from my protracted bike efforts after a whopping six hours and forty-five minutes, well over an hour off the leading women. My tummy isn't happy.

What do you want, tummy? I plead.

For you to get a lobotomy, it answers.

Here, have an orange slice.

I don't wa—frrrlllmp.

My run, for which I've trained at an eight-minute mile pace, immediately slips to a ten-minute pace. Then twelve. Then I lose track. At the eleven-mile mark, I see another pro on her way back from the marathon turnaround. She is walking and lamenting to a friend about being the last pro. I call out and show her my faded pink race number, which only the female pros have.

"Don't worry," I say. "I'm picking up the night shift."

She immediately brightens and her pace quickens. "All right. Hey, thanks!"

Halfway into the marathon, volunteers hand us our special needs bags, in which each racer has previously packed food items they might want midrun. The sun is beginning to set. A young girl calls out to me,

"Hey mister, want your special needs bag?"

At this point in the race, I'm just happy to be recognized as human. The sun goes down. A volunteer hands me a glowstick which I bend into a halo around my head. In its pale fluorescent light, I take note of the silhouettes passing me. Four men, each missing one limb, have run by me in the last hour. I have collectively been passed by a torso. Is that a raindrop? I'm now tired and grouchy and a good two-hour's limp from the finish line. Everyone says Ironman Hawaii is magical, and I'm trying to remember this as I run down the crumbled shoulder of a dark highway with cars on my right and lava rocks on my left and rain pouring down and blisters forming on unmentionable body parts. It's magical, all right. Like a page right out of the Wicca handbook.

When I finally make it to Alii Drive, I see my dad and Steve and Debora from Jelly Belly all wearing matching Sport Beans T-shirts and standing soaking wet at the finish line. Despite waiting/wading through a downpour, they're still smiling and offering to hug me at the end of a very long, sweaty, smelly thirteen-hour day. The hugging hurts, but I welcome it anyway. My father tells me that in the Navy, both the first- and last-ranked man of each graduating class gets a standing ovation, so he claps for me. Dads are awesome.

We head to the med tent (which looks like a MASH unit) for a quick blister bandage and then weave our way out of the race area. My day here is done. So too is my triathlon career, at least until after 2008. Perhaps I can get a stomach transplant by then. Or a lobotomy. While the day hasn't gone as planned, I'm still in awe of how much I learn at each race, even after eight years of competing. Here is what I' learned at the 2006 Hawaii Ironman World Championship:

I'm capable of racing terribly. I'm capable of finishing proudly. After 140.6 miles of exertion, I look like a dude. My boyfriend disagrees. Darkness makes everyone look faster. Madame Pele doesn't like fruit punch. My father is the original St. Peter. Toenails aren't really necessary. I need a month of sleeping in until noon. I'm ready to put swimming and running on hold and pour all my energy into the bike. Becoming a world-class cyclist won't be easy, but if I can get through a day like today, then maybe I'm stronger than I think.

WATER BREAK

THE HYDRATION GAME

On a Sunday afternoon, not unlike most of my Sunday afternoons, I find myself lying on the couch deeply involved in game of Hydrate That Athlete. I'm losing. Here's how to play: On the coffee table, which is two and a half feet away from me, is a glass of water. The object is to get the contents of the glass into my stomach. Rules: I can use my hands and all ten fingers. I can use my lips. I can even use a straw. There is an abundance of successful strategies. The sit-up-and-reach is foolproof. The lean-and-stretch also works well, as does the lean-recline, though spillage can occur, costing the contestant valuable points. If the above strategies are overwhelming, there is the honey-can-you-come-over-here-and-hand-me-that-glass maneuver, but some players consider that cheating, or at least annoying.

This is not a difficult game, but the opponent is ruthless. Its name is Exhaustion, and unless you do what I do for a living, it will be hard for you to imagine what a formidable opponent it is. Exhaustion's goal is to do everything possible to keep the athlete from replenishment and recovery.

Before starting the game, I warm up with some motivational phrases. *The water is good for me. I need the water. The water is my friend. It will make me a better athlete.*

Lying on the couch, I let my arm hang over the edge of the cushions and gesture vaguely in the direction of the coffee table. Deciding against the sit-up-and-reach method, I first try telepathy, mentally willing the glass to move closer. I concentrate on the whole glass. When this proves tiring, I shift my concentration to the glass's decorative stripes and will each color individually. *Come on, wide blue stripe, you can do it … closer … closer. Move your ass, skinny green stripe.* Wondering if this negativity has an impact on telepathy, I switch tactics. *Nice glass of water, come this way! Pretty water, good water!* Nothing happens. Exhaustion 1, Athlete 0.

I switch to a moaning strategy. Moaning indicates that I not only want the water but understand its importance. Moaning should be low and steady, so as not to frighten the glass. I add finger stretching toward the coffee table, but keep my shoulder in place. Still the glass doesn't budge. Exhaustion 2, Athlete 0.

Steve, who is visiting from New York City and enjoying the Tucson backyard garden, cannot hear my moaning or see my valiant effort. Surely, if he were closer, he would rush to my aid and hand me the victory. As it is, I retract my aching, dangling arm. A setback. I tuck my arm beside me and my eyelids lower. Exhaustion 3, Athlete 0.

The back door slams. Steve has come to my salvation! I quickly decide on a strategy of whining with loving undertones.

"Hi, honey pie, can you come here for a sec? You look so rugged in those pruning gloves. Hey, hon, could you do me a favor? Could you hand me that glass of water?"

"The one right in front of you?"

"Have you been working out? You look so strong!"

"That glass? Two feet away from you?"

"Kiss me, you gardening god."

"Kathryn, reach over and drink the damn water."

Exhaustion 4, Athlete 0.

After another fifteen to twenty minutes of semiconsciousness alternating with short naps, an odd sensation of divine intervention courses through me. Without warning, I sit up, reach over, drink the glass of water, put down the glass, and fall back on the couch. With five points for my last-second heroics, I nip my opponent 5 to 4.

"Steve, I won!" I call toward the kitchen.

"What were you playing?"

"I don't really know."

"What did you win?"

"Water."

"Good job. You should nap."

Other versions of this game are available as *Nourish That Athlete!*, *Bathe That Athlete!*, *Nap Athlete Nap!*, and, coming soon, *Cranky Athlete III: Lactic Acid Warriors.*

6

TWO AND A HALF WOMEN

November 2006

Which of these objects weighs 10,805 grams?

a) Nicole Ritchie
b) A 1987 Yugo
c) My left leg
d) All of the above

The answer is d) All of the above, although c) My left leg, is really the only one I can prove. And my 10,805 grams o' leg do not even include the weight of the bones; it's just the muscle, fat, and tissue of that particular limb. And my entire body? A whopping 59,431 Olympic hopeful grams of potential, baby. Which is far more interesting than saying I weigh 134 pounds.

I obtained my left leg's precise weight by way of:

a) Whiskey, a sharp saw, and strong sutures

b) A psychic

c) Spam

d) The DEXA Body Composition scan at the Canyon Ranch Peak Performance program in Tucson, Arizona

It's d) again! I could easily spend the rest of this book talking about the body fat percentage of my fourth toe or the muscular circumference of my armpit, but I fear sharing such fascinating knowledge would cause the rest of my readers' lives to feel boring. And I don't want that. The story of the Canyon Ranch Peak Performance program, however, is too interesting to keep to myself.

Elite athletes—if I may be so bold as to include myself—are pretty good when it comes to knowing our bodies. We're like big babies. We know when we're tired, hungry, cranky, and need to be changed. Usually, we know how to meet these needs in the heat of competition. But medical technology has developed so much over the past few decades that "knowing the body" has risen to a whole new level. For example, I always knew I needed to consume food during a long bike ride, but I had no idea I needed exactly 61 grams of carbohydrates, 200 milligrams of sodium, 210 calories, and 36 ounces of electrolyte-enhanced fluid per hour for my particular 59,431 grams of self.

In November 2006, I spent four jam-packed days at the Canyon Ranch Peak Performance program in Tucson getting poked, prodded, and X-rayed by the best sports medicine team in the country. After all, if I'm trying to be an Olympian it's probably a good idea to see if I'm physically capable of meeting such demands. Before I went any further in my quest, both ESPN and I thought it was a good idea to measure my athletic capacity. Finding out I have some genetic inability or some rare disease would definitely be a bummer, but likely something I should know now rather than later.

The athlete side of my brain was confident the tests would turn up good things. The creative writer lobe, however, envisioned ultrasounds showing alien gene mutations and large orbs of inexplicable debris clawing through my half-human bloodstream. I'm not sure the

IOC allows extraterrestrials to compete at the Olympics, so you can understand my concern.

In addition to getting my body physically examined, my ego was in need of an evaluation, too. After pentathlon, team handball, track cycling, and the Ironman World Championship stuck their daggers into my athletic pride, I hoped a Canyon Ranch psychologist might cauterize some of the wounds.

I was generously welcomed as a guest to the Canyon Ranch ultra-lovely spa resort in the foothills of the Catalina Mountains in Tucson. Not only did I get free meals and board (courtesy of ESPN), but I was allowed free cookies at the cafe any time I wanted! At the Peak Performance center, medical director Dr. Steve Brewer and sports medicine specialist Dr. Rich Gerhauser examined my blood, bones, muscles, and organs. Registered dietician Hana Feeney broke down my nutritional needs. Life management therapist Peggy Holt bravely wandered into my psychological territory. Director of exercise physiology Mike Siemens set me up with a cycling-specific weight training program and physiologist Teri Albertazzi kindly explained all their data to me in slow, easy terms after I asked her to speak to me like a four-year-old. (There were a lot of numbers with decimal points and really big, science-y terms like "ventilatory threshold capacity.") The stats basically measured how much athletic potential there is inside my muscles, heart, and mind. And it turns out I don't come from the planet Gixtharoog after all. Which is too bad, as that would have explained a lot—even more than getting kicked in the head.

The DEXA body scan contraption is a giant slab of plastic and metal that resembles a human-size photocopy machine. I strip down and put on two long, flowing hospital gowns that make me look like some sort of religious figure, then lie on the scanner. A motorized bar slowly travels over the length of me, not unlike the metal detecting wands used by airport security agents. Five minutes later, this machine knows more about me than I do, from the weight of each vertebra to the density of my entire skeleton. This funky little scanner has deduced that I am rather healthy inside. "Actually, your bones are twenty-five times denser than most people your age," Dr. Steve tells me. The knowledge of my super-strong bones deposits some positive juju in my overdrawn ego account.

"So I'm kind of like Bruce Willis in *Unbreakable*?" I ask.

"Um, no."

Well, it's something to work toward. Olympics first, superhero later.

Next, I head into the nurse's office for a look-the-other-way-while-I-stick-this-foot-long-needle-in-your-arm blood test. Usually, blood tests provide stats on iron levels, red and white blood cell counts, and whether or not someone partakes in various naughty activities. The peak performance blood test goes so far as to spit out three sheets of data filled with words like globo-oxy-oloride-ochine, measuring sixty-seven different components of my blood and whether or not such things should even be in my blood. It even tests for something called homocysteine, which could tell me if I'm at risk for cardiovascular diseases. Like my dense bones, my blood seems to be problem-free and nothing unexpected has been found swimming among my cells. Just some good old DNA, platelets, and sugar.

Then, trading my Medical Jesus robes for gym clothes, I meet up with exercise physiologists Mike and Teri (a fellow cyclist and triath-lete, and a training partner of mine) to determine my physical strengths and weaknesses in a muscle-function assessment session. I flashback to my team handball experience, wondering if Mike and Teri are going to make me do manly-man pull-ups or attack me with fat calipers. Instead, they put me on a leg press machine that is hooked up to a computer.

"We're going to do three tests," Mike informs me. "The first is a four-second leg output drill."

Four seconds? My kind of test!

Mike has me push the computerized leg press machine with all my super dense might for four seconds, one leg at a time. The machine goes nowhere, but a little line on the computer screen chart dips and climbs with every molecule of my effort. After just four seconds, each leg is exhausted. Naturally, we do it over and over again.

Drill number two is more traumatic; I'm asked to do twenty leg press repetitions of sixty pounds, as fast as I possibly can. This time the machine moves like a regular leg press. The weight blocks zoom up and down and the computer displays colorful zigzagy data and shiny numerical outputs that English majors like myself don't comprehend, but are visually stimulated by. Sixty pounds is not all that heavy for a leg press exercise. But doing it in time to the frenzied pace of Richard Simmons on crack proves rather exhausting. Of course, we do this again. And again.

The most entertaining evaluation, however, is the one that measures my muscular coordination. On the computer screen is an image similar to the old Atari game Breakout. A little ball bounces up to the top of the screen, then down again, and my job is to move the little dash mark beneath the ball so that it bounces back up again. But this is no hand-eye coordination test. I have to move the dash mark by pushing one foot against the leg press platform. It's a video game for my thighs. After Breakout, we do two more coordination tests similar to Frogger and Q-Bert, and it is soon obvious that my right quadriceps easily outplay my left quadriceps. Actually, my left leg really tanks. I ask Mike and Teri what the normal difference is for left-right strength and coordination.

"Most people have about 10 percent discrepancy between their right and left leg strength. Elite athletes usually have between a 3 and 5 percent difference," Mike says.

"And mine?"

"Your right leg is 13 percent stronger than your left." Instant ego bank withdrawal.

"Thirteen percent?! I'm that abnormal?" Must have been my fifteen-year figure skating career, with all that g-force from a million right-leg landings. And two million crash landings.

"Yeah, but we'll fix it."

I envision myself carrying a brick in my left pocket for a year. Or cycling with one leg. Mike assures me I'll "even out" on a weight-training program. He gives me a sheet of graph paper on which are written various weights I'll lift every other day for the next two years: bench presses, calf raises, squats, lats, bis, tris, back, abs, hips, and flexibility intervals. My eyes feel stronger just looking at it.

Taking a break from the physical testing, I spend an afternoon session with Peggy, Canyon Ranch's very talented sports psychologist. She asks me about any insecurities or issues I have with competing. I tell her that the mental side of competition is one of my stronger areas, but that I've been very bummed out about my digestive issues during Ironmans (which have forced me to walk marathons). After suffering heat stroke in a half-Ironman race 2001, my stomach tends to rebel in all races warmer than eighty-five degrees. Usually the difficulty starts on the running portion of an Ironman. I tell Peggy I'm concerned this could affect my cycling races. Peggy asks me to think about a stomach-suffering race and then re-imagine the scene so the problem is fixed. I hesitate, unsure if Peggy has the authority to put me in a psych ward. I risk it.

"Okay, Peggy," I begin haltingly, "so there I am, on the bike at the Hawaii Ironman. It is very hot and my stomach is not tolerating food or drink. I fear my run will be a disaster. Then, all of a sudden, a deafening screech echoes through the sky! I look up, and a griffin—half eagle, half lion—is barreling toward me just like it did toward brave Perseus in my favorite eighties movie ever, *Clash of the Titans*. The griffin claws my stomach out with sharp talons and drops my entire intestinal tract onto the hot Hawaiian lava rocks adjacent to the bike lane. My intestines sizzle. The gaping hole in my torso magically heals. And I haven't stopped pedaling once during my entire disembowelment! The griffin gives me a high five (with its wing, not its talon) and I head into the transition area, then cruise to a victorious marathon and my newly grown stomach never, ever bothers me again. The end."

Peggy looks at me oddly for a moment before saying, "Next session, let's try some hypnotherapy."

"Okay!" I agree. That should turn up some fun stuff. But she'll never get my griffin. He lives very deep inside my mental happy place.

My final evaluation in the Canyon Ranch Peak Performance program is a fitness test that will measure my VO2 max—the maximum volume of oxygen that an athlete can use while giving total physical effort. It will be assessed by the dashing Dr. Rich. Every doctor at Canyon Ranch happens to be dashing and healthy, which I do not believe is a coincidence.

"This test will tell you how much oxygen can be absorbed into your blood and thus utilized by your muscles," Dr. Rich explains.

"Pardon?"

"Your VO2 max will tell us whether you've got the horsepower of a Ferrari or a Pinto."

To find my VO2 information, Dr. Rich gives me a cardiometabolic stress test. After the nurse sticks six electrodes in various locations around my torso, I climb on a stationary bike that is programmed to record watts, heart rate, revolutions per minute, and other medical and cycling data.

"Every minute, I will increase the wattage of the bike, making it harder for you to pedal," Dr. Rich says. "Keep going until you can no longer keep the pedals moving above sixty revolutions per minute."

"Okay!" Finally, a fitness test with no horses, swords, balls, or push-ups. I'm beyond psyched.

"The nurse will take your heart rate and blood pressure every minute. I will hold up a chart and you will point to your perceived exertion." Dr. Rich shows me a chart with categories printed in block letters: very easy, easy, moderate, difficult, very difficult, extremely difficult.

"How long do these tests usually take?" I ask, thinking I'll be on the bike for an hour or two.

"About fourteen minutes," he says, "maybe fifteen."

Ha! You think I'm going to exhaust myself after fifteen minutes?! Hellooo, I'm an endurance athlete, doc!

Clearly, my ego has learned nothing from pentathlon, handball, and the flying five-hundred-meter sprints of track cycling. Everything that sounds simplistic turns out to be the devil's wrath bestowed upon me.

Before getting on the bike, I'm given a breathing test, where I have to exhale as hard as possible into a little white tube. I do as I'm told, and instantly find a new respect for breathing. It is a lot harder to do when people stand over you, taking notes. I am then outfitted with something that goes over my face and resembles a jock strap. The plastic seal around my mouth and nose are to ensure I breathe directly into the machine that calculates my oxygen use. The test begins. I pedal. My brain comes along for the ride.

MINUTE 1: *Easy squeezy! Feels like they haven't even turned the bike on.* I point to "very easy" on the clipboard.

MINUTE 2: *Are you kidding me? I could do this with one leg.* Very easy

MINUTE 3: *I wonder if Letterman will want to interview me?* Very easy

MINUTE 4: *I'm going to blow these doctors away, yo.* Very easy

MINUTE 5: *Finally, a little resistance to the pedals. Still, too much leg flailing.* Very easy

MINUTE 6: *Okay, this is my three-hour pace. Nooo problem.* Easy

MINUTE 7: *"It's the eye of the tiger, it's the thrill of the fight, it's ..."* Easy

MINUTE 8: *And in first place, from the United States, Kaaaaathryn Bertiiiiiiiine.* Easy

MINUTE 9: *Letterman first, then Oprah. Maybe Conan if my schedule clears.* Easy

MINUTE 10: *Yeah! Okay! I was wondering when the sweat would start.* Moderate

MINUTE 11: *Whoa, did he just triple the watts?!* Moderate

MINUTE 12: *I ... will ... not ... point ... to ... "difficult."* Moderate

MINUTE 13: *Wih ... nu ... poi ... tu ... dificuh ...* Moderate

MINUTE 14: *Ghunhhh ... ghunhhh ... ghunhh h... You want me to try to lift a finger and point to that freaking clipboard? Are you out of your extremely intelligent mind, Dr. Jekyll?*

MINUTE 15:30.2 ... Difficult

I slouch over the handlebars, heaving whatever oxygen I can get into my strappy little jock mask. After nine minutes, my pulse—which reached 190—settles to 108 and drops slowly from there. I'm spent. Exhausted. Toast for the rest of the day. Later, in Dr. Rich's office, he presents me with the evidence.

"Most women your age [thirty-one] have a VO2 max of about thirty," he says.

I shudder. Memories of high school math teachers flood my brain: *Most students in this class average about eighty-five. You average thirty, Miss Bertine.* Great. My VO2 max is about to go for the jugular of my Olympic dream.

"Your VO2 max is seventy-one."

"Seventy-one? So that's like a C-minus?"

"No, it means you have the lung capacity of two and a half women."

Oh. What? Really? *Two and a half women?!*

Dr. Rich proceeds to tick off the names of Olympic women with VO2 maxes in the low seventies: Grete Waitz, Joan Benoit Samuelsson, Mary Decker Slaney.

"Lance Armstrong has a VO2 of eight-five, but he's got more height and mass than you," he says, "so comparatively you're not that far off from him."

I get the happy shivers. Later, I race into the lobby and call my boyfriend.

"Steve! Both our dreams have come true. I'm two and a half women!"

"Fantastic, hun!"

"And a griffin tore out my stomach!" I add.

"That's most excellent. Well done!"

"And I get to come back to Canyon Ranch once a month for psychological evaluations!"

"Right then, luv!"

While Steve's words are supportive (and very British), I'm starting to notice he may be somewhat disengaged from my quest. We've fallen into a pattern in which I tell him all about my crazy athletic days and he offers comment, but not much in the way of questions, nor does he share much of his own thoughts and desires. However, after a relationship in which my inebriated ex-fiancé enjoyed dishing out slurred diatribes on the subject of my general worthlessness, the immediate consequence is that I act like I'm grateful for anyone who says hello to me. I keep these new thoughts to myself, but make a private vow to dig a little deeper into the actual Needs, Wants, and Will Not Tolerates of my relationships. That should be fun. Maybe my inner griffin can tear into that one.

VO2 tests, blood samples, body scans, and thigh games. At the end of my Canyon Ranch stay, I feel ten times more confident of my abilities as an athlete ... and pretty darn psyched about finally writing an ESPN column where I don't end up losing, falling, or sucking at my given task. Despite my inability to throw, block, swordfight, sprint, or steer horses, it turns out I *do* have potential as a high-performance athlete. I just needed to get my horsepower in the right vehicle, and it's looking like that'll be a bike. So, I'm going to take all of my 59,431grams of flesh, my heavyweight bones, and my oxygen-happy lungs out for a training ride and see if that gets me one step closer to my Olympic dreams.

🚲   🚲   🚲

When I leave Canyon Ranch, it takes me only a few minutes to get home. I live just five miles from the Canyon Ranch resort, and I'm easing into my new life in Tucson. After a year of friends' couches, I am finally beginning to feel settled—settled enough as an Olympic hopeful can be, between bouts of travel, racing, and training. I rent a small house on the east side of the city, where it takes less than ten minutes to bike my way out of traffic and head to the hills of the Saguaro Monument or the base of Mount Lemmon. The house comes mostly furnished with a few tables, beds, lamps, and so forth. Sitting is tricky, however; I do not own a couch. I've spent the past eight years in the often squalid world of dream-chasing, surviving on a four-figure income and carting my life around in cardboard boxes. I'm not complaining. I've never been big on bourgeois assets. But at thirty-one, somehow I've amassed three bicycles, yet until now haven't owned one single chair or other sitting apparatus. Desks have come and gone, always of the plywood kind that require assembly. Solid oak and maple seem so flashy. I had a futon once. That was nice. Those were good times.

So now I have a roof over my head, non-ramen food in my cupboards, and a game plan to cycle my way to Beijing in 2008. It is time to make my first grownup purchase. A bed? Nope. A dresser? Nah. Like Ralphie and his coveted .22 Red Rider air rifle in *A Christmas Story*, there was only thing I wanted: a La-Z-Boy convertible recliner couch, model number 2342, otherwise known as "the Beverly." She is the most beautiful thing I've ever seen.

There's a creed among endurance athletes preparing for competition: If you are standing, sit down. If you are sitting, lie down. If you are lying down, elevate your feet. Order a pizza when available. Rest is a vital component among the endurance crowd, so sofas and ottomans are just as vital as gym memberships and protein powder. To be able to physically give all we have, we need to conserve all we have in between bouts of giving. So one day, in a furniture gallery in central Tucson, Beverly called out to me. "Kathryn, sit on me. Rest your weary gluteus maximus." I have a rule that I always obey furniture that speaks, so I wandered over to Beverly and sank into her invitation. Cushions so deep and fluffy! Armrests so soft and inviting! So different from the stiff-backed furniture I grew up wi— what's this?

And there it was. On the side of Beverly, a wooden handle jutted from her velvety, microsuede flank like a lever of forbidden pleasure.

I pulled. Suddenly the couch let go of all inhibitions and ricocheted into a deep recline, swinging forth a foot stool with such command that I had no choice but to elevate my fatigued calves and aching feet. Somewhere overhead, angels began to sing.

"Do you offer same-day delivery?" I asked the sales lady.

As if having furniture wasn't joyous enough, I had a kitchen too. For the past year of my Couch Tour, cooking full meals was a luxury I could not often afford. I got by with minifridges, microwaves, portable electric kettles, and leftovers. Truthfully, these things suited me just fine. Meeting my nutritional needs as an athlete is always a priority, but I am a rather uninspired chef. I like eating, but I don't like spending time in the kitchen. I don't understand people who find kitchens peaceful and cooking relaxing. These are often the same people who think fruit qualifies as a dessert. I cannot relate. What on earth is relaxing about open flames, sweltering ovens, sharp knives, and constantly watching pots to see if the contents are about to escape, implode, or evaporate? How is *that* fun? And while we're on the topic, fruit can go on dessert. It can go next to dessert. It can go in dessert. But fruit cannot be dessert. It is *fruit*. So until the day comes when we mix Raisinettes, Goobers, and Sno-Caps together and call it a salad, don't tell me fruit is a dessert. Fruit is fruit. Dessert is dessert. How is that *not* understood?

I am not a normal person. I am reminded of this on the first night I try to make a meal in my Tucson home. I have a slab of frozen salmon from Trader Joe's. All I had to do was put it in the oven. I did that well. Even remembered to unwrap it. The problem arose in taking it out. Outwitted by my oven mitt, my finger touched the metal pan. I yelped and watched the salmon slip slide to the floor. Kerplop. A normal person would get a mop and a garbage pail. I got a fork and a cushion. A normal person, upon dropping dinner, thinks, *Bummer.* They do not look at the salmon and think, *Play it where it lies.* But I am not a normal person. I am an endurance athlete. And when an athlete is hungry, an athlete is hungry. Besides, throwing away the salmon would not only be wasteful, it would force me to admit defeat. And I'm far too competitive for that, be it an Ironman or a linoleum salmon. I will not admit defeat, even if I am alone in my own kitchen. Not this year. Not ever. No way. I am Kathryn Bertine, Olympic hopeful, persona non normal, two and a half women, occupant of a home with furniture. I am an athlete. There are no shortcuts to greatness. There is only one way to be the best: to own up to adversity and play it where it lies. Dinner included! Telling sports psychologist optional!

WATER BREAK

FAN MAIL

The top five comments or questions I received from my ESPN readers:

1.

Good luck making it to the Olympics.
I hope ESPN doesn't make you work out too hard.
—Justin H., Wheeling, West Virginia

2.

I have two questions.
Do you have a six-pack and are you stronger
than a Denver Broncos cheerleader?
—Drew B., 12, Westminster, Colorado

3.

If the Olympics don't work out for you,
you should try to be a writer.
—Dan P., Oakland, California

4.

Try not to wear a ponytail too much.
You'll go bald.
—Mom, Bronxville, New York

5.

I think you should try to get to
the Summer Olympics in luge.
—countless readers across the world

7

SACK OF POTATOES

December 2006

After my first few articles were posted on espn.com, there was an outpouring of support. Total strangers apparently enjoyed reading about me falling down on handball courts and shriveling up like a prune in Kona. These nice folks, and the occasional weirdo, wrote in and offered suggestions on what Olympic sports they believed I should try. Many encouraged me to go for cycling, some thought I should stick to Ironman triathlon (overlooking the fact that it isn't in the Olympics), but the most popular suggestion was that I should try the sport of luge. *How hard could it be?* people asked.

Pretty hard, seeing as luge happens to be a winter sport and therefore is not part of the Summer Olympics in Beijing. Or any other summer games, for that matter. So I responded with thanks and let the matter slide.

Until I received an angry e-mail from the head representatives of USA Luge. This was a direct result of one of my earlier online columns, in which one of my ESPN editors had made a quip about luge, writing, "Bertine's chances of making it to Beijing require her to find an *easy* sport that is the summer equivalent of the two-man luge."[1]

Well now. After getting my ass handed to me in four little-known sports, I knew better than to call any sport easy. My editors, though, went for the punchline. The remark was certainly not lost on USA Luge's Fred Zimny, the national team manager. He wrote:

Kathryn,

I would like to invite you to come and try the "easy" sport of doubles luge this winter. In fact, doubles is actually more difficult than singles luge, so I would love to have you even come try singles. We have two tracks in the USA, in Lake Placid, New York, and Park City, Utah, where you could experience luge first hand. I hope you will take me up on this offer so that you will be able to write an informed and educated review of your experience rather than the off-the-cuff, titillating comments in your most recent ESPN article. I hope to hear from you but I do not expect to.

Fred Zimny
National Team Manager, USA Luge

Fred's psychology worked, and his timing was even better. The start of the road cycling season was still weeks away. Even my new cycling coach was for it. "Dude, you gotta try the luge, man," Jimmy Riccitello said. "They go a hell of a lot faster than cyclists. Luge. That's some crazy lookin' shit."

In addition, ESPN thought it would be a great idea to show the world just how "easy" luge is … or isn't. Even better, I could somewhat

---

1 After the tragic death of Georgian slider Nodar Kumaritashvili at the Vancouver Winter Games in February 2010, it's undeniably clear that "easy" and "luge" don't belong in the same sentence. I hope this chapter helps educate those who dare judge a sport before trying it.

please all those readers who wanted me to luge myself to the Summer Olympics. Also, my curiosity about the sport awakened a sleeping What If: *Hey, what if you're actually good at this sport?* Okay, then. Luge time.

In mid-December, I head to upstate New York to see what kind of skill it takes to slide down a 1,455-meter ice track, and whether I possess any of that particular skill. The USA Luge organization kindly houses me at the Olympic Training Center in Lake Placid, which is a cozier version of the larger OTC in Colorado Springs. Lake Placid's facility incorporates the dorms, cafeteria, gyms, courts, and weight rooms in one long, ranch-style building, unlike the spread-out campus of Colorado Springs. Fireplaces and snowflake decorations and people at the front desk who know all the athletes by name make the Lake Placid center very homey. There are posters of the 1980 U.S. hockey team on nearly every wall. The cafeteria does not have a dessert carousel (sad!), but it does have stationary shelves of cake and pudding (happy!). The dorm room hallways (this week filled with a gaggle of European, male, teenage Nordic skiers who keep their equipment in their rooms) have lingering bacterial fumes that trump the New Jersey Turnpike and the Handball House, combined. Unlike the OTC in Colorado, there is no iron fence around the Lake Placid complex. Just snowy fields and a single-lane road with very little traffic that leads to the off-site winter sports complexes that hosted the 1932 and 1980 Winter Olympics.

Jon Lundin, the PR manager for USA Luge, is in charge of shuttling me to practice. He is very nice to me. This makes me uneasy in light of the ESPN editors' luge insult, which goes unmentioned. I get the feeling that Jon and I both know the karma monster is lurking nearby. At 8 A.M. on a chilly, northeastern winter morning, Jon brings me the appropriate luge attire, which I am instructed to put on over my long underwear: a shiny yet slightly rubbery Lycra body suit with *USA Luge* emblazoned on the shin, funny little crooked booties, hole-ridden gloves no thicker than the gardening kind, and a tight-fitting black helmet—with no face shield. We drive the ten-minute route to the Olympic Sports Complex track at Mt. Van Hoevenberg.

What unfolds before me is a mile-long jumble of large, whitish-gray tubing that snakes its way up a steep Adirondack mountainside. The structure looks random, as though Paul Bunyan (or possibly a vegetarian Yeti) had dropped a strand of spaghetti onto a cliff. The track has a vertical drop of three hundred feet and seventeen curves, which have comforting names like Devil's Highway, Shady, and The Labyrinth.

Jon puts his Ford Ranger into four-wheel-drive and we creep up the snowy mountain. He takes me to Start Five, which is only a third of the way up the track. I'm surprised USA Luge isn't pushing me off from the top with a heavy slap on the back and a sarcastic "Have fun." Before I'm even out of Jon's truck, I realize the grave mistake of referring to luge as simple. My editors must have felt very brave sitting there at their desks, which have a vertical drop of two and a half feet.

While still in the car, Jon entertains me with a story about a female reporter from a Los Angeles morning news show who came to try the luge a few weeks ago. "We took her up to Start Five, got her on the sled, and she sat there ... and sat there ... and sat there. Then she got up and drove to the airport. We haven't heard from her since."

At Start Five, I meet my coach for the week, Lake Placid native Duncan Kennedy, who is a three-time Olympian, a World Cup champion, and a three-time national champion. With a record like that, I expect some level of egotism and definitely some sort of revved-up extreme personality, which I imagine goes with the territory of people involved in eighty-mile-per-hour sports. Duncan fails all these expectations. He is not only egoless and übermellow, but he is an extremely talented coach and kind person who speaks soothingly when pushing someone down the icy death chute. In the Olympics, Duncan placed fourteenth in 1988, tenth in 1992, and was heavily favored to medal in 1994 when he crashed on his third run and was out of the competition. His second run would have placed him fourth overall. He speaks of his results positively, without disappointment and without regrets. For many athletes, coming in fourth is almost harder than coming in last. Fourth place is so close to a medal, so close to the record books. But Duncan has no regrets.

"To win," he tells me, "I knew I had to drive aggressively. There was a high risk factor. I crashed. But I went for it." That's a true athlete, the one who takes risks to be the best. And, when those risks involve life and death, a true athlete will reevaluate his or her goals. Duncan stopped his career after the 1994 Olympics because of a condition called arterial vascular malformation (AVM), a congenital problem that in his case resulted in an enlarged artery in the neck. Scar tissue developed to the point where dizziness and sickness could become so severe that temporary partial paralysis set in. "Sometimes I was so incoherent it became impossible to tell the difference between dreams and reality," Duncan explained. When traveling eighty miles per hour and clothed in nothing but Lycra, that's not a line one should blur. When he got the diagnosis, Duncan retired and refocused his energy on coaching.

As I put on my flimsy, shiny luge outfit in the little warming hut near the start (it is twenty-seven degrees outside), there is a knock at the door. It's the karma monster! And she's brought a basketful of anxiety! I am suddenly fully aware that I'm about to get on a sled with sharp runners and hurl my Lycra'd body down an ice track. My nervous willies and my inner athlete battle it out for mind control:

What If I flip the sled? Flip it back and keep going.

What If everyone laughs at me? They already laugh at you.

What If I break myself in two? That would make a very good article.

I step out of the toasty hut and slip-slide along the snow in my slick rubber luge booties, which are only twenty millimeters thick, have no tread, and are turned inward. They're designed to keep the slider's feet in an aerodynamic position while racing. Bedroom slippers offer more support than luge booties, and I fear the consequence of any upcoming crash involving my feet.

Duncan shakes my hand and shows me the sled, a rickety looking thing of red and blue metal with a fabric seat the color and consistency of duct tape.

"This is a training sled," he says. "It sits up a little higher and doesn't go as fast as the others."

"How fast do the real sleds go?" I ask.

"About eighty to ninety miles an hour."

"And my sled?"

"About fifty. Sometimes more, sometimes less."

I try to think positive thoughts about going fifty miles an hour. This is the best my brain comes up with: *I bet a dog would love to stick its head out the window of a luge.*

Duncan shows me how to lie back in the seat cradle (pod) of the sled, keep my shoulders down, my neck up, and apply slight pressure against the runners (kufens) with my legs. He advises me not to try to steer just yet. I assure him I don't know how. Ahead of me, all I can see is the banked curve of the icy tunnel, which looks like some yellowish, intergalactic wormhole. From my adolescent waterpark experience, I'm pretty sure there is a nasty dropoff and a few hairpin turns in my very near future. Every now and then something dark and speedy shooshes by with a roar; it is one of the junior national team members, launching themselves from another starting area farther uptrack from me. The hollow, tunnel-like sound of the track is just as intimidating as the sight of it, and I can feel the rumbling quakes of the sliders' sleds rushing past Start Five. A tinny, vibrating voice comes over the loudspeaker, announcing the coordinates of each slider as they make their way down the track. "Sliding into Devil's Highway, coming through the Chicanes, into the Heart …" I suddenly feel like a racehorse at a derby—the idiot one that doesn't move when the gate opens. The loudspeaker says, "Track clear for Start Five, Kathryn."

Duncan says, "You ready?"

"For what?"

"To go down the track."

Okay. Hang on a minute. Usually, when we first begin a sport, we're given a watered-down version of the real thing. We play catch before we play baseball, we splash around in a pool before we do laps, we tackle the bunny slope before the black diamonds. But in luge, you're telling me the introduction to this sport involves sending a first-timer on a lone voyage with an eight-hundred-foot drop down the Olympic track wearing a Lycra outfit, booties, and gardening gloves, with the advice to "just relax and hold on tight?" Excuse me, Mr. Olympian, but aren't I supposed to have a formal lesson much longer than two minutes? Aren't you supposed to hold my hand? Perhaps assure me of a long and prosperous life?

Duncan notices my hesitation.

"Look, I could talk to you about steering, negotiating turns, and all that stuff but you'll have no idea what I'm saying until you understand what it's like to go down the track. You'll be fine." He motions to my scrap metal training sled. "A sack of potatoes could make it down on that thing."

I'm assuming he means whole potatoes, yet I'm envisioning mashed. Possibly scalloped. "How do I stop?" I ask.

"Someone at the bottom will catch you."

Catch me? I hadn't planned on being airborne. I picture a large man with a very strong butterfly net standing at the base of the track. As I settle into the pod, Jon comes running over and hands me some elbow pads.

"Here," he says. "If you friction-burn through these we'll get you new ones." I am unsure if he means new pads or new elbows. This seems like the right time to ask ESPN for a raise.

"Oh, and if you crash, try to hold onto the sled so it doesn't slam into you because that's really dangerous," Jon adds.

A raise *and* health insurance. Possibly dental.

"Ready?" Duncan asks again.

I spasm, which he interprets as a nod. Duncan gets behind the sled and pushes gently.

The following is a transcript of my thoughts and speech during my first thirty-three-second luge experience:

AAAAAAAAAAAAAAAAHHHHHHHHHHHHHHHHHHHH! SkofpotatoesSackofpotatoesSackofpotatoesNervousGigglegigglegiggleAH-HHHHHHHEEEEENervousGigglegigglegiggleAhhhhhhhhhhhhhhhhh-hhhhhIhateyouESPNWhoooooheeeeeeehaaaaaRickyBobbyGigglegigglegig-gleIloveyouESPNAhhhhhIhavenoideahowtostopthisthingAHHHHHHHH-HHHHSackofpotatoesSackofpotatoesGigglegiggle......

The roar of the wind dies out in my ears, my velocity slows to a dribble, my innards realign, and I notice I am neither airborne nor caught inside Paul Bunyan's butterfly net. The sled has calmly slowed down. My brain catches up with my body and lets loose a word I did not expect: *AGAIN! AGAIN! AGAIN! I wanna go again!!!!*

My half-minute run is over, and as I sit up on the sled, a track employee jumps into the icy shaft and stops my duct-tape-mobile with his foot just as I start to slide backward down the embanked finish chute. I ungracefully scramble out of the track, giggling stupidly. Jon, smiling, takes my sled and asks, "How was it?"

"I need to do that again. Now. Right now. I mean … please? Please, Jon? Can I go again? How many more times can I go?" One hit and I'm a luge junkie. All hail sport, the greatest, baddest dealer of pure endorphins.

That morning, I get to take three more runs down the frozen track; use rotates on a tight schedule among the athletes of luge, bobsled, and skeleton. I continue to make it down in one piece, all my potatoes un-scalloped. My nerves subside only a fraction and my heart rate gallops ridiculously each time Jon drops me off at the start. Of all the sports I've ever tried, luge is the only one where the euphoric endorphin high is instantaneous and present *during* the event. Not after, not due to victory, not before due to nerves, but during. Luge, however, isn't all wheeeeeeee. Before the chutes and tunnels and turns, you must conquer the most technical element of luge: the start.

Housed in what looks like a glorified garage in back of the luge corporate offices, Lake Placid also boasts an indoor luge track, one hundred meters long, where sliders practice their start techniques. The mini track resembles a skateboarder's halfpipe: two high ends with a dip in the middle. One end of this start track is frayed into three sections so that three athletes can set up their starts simultaneously. Coach Gordy Sheer, who, with his partner Chris Thorpe, won the 1998 Olympic silver medal in doubles luge, shows me the six parts of the luge start: block, compression, pull, extension, push, paddle.

"The start is like a golf swing," Gordy tells me. "You could spend your whole life trying to perfect all the variables."

Yay! Another sport that requires lifetime participation to achieve greatness! He gives me a pair of proper luge gloves with tiny nails in the fingertips, which help grip the ice during the "paddle." They look like something a young Freddy Krueger would enjoy, and I learn the hard way not to scratch my face while wearing them. Within minutes, I also understand how intricate, technical, and vital the start is to the rest of the run. Not only are my starts slow, but I am unable to keep the sled straight after pushing off. I bounce between the halfpipe borders, causing no external damage but surely adding to my various internal dislodgings. I have not mastered one bit of skill in the hour-long luge-start practice, and can only imagine how many years it must take to get it right.

Duncan and Gordy agree. Luge is such a difficult, intricate sport that, while it takes years for an athlete to become proficient, luge also expects a lot from a person right off the bat.

"This is a sport where you have to commit immediately," Duncan says. "You can't go easy, you can't go slow, and you can't put on the breaks. There is no hit-the-reset-button-and-start-over PlayStation mentality."

After my session at the start track, Jon takes me to the weight room of the Lake Placid OTC and introduces me to Brenna Margol, twenty-five, a two-time U.S. and North American luge champion with two Junior World Championship medals under her bad-ass luge belt. The minute I see her I know I'm in trouble. Brenna has a powerful build with thick shoulders and jacked arms. Like a team handball player. Oh no. My worst fear is realized—luge is an upper body sport. We spin for ten minutes on the stationary bikes to warm up before Brenna takes me through a typical luge weight circuit. I ask her where the other national team women are.

"Germany," Brenna says. "We could only have three women on the International World Cup Team, and I came in fourth by one one-thousandth of a second."

Wow! I had no idea time be broken down that small. Apparently, luge is the only sport that records times in thousandths of a second, whereas "slower" sports like bobsled, skeleton, speed skating, and swimming only deal in hundredth-of-a-second increments. It takes a certain strength of character to be involved with a sport that differentiates winners and losers by a nanosecond. Imagine training your whole life for the Olympics and missing it by half a blink. That would just plain hurt.

"It happens all the time," Brenna says.

In the Olympic Training Center weight room, we start with pull-ups. But not regular pull-ups. *Luge* pull-ups. A luge pull-up requires an extra wide grip that mimics the starting motion on the track (a vital component in saving every possible thousandth of a second). The proper stance for a luge pull-up is to detach one's arms from their shoulder sockets, place one arm at either end of the gym, and attempt a pull-up from there. At least that's how it feels. I manage five pull-ups, spotted. Brenna cranks out about fifteen, unspotted. This is before she attaches weights to our waists, and then I can barely eke out one.

"Don't worry," Brenna says, "I couldn't even do one when I first started."

"And how old were you then?"

"Eleven."

We then do extra wide push-ups, clean and jerks, bench presses, shoulder presses, triceps, biceps, abdominals, and neck strengthening. "We do a lot of neck work because there are some tracks in Germany that snap your head back with over four G's of force," Brenna says. From what I understand, four Gs is the equivalent of having a baby elephant camp out on your forehead. We also do some lat pulls specific to the luge start. Near the lat pull machine, an object catches my eye: A plastic figurine of Yoda hangs from a string tacked to the wall. It is a very random yet obviously prophetic sign that I'm on the correct life journey. Next to Yoda, Batman also dangles by a thread. I can only imagine what they talk about when no one else is in the weight room. Probably past dreams.

BATMAN: "Mr. Yoda, did I ever tell you I wanted to be an Olympic bobsledder?"

YODA: "Good at that you would have been."

BATMAN: "What about you? What would have been your Olympic dream?"

YODA: "Coxswain."

By the end of the circuit, I can feel my muscles coagulating and I understand tomorrow will hit me like a sledgehammer. What I don't yet understand is that tomorrow will also bring my formal physical evaluation, to see if I have the strength it takes to make the national luge team. Even though I'm dedicated to road cycling through 2008 and luge is not on the roster of any Summer Olympiad, the word "evaluation" immediately revs up my competitive drive. If there is to be a luge evaluation, then I want nothing more than to pass it. I can't imagine what, exactly, is on a luge evaluation, but I have learned enough not to predict such things, as I am always wrong.

Tomorrow arrives with its promised soreness. Before hitting the luge track, Brenna administers my physical testing program, which includes the standing long jump, overhead medicine ball toss, pull-ups, push-ups, sit-ups, a sit-and-reach flexibility test, and a three-hundred-meter run. Brenna decides to skip the outdoor run because it's snowing outside, and it's probably snowing outside because the karma monster knows I like to run.

Let me make this painfully brief: Out of a possible 128 points comprising the luge physical testing program, I get a zero. I get no credit for my dribbly pull-up (so sore from yesterday I could only do one today), no credit for my eleven wide-stance push-ups (twenty-two minimum requirement), no credit for my forty-three sit-ups in one minute (sixty is the mandate), and zilch for my nonexistent sit-and-reach test because I am too inflexible from yesterday's lifting to touch my toes. Or my knees. My ball toss and my long jump might have set an elementary school record, but it impresses no one in the national luge department. Zero.

I am a professional triathlete and I just scored a zero on a physical examination for the luge. Take that, you ESPN smarty-pants editors. We go back into the weight room, where I hang my head as I walk past Yoda and Batman. Brenna kindly tells me these tests are sport-specific skills and not many people start out doing any of them well. I have acute, sudden déjà handball vu.

"Let me guess, the luge federation would have gladly accepted me if I were twelve."

"Definitely," Brenna assures.

Pop quiz: Out of all the sports I've ever played in my life—figure skating, softball, track, cross country, ice hockey, rowing, modern pentathlon (swimming, running, shooting, fencing, horseback riding), team handball, track cycling, triathlon, road cycling, and luge—guess which one has left me the most bruised, battered, and sore? Fencing perhaps, with all those sword welts? Equestrian events, with all that chafing? Running and its injuries? Cycling, with its spectacular wipeouts? Skating collisions? Hockey checks? Attack of the giant handball women? No. My third day of attempting to simply lie down on a sled has left me looking like I went nine rounds with Mike Tyson. Or perhaps dated him.

Two things are now exceedingly clear: One, luge requires intricate and demanding skills. Two, I possess none of those particular skills. Never, in a million years, would I have guessed the sport of luge would kick my ass. Actually, it kicked my shins, my elbows, my shoulders, my ankles, my neck, my back, and it then beat the living daylights out of my knuckles. My rear end is just about the only body part to remain intact. Despite my shortcomings, I'm still hooked.

On this morning of luge practice, I decide to try to steer rather than just lie there like a beginner sack of potatoes. Like most of my decisions involving Olympic dreams, this proves to be bad. I apply what I think is gentle pressure to the right kufen with my right foot as I hug a right-hand turn. I immediately learn that "gentle pressure" is a relative term when one is traveling at the speed of light. The sled replies to my push with a quick and fast jolt and before I know it, I'm slamming back and forth from wall to wall like a reluctant pinball on its way down the Game Over chute. Each collision comes more painful than the last, thus obliterating my theory that hitting icy walls at fifty miles and hour might just feel slippery and painless and perhaps even ticklish. Yeah, and concrete is soft and fluffy. Just as I'm sure I'm going to "eighty-one," which is luge-speak for crash, I stop bouncing off the walls and trickle to a stop. The brunt of each impact is absorbed wholly by my knuckles, which stick out past the edges of the sled. I take off one of my wafer-thin gardening gloves. The topography of my right hand has changed instantly and dramatically. My formerly flattish knuckles have ballooned into purple mountain majesties. With ample waves of pain.

"Hey, *rodel* knuckle!" Jon proclaims. Apparently this knuckle battering happens often enough to have its own name. *Rodel* means "sled" in German, Jon informs me. I wonder how Germans say "I prefer cycling."

Although my wall-slamming excursions have been sufficiently punishing, the next few runs nearly *rodel* me to death as I come to understand the mental aspects of luge. If the mind is not relaxed, neither is the body. And neither is the sled. After nearly maiming my hands, I immediately comprehend the fortitude and courage it takes for a luge athlete to put such a physically painful instance behind them and slide down that death tunnel over and over again. That takes some crazy guts and hardcore devotion. Despite my beginner status and full body welts, Jon decrees I'm ready to go up to Start Four, a couple of hundred feet higher up the track.

"You'll definitely have to steer from Number Four, or you could hurt yourself," Jon informs me.

"But I've been *trying* to steer and I hurt myself," I lament.

"Oh," Jon says. "Well then, this shouldn't hurt that much more."

As I fling myself down the frozen chute quietly babbling about potatoes, with G-force tears streaming out of my eyes, my head shaking like a bobblehead doll, unable to see anything other than the vibrating, stumpy booties that are my feet, and contemplating the physics of decapitation, I feel an overwhelming desire to sing the praises of luge. This sport doesn't get an iota of the credit it deserves. The media only pays attention to luge for a few minutes every four years during the Olympics. As Duncan says, "A sport like luge is in a thankless environment. There are no endorsements, no multimillion-dollar contracts. There is no such thing as a luge groupie."

Duncan is right. While it is true that most people could make it down the last eight hundred feet of the track on a tourist-friendly training sled, the skill, power, strength, flexibility, and guts it takes to be good at luge is a whole other ballgame. And, unfortunately for me, it's a ballgame best started in childhood. Which is exactly when USA Luge is trying to get American kids hooked.

In the past five years, the luge federation has begun to actively recruit kids between the ages of eleven and fourteen, often traveling to ski mountains and setting up slalom-ish courses that kids go down on a safe, snow-adapted luge.

"You need to build people as much as athletes," Duncan believes. "Kids who commit to luge come home more disciplined. Parents want to know, 'What's in it for my kid? What are they gonna get out of this?' Well, there is extreme joy in seeing a fourteen-year-old kid going through a clean turn at seventy-five miles an hour, but it is the personality-building side of the sport that is underrated. I love it when parents tell me their kid came back from luge and cleaned up their room or helped with the dishes," Duncan says.

"We have a dream of opening small luge tracks—one hundred meters long—all around the country," "Duncan explains. "If someone wants to get into auto racing, they don't just hop into a Formula One car. Usually, they go to a go-kart track as a kid. We want to offer the same type of opportunity. Look at Germany—they've got five full-length tracks and their Olympic slider, Georg Hackl, is a national hero."

Like other "fringe" sports on the Olympic roster, a lot of internationally celebrated sports have very little exposure in the United States. After experiencing the rush of luge, I have no doubt this would be a wildly popular sport if ice tracks were as accessible as fields, pools, courts, and rinks. But until the spirits of lugers past materialize out of an Iowa cornfield, luge needs—and deserves—some serious financial and social attention. Duncan sums it up perfectly: "The most frustrating thing about the Olympics is that it is our only chance to showcase to the world what we're doing. The world's attention to our sport comes down to four runs, a total of three and a half minutes. The media comes in and bases an entire picture of the sport on a few pixels of information. Where were the cameras and the press when I was busting my ass to get there? That's where the heart of the sport lies."

I tell Duncan I'm going to work on a list of marketing ideas that will draw the American public irresistibly to the sport of luge. By the end of the week, this is what I've got:

- Sleds will be henceforth known as Rocketpods.
- Replace "booties" with Black Sox.
- The Lycra bodysuit will be referred to as the G-force Shield.
- The nail-infused gloves shall be Death Grips. Or Kruegers.
- Instead of referring to crashes as "eighty-one," overturned sleds will be referred to as Ice Hawk Down.
- The sport of luge, being a French term, should most definitely be renamed Freedom Sled.

On my last day at the luge track, Jon calms my nerves with a lovely story as we drive to Mt. Van Hoevenberg. He points to the old bobsled track just a few yards away from the one I've been sliding down. He tells me about the horrible fate of Italian athlete Sergio Zardini, an Olympian who, in 1966, was training with a Canadian bobsled team. Losing control while driving the bobsled, Zardini headed into a turn on the old track and flipped his sled. He was instantly decapitated.

"Don't worry, nothing like that has happened on the new track," Jon says, and then abruptly changes the subject. "Do you remember your comment about doubles luge being easy?"

"Um, no," I lie.

"Well, today you're going to slide doubles with Chris Mazdzer, our junior national champion."

"Will I hurt her?" I don't want to *rodel* anyone, especially a legitimate Olympic hopeful.

"I don't think so. Chris is 212-pound male teenager, and you'll be on the bottom," Jon informs.

"Is this legal?"

"Sure."

Chris Mazdzer, nineteen, and his eighteen-year-old doubles partner, Jayson Terdiman, are the reigning 2007 junior doubles World Cup bronze medalists. They are also two of the nicest and handsomest teenagers I've encountered—two more reasons luge should have groupies. Jayson gives me a quick lesson on doubles luge, emphasizing that the bottom man—which I will soon be—is in charge of stabilizing the sled, while upper-level Chris is in charge of steering. I assume I'm also in charge of not passing out. Or screaming hysterically into Chris's ear. Jayson agrees these things would be detrimental.

We walk over to Start Five and Jayson helps me settle into the flatter but wider doubles sled. I notice there is an indentation where Chris will rest his butt/lower back, and I'm relieved I won't be carrying all 212 pounds of him. Little do I know that I will still be carrying two persons' worth of G-force on my wimpy neck, which will result in my head bouncing along the ice more than once. (A coach will later tell me he thought I was unconscious during the doubles runs). Chris takes his place on the sled and leans back on me. I immediately notice that doubles luge is much warmer than singles luge. Jayson pushes us off, and all I see is sky, lights, tunnel ceiling, tarp, and the back of Chris's helmet. I make mental note to find out if tandem cycling is an Olympic event.

Chris and I make it down the track twice without glimpsing the Grim Reaper (although I make good friends with the Kneecap Rodeler), so we decide not to push our luck. After twenty runs and four days of luge, pull-ups, bruises, and frozen nostril hairs, my time as a slider has come to an end. I thank Jon, Duncan, Gordy, Brenna, Chris, Jayson, and manager Fred Zimny for such a terrifying and enlightening experience, and I promise to help spread the good word of luge, adding that I know lots of people who would probably like to push their preteen child down a luge track and thus get them involved in the sport. I apologize for myself and ESPN for ever referring to their sport as "easy" and promise not to do so again. They accept, and wish me luck in cycling.

Driving from Lake Placid to the Albany airport in my wicked purple Chrysler rental car, I get pulled over for going over eighty miles and hour on the New York State Thruway.

"Do you know how fast you were going, miss?" the trooper asks.

Seems that after a week of luge, my sense of speed is completely distorted. I wonder if the officer will find that funny? I pause for a moment, then decide to tell him the truth.

"Officer, I had no idea a PT Cruiser could go that fast."

He lets me go. So does the karma monster. For now, anyway. While my athletic future is a continuous gamble, this I know for sure: I've got seventeen months to make the Olympic trials, a million more lessons to learn, and one hundred more body parts to *rodel*. I have a feeling the bike will be kinder than the sled.

I mean, the Rocketpod.

8

BLOODY BIG FREAKIN' JELLYFISH

January 2007

My dropped salmon dinner in Tucson may or may not have been a foreshadowing of the next phase of my Olympic quest. I'm going to be an open water swimmer. At least for one day.

While my commitment to road cycling is still fully intact, the 2006 cycling season just ended and there is another month or so until the 2007 season starts. Wanting to keep my fitness level high during the winter months, I wondered if there were some cross-training options that would fit into my training schedule. Also, in the back of my mind lurked another quiet What If. *Yes*, the What If silently pointed out, *you are good at cycling. But you're not a terrible swimmer. Remember the pentathlon tryout and your sub-hour Ironman swims? What if there's something for you in swimming? This is your only time to see if swimming would be a better choice than cycling.* I know my What Ifs well. They don't go away until I live their questions.

As luck would have it, while visiting the Olympic Training Center for track cycling camp back in August, I happened upon *Olympic Beat*, a newsletter for resident athletes. Articles on the 2008 Beijing Games listed some interesting facts and statistics, such as that there will be twenty eight sports and 303 medals to win and roughly ten thousand McDonald's hamburgers to be consumed in the athletes' villages. Also mentioned was the fact that the sport of open water 10-kilometer swimming will make its Olympic debut in China.[2] Hmmm. Swimming is one of the two remaining sports on my I-already-know-how-to-do-this-sport-so-why-not-give-it-an-Olympic-try radar. Open water swimming … does anyone in the United States even know what open water swimming is? Could this first-time Olympic sport have so few U.S. participants that I'd possibly get a shot at the Olympic trials? A mental picture emerges. There I am, clambering out of the ocean and onto the beach, where I break into a Baywatchian sprint to the finish banner just a few yards up shore. Behind me there is no one, because that's how many other people have entered the Olympic trials. I win and—scene change—I'm stuffing my USA duffel bag into the overhead compartment of Air China flight 2008 while an attendant waits patiently to hand me a hot towel and the other first-class passengers point and whisper, "Isn't that the ESPN Olympian? Wow! She looks even weirder in person."

Unfortunately, it turns out the USOC is indeed aware of open water swimming, and USA Swimming has been cultivating talented distance swimmers for the open water event for quite some time. A bit more research turns up a difficult qualifying procedure for getting to trials, and I'm disheartened to find I'd need to swim 1,500 meters (in a pool) in less than sixteen minutes and fifty-four seconds, which is slightly faster than most fish. Rats. Once again, I'm a day late and a dollar short for my own dreams. But my curiosity remains piqued. I

2 The other four sports debuting in Beijing 2008: BMX cycling, women's steeplechase, women's team saber and foil fencing, and table tennis team event.

swim 2.4 miles under one hour for my Ironman races, but I've never actually swam ten kilometers (six miles) in open water before. Hmmmm. Could a six-mile ocean event be all that different from a two-hour pool workout or an Ironman swim?

I Google "open water swim races" and am not surprised when an Australian web site pops up. It is winter in Tucson and the rest of the United States. I'm going to have to venture across the equator if I want to attempt open water swimming before my cycling season begins. Leave it to the swim-crazy Australians to come up with an incredible aquatic event: The Bloody Big Swim, a 11.2-kilometer (7-mile) marathon swimming event just outside of Melbourne on January 11, 2007. The event's logo is a smiling shark wearing a yellow Speedo. I click on the entry tab and within twenty-four hours, race director Bruce Dixon has comped my entry, secured me the mandatory safety boat and kayaker to accompany me, and invited me to stay with his family the week before the race.

"I'll be there, Bruce!" I say. I love Australians. They are amazingly generous people.

"Wonderful!" he says. Then, in a failed attempt at lighthearted banter, I ask, "Bruce, there aren't any sharks where we'll be swimming, right?"

"Well, it is the ocean, Kathryn. But don't worry about that. We keep our sharks very well fed here, so they shouldn't bother you."

🚲   🚲   🚲

Two days before the race, I arrive in Melbourne and watch airport television as I wait for Bruce to pick me up. Three topics dominate the news stations: the tennis results of the Australia Open, George Bush's latest war "strategies," and the medical condition of a local man half-swallowed by a great white shark earlier that morning. The man was apparently spat out after repeatedly poking the predator in the eyes, presumably with the half of his body not yet inside the shark. If not, I make a mental note to check where exactly a shark's eyes are located and how best to reach them while inside the esophagus.

Bruce arrives and takes me to his home, where I meet his lovely wife, Vicki, and the three stunning Dixon daughters, Sari, Talia, and Romony. They are so beautiful that my ESPN photographer, Lucas, starts telling me that my Olympic dreams are the best thing that's ever happened to him.

The Dixon household is abuzz with pre-race chaos. There are 181 swimmers registered for the 11.2-kilometer Bloody Big Swim, and entrants are making last-minute calls to ask if they can still sign up or drop out, and what the weather forecast is for the race. It doesn't look good for Saturday morning, and Bruce is nervous.

"The winds are predicted to be over twenty knots with meter-high waves," he tells me.

I'm not fluent in knots, but I understand that nautically, lots of them are bad. As with hair or string. I try to say something positive and cheery. "Well, that'll be a good, athletic challenge for the swimmers!"

"Kathryn, look outside," Bruce says sternly.

Through the large picture window I see Port Philip Bay, where The Bloody Big Swim will take place. The water is crinkled with a heavy chop and the dark, rolling waves are breaking with frothy white caps. There are no swimmers bobbing about, let alone boats. Someone has clearly pissed off Poseidon. That, or Madame Pele from Hawaii has informed Bruce of my intention to race.

"It's supposed to be worse in the morning," he sighs.

I pat him on the shoulder. One thing I've learned about weather: You can't do a damned thing about it so there's no use worrying. Or so I tell myself from the nice, cozy couch in the warm, dry living room. Besides, what's so bad about wind? Or rain? We'll be underwater anyway. It all feels the same.

My swimming career started and ended the same day, back in 1986, at a local Westchester, New York, summer swim league meet. A teenage coach entered my eleven-year-old self in the 50-yard backstroke event. I won, and then was promptly disqualified. The coach explained that stopping at the shallow end to stand up and wave at parents was not permitted. I decided I liked figure skating better, where standing was encouraged, waving optional. Sixteen years passed before I took up swimming again, as a triathlete, and I fell in love with it once more.

But seven miles across an ocean bay was a whole new experience. How would I stay hydrated? Fueled? Motivated? What would it feel like to pull my arms and kick my legs for so long, and would certain aquatic mammals interpret my movement as that of dying prey? Before heading to Australia, I had consulted my friend Heather Royer, who successfully swam the 23.7-mile-long English Channel. If anyone had tips on how to swim a mere seven miles, she was the go-to girl. Along with advice on staying relaxed, hydrated, and stroke-efficient, here's what Heather recommended:

• Tying my water bottles to a rope so the kayaker could throw/ pull them as needed. This would save me time and energy not having to swim back and forth to the kayak.

• Using mouthwash to combat the effects of saltwater throat constriction and tongue swelling. (Also, it ensured fresh breath should a hot Aussie lifeguard give me CPR.)

• Eating an energy gel or other chewing-optional food every thirty to forty-five minutes to keep up my strength.

• Attaching a fun, colorful helium balloon to my escorting kayak to distinguish it from the others.

The idea of participating in a sport that uses happy, cheerful balloons immediately put me at ease. Little did I know there would be no need to distinguish my kayak from anyone else's.

That night at the pre-race meeting I find out I will be one of seven female competitors and one of twenty-five solo swimmers—the rest of the 181 entrants are swimming in teams or two or four, relay style. In the meeting hall, Bruce goes over the swim course, which begins off the town of Mornington and ends on the beach in Frankston, 11.2 kilometers away. There is a nervous but familiar energy among the competitors; a feeling of pre-race excitement ripples through the room. After a high-carb pasta dinner I head to bed early, like a good little competitor. I have strange dreams of sea life, likely brought on by my nerves and by the toilet paper in the Dixon's guest bathroom that is printed with pastel-colored jellyfish. At 5:30, I wake to the sound of pounding rain and howling winds. The race is scheduled for 9 A.M., so I return to my nocturnal jellyfish, confident the race will go on, seeing as

I flew seventeen ankle-swelling hours to get to Australia and weather patterns, of course, reward us when we go to such lengths.

At 7 A.M., when I saunter into the living room, the Dixon family is already awake and staring at the roiling bay through their incredible picture window.

"We've cancelled the race, dear," Vicki tells me.

For a minute I think she actually said they've cancelled the race. I smile at them. No one smiles back.

"Postponed, anyway. Until next weekend, dear," she continues. "Would you like to stay with us?"

I stammer gratefully for the invitation, but explain that I have my first bike race next weekend. There goes my bloody big swim, my foray into open water swimming, my attempt at ruling out (or in) another Olympic sport.

The next few hours at the Dixon household are manic. The weather clears, the race is back on, the weather worsens, the race is off again. I drink tea, read Australian tabloids and try to stay out of everyone's way. At 1 P.M., the waves are still plump but the wind has died down and the sun has come out. By 2 P.M. I'm restless, with a bad case of unreleased endorphin cooties. By my fifth issue of *Hello!* I have learned four valuable pieces of information: Lindsay Lohan needs rehab, Kiera Knightly needs a milkshake, Paris Hilton needs a purpose, and I need to swim. For once, my chances actually seem best. I go into the next room and approach the weary race director.

"Bruce, if the weather holds this afternoon could I do the swim anyway? By myself? Just to see what this open water distance is like?"

"Kathryn, I can't let you swim eleven kilometers alone," Bruce says, shaking his head.

I sulk.

"I'll do it with you!" he suddenly declares with unparalleled Aussie enthusiasm.

At 2:30 P.M., under graying skies, with twenty-five-knot winds and five-foot waves, Bruce and I enter the water of Port Philip's Bay at Mornington Beach. I'm sporting my snazzy new sleeveless wetsuit the wonderful folks at 2XU have given me. Wetsuits are vital for a race of such a distance, not only for creating buoyancy but also for warding off hypothermia. Bruce is in a full wetsuit, arms covered by the rubbery black material. I don't like sleeves; they feel too hot and claustrophobic. My entire triathlon career has been sleeveless. I like swimming this way. A few yards out to sea, Vicki sits in a kayak. She'll guide our course as an escort paddler. An emergency motorboat accompanies us, just in case we encounter dangers like fatigue, illness, or dorsal fins. The boat holds a crew of five: The emergency personnel, plus Bruce's daughter Sari, Lucas the photographer, and co-race director Leon Cox, who will switch on and off in the water with Bruce every fifteen minutes so I won't ever be alone. As we wade into the surf, I notice scores of strange, burgundy-colored squishy looking orbs floating in the tide.

"Bruce, what are all these red things?" I ask.

"Seaweed! Let's go!"

We dive into the surf. Underwater, I notice the reddish "seaweed" moves freely and comes equipped with tentacles. A few moments later, I feel a stinging sensation on my left, sleeveless arm. Then on my right shoulder. Then my face. And ankles. For the next three hours, I do not go more than five seconds without seeing or colliding with a *Stingmius oftenus*[3] jellyfish. While most of the jellyfish slapping upside me are between the size of a teabag and a tennis ball, every so often I have a close encounter with what must be the mothership of these numerous floating druids. The giant jellies are clear and scary and look like brains and are about the size of a medium Domino's pizza. Terrified, I sprint over to Bruce and swim so close that our arms entangle every few strokes. Instead of keeping my head down in good swimming form, my neck is strained upward, on the lookout for all things with tentacles and teeth. I can feel the wetsuit rubbing a divot into my ill-positioned neck. Blood in the water would not be a good thing. I call to the safety boat and ask Leon to bring the Vaseline jar on his next shift. That should keep the chafing down and lessen my chances of becoming chum. Unfortunately, I've brought no salve for my nerves and the jellyfish are wearing away at my mental state. I pop my head out of the water and whimper to my kayaker.

"Vicki, they're everywhere—"

---

3 With more than two thousand species of jellyfish, I was unable to find the actual scientific name of this particular red, squishy orb.

"I know, dear, I know," she says in a soothing maternal voice, then commands, "Keep going!"

Despite my low freakout factor, I'm now registering a solid nine out of ten on the Freak Outometer and no college theater minor acting tricks are helping. Unable to relax, my usual gee-I-love-the-water enthusiasm has dried up like a salted slug. I think about my last session with Peggy, the sports psychologist at Canyon Ranch. She advised that if I feel tired while swimming to envision a giant hand of a loved one pushing me through the water, speeding me along. I conjure up a bizarre image of British Steve in which his hands are the size of yachts. I use his gargantuan palms not to push me but to part a path through the jellyfish. It works for about two seconds.

"Why are there so many of them?" I call out to Vicki.

"The wind brings the jellies in," she explains. "And they like to eat the sea lice."

Sea lice? I'm swimming through sea lice? Great. Now I'm terrified *and* itchy. I dream up an itty bitty Steve with microscopic palms to filter out the lice. Not happening. Still itchy. Still scared. The little red buggers keep on zapping me, often in the face. Their venom feels stronger than mosquito bites but less painful than wasp stings. The itchy, ouchy sensation lingers and drains me more mentally than physically. Not a nice feeling, but I try to tell myself there are worse kinds of pain. Like electrocution. Or flogging. Or fatal knife wounds. The folks at USA Swimming better make sure their pool-trained Olympic hopefuls are ready to trade in their flip turns for tentacle burns.

I've been in the water less than ten minutes, probably not even past the first of my eleven kilometers. I begin to miss cycling terribly. Through one particularly bad swarm of jellies (not unlike Dory's near-death scene in *Finding Nemo*), I call over to Bruce, nearly stingless in his full-sleeve wetsuit, who seems completely indifferent to that which lurks beneath.

"Bruce, I'm having a hard time with the jellyfish," I admit, hoping the wind will disguise my sniveling. Bruce looks beneath the waves.

"What, these?" He points to a particularly large floating brain. I nod. "Look, these won't hurt you one bit!" Bruce thrusts his left hand into the water, grabs the pizza-size brainfish, pulls it out of the water, shakes it about, then puts it back in the water, and inserts his foot fully into its clear, plasmic entirety and jiggles it around some more. I have just witnessed a grown man do the hokey pokey with a jellyfish.

Bruce lives. I decide I will too. I put my face back in the water and keep swimming. Apparently, that's what it's all about.

After an hour or so (I've taken off my watch so as not to attract any fish with the shiny, reflective face), my energy level is still strong and I've adjusted my attitude from *AAGGHH! JELLYFISH!!!!* to *Oh. Jellyfish.* The water is clear enough that I can see the ocean floor nearly the whole time. Reefs rich with sea vegetation melt into rippled sand patterns, interrupted by the occasional bottomless abyss of darkness. Oddly, I see no fish whatsoever and logically push the thought of sharks out of my mind. After all, if there are no fish, then sharks have nothing to eat, so why would they hang around here? This logic then turns on itself, suggesting that there are no fish because the sharks have eaten them all and are looking for more. What a treat for them to happen upon a black, shiny, struggling, seal-looking thing with really big flippers! (I have size ten feet.) I do what I can to push this out of my head, choosing to focus on the scenery of the shore. Bruce or Leon and I cruise along for a while with the tide in our favor. Then, about two-thirds of the way through, the tide turns on us and we have to muscle through the current. At one point, I see a cute little house on the shore. A half hour later, I'm still eye level with that cute little house.

"We haven't moved for quite a while," Vicki says, confirming my worst suspicions. She is cold and drenched in the kayak, as the waves have become higher and stronger. "If we don't make any progress in the next twenty minutes, the tide will take us out. We'll have to take the boat to shore."

With that, my adrenaline kicks in. A canceled event is something I can live with, but not finishing an event in progress just isn't an option.

Leon and I rev up the power and intensity of our stroke, driving our now fatigued shoulders into the waves. Because I've been preoc-cupied with my place in the food chain, the act of swimming has barely entered my mind. My body feels relatively good in the cardiovascular and muscular sense, though my neck is stiff and the sixty-nine-degree water is starting to feel cooler and cooler. I cannot sense how long I've been in the ocean, but my tongue feels thick and my hands feel rubbery. I'm ready to be done now. I've ingested two of my three water bottles and two energy gels, and estimate my time in the bay to be three hours. Maybe more. Little by little, the shoreline changes and soon a landmark appears; the pier of Frankston beach slips into view. Bruce, Leon, and I are finally in the homestretch, our three fluorescent-capped heads bobbing slowly through the waves. The fishermen on the pier look at us quizzically.

Finally, the sand comes up to meet us and we wade onto the beach. Bruce's daughter Romony presents me with a finisher's medal and Vicki and I waddle off to the hot showers kindly offered by the lifeguard station.

"Kathryn, guess how long the swim took?" Vicki says.

"Oor dan thee howerth? Maee fou?" which is my attempt at saying, "More than three hours? Maybe four?" with a tongue that has swollen to the size and texture of a sea urchin.

Vicki shows me her stopwatch. "Two hours, forty-nine minutes!"

"Weewy? Unna thee howerth? Thweet!"

But within minutes of emerging from The Bloody Big Freakin' Jellyfish Swim, two things are abundantly clear: My love of swimming is still buoyant, but my Olympic dream of open water greatness has gone belly up. While I think I might be able to handle racing a 10-kilometer swimming event now and then, I have too little skill—and too much imagination—to consistently practice in an ocean environment. While 2:49 is a respectable time, the women's Olympic field is expected to turn in results much closer to the two-hour mark. (Open water swimming is often called marathon swimming because elite swimmers often finish a 10-kilometer swim in the time it takes elite marathoners run 26.2 miles.) Alas, selections and trials for the U.S. Olympic open water team begin in September 2007 and dropping close to an hour off my time is probably not going to happen within the year, or even within the millennium.

It's at moments like these that I get a little frustrated with ESPN. Why two years? Why couldn't they have given me six years to train, so I could have a legitimate shot for London 2012? In reality, though, how frustrated can I be with a corporation that's enabling me to travel to the ends of the earth in search of this dream? I would have taken this assignment if they gave me two days to try to be an Olympian.

I have too much respect for sport to be disappointed in my Bloody Big Swim. I'm proud of my efforts, happy with my ability to thwart jellyfish and fear for nearly three hours. My competitiveness wants me to succeed immediately, but I understand how much work goes into making a champion. After my experience with pentathlon, track cycling, and team handball, was it arrogant to think I could compete against the best swimmers in the world in a sport I've tried only once? I've been swimming as a triathlete for nearly a decade, but open water swimming is to triathlon swimming as track cycling is to road cycling. A similar sport, but a whole different animal. I know this now. I get it. I respect it. Swimming is out. But what about a sport I competed in for more than four years? There is still one sport where I have an inkling of my potential, one last stone—or so I think—to turn over before getting back on the bike.

WATER BREAK

MENTAL EARPLUGS

What the world says:

You want to do what? Try to make it to the Olympics? You're too old. That's an impossible goal. There are so few people who ever get that far, there are no guarantees, you have to give up so much. Think of the sacrifices, the early mornings, the hard work, the exhaustion. You'll be disappointed if you don't make it. Why bother? Not many athletes ever make it to that level, and even fewer ever make any money. It doesn't matter how hard you try, there will always be someone better than you.

What an athlete hears:

Do ... make it ... possible ... people ... get that far ... give ... think ... work ... make it to that level ... money ... doesn't matter ... try ... always be someone better.

9

TO BE
OAR NOT TO BE

February 2007

My dad got me into the sport of rowing. As a kid, he drove me to figure skating practice at 4:45 A.M. in Yonkers, New York, and then took himself to a boathouse in New Rochelle, where he rowed until it was time to pick me up. When I got to Colgate University, I wanted to find some cross-training for my figure skating.

"Try rowing," dad said.

After one floaty hour rowing on little Lake Moraine in Hamilton, New York, I developed a whole new endorphin addiction. I rowed all four years for Colgate and loved every godforsaken predawn practice. So why don't you try to get to the Olympics as a rower, dumb ass?

Well, being dumb isn't the problem. My ass, however, is. There are two categories in rowing. Lightweight, for women under 130.0 pounds, and open weight, for women over 130.1 pounds. (For men, the cutoff is at 155 pounds). Unlike wrestling or boxing, where there are numerous weight categories at ten- to fifteen-pound increments, rowing gives you only two choices. You're either "lightweight" or "open weight"—which is a politically sensitive alternative to "heavyweight." The euphemism notwithstanding, the national open weight women's team averages six feet tall and nearly two hundred pounds, and the majority of the elite lightweight women ring in under five-foot-five and one-twenty-five. At five-nine-ish and one hundred thirty-four, my ass and I seem to be caught smack dab in rowing purgatory.

On top of all that, while heavyweights enjoy five events (singles, doubles, pairs, fours, and eights) there is only one event for lightweight rowers at the Olympics—the double sculls. So every four years only two rather emaciated-looking women and two willowy, gaunt men qualify for this event. And I just had to go ahead and wonder if I could be one of them. For starters, dropping six to ten pounds seems doable, right?

Depending on certain times of the month, I weigh between 134 and 137 pounds and have been in this range for the past ten years. This is my weight after years of twenty-five-hour-a-week aerobic-based Ironman training. My body likes to be this weight. My body feels happy here. I give it carbs and fat and protein and dessert and we get along famously. My ass and I consider dieting to be a load of horsepoo, unless it is the "Are you gonna finish that or can I eat it off your plate?" diet, to which most distance athletes happily adhere. I don't have six to ten pounds I can lose without sacrificing my strength. Of course, I could try to force rowing's glass slipper to fit via dehydration and starvation, but somehow that doesn't seem right. Forced things usually end up cracking, and I'm not really up for going to the Anorexia Olympics.[4]

Yet, having vowed to leave no stone unturned in my Olympic quest, I looked into lightweight rowing anyway. Perhaps the women's lightweight requirements have changed since they were first implemented in 1985. Maybe FISA (the international governing body for rowing) now uses body mass index testing or incorporates a healthy height-to-weight ratio to determine who can row lightweight. After all, it's been ten years since I've been in a boat. Colgate University did not

---

4 While I could rant for hours about the ideas of strength, slimness, and eating disorders in female athletes, I've already done this. My first book explores this topic in depth. You can buy it used on Amazon for about forty-seven cents. Makes a good coaster.

have a lightweight crew, so I rowed with the big girls and held my own. I even sat in the "engine room" of our silver-medal-winning boat at the collegiate championships, sandwiched between two six-foot queens of strength.

But that was a decade ago. To know exactly where I stand now among the best lightweights in the nation, I needed to go to the CRASH-B World Indoor Rowing Championships in Boston. The twenty-five-dollar entry fee allows me to "race" a 2,000-meter sprint (the Olympic distance) on an ergometer (otherwise known as a rowing machine) and compare my time with the hundred best lightweights in the world. The race takes between seven and eight minutes at a highly anaerobic pace, which is athletic terminology for the body going so hard and so quickly that puking seems inevitable. As an added bonus, the lightweight limit for the CRASH-B race is set at a hibernation-friendly 135 pounds, not 130 pounds. Perfect. I wouldn't have to lose an ounce for the race. *Come on, ass! Let's see what we've got!*

At my local gym in Tucson, where I've begun lifting weights for cycling, there are three rowing machines. Despite their landlocked nature, ergometers mimic the motions of rowing on water. I walk by them every day, telling myself I'll get on one tomorrow. Cycling has taken up the bulk of my training, so there's not a lot of time left for extracurricular exercise. However, the two sports rely heavily on the same muscle groups, namely the quadriceps. A curious and potentially stupid idea forms in my head: What would happen if I showed up at CRASH-B without having pulled a single stroke in ten years? Would my hamstrings tear free from their ligaments and my bones pop from their sockets or would my cycling training hold everything together? Well now, wouldn't that be fun to find out! In the name of sport and the science of jackassness, the ergs at Gold's Gym remain ungraced by my presence in the weeks leading up to the race.

The week before the race, I check my daily weight. The scale reads Wednesday, 134; Thursday, 136; Friday, 134; Saturday, 134.

"What will you do if you're a pound over on race day?" Steve asks me over the phone. We've been dating nearly a year, long distance, which works out to be about two months of live-and-in-person dating.

Visits happen every five to six weeks and usually involve me going to New York on a stopover from a race or training camp. Not ideal, but there has been much talk of Steve moving out west. In any case, he's meeting me in Boston.

"I'll just row in the open weight category," I tell him. "Not like I'm gonna go berserk trying to lose a pound or anything. Geez."

I arrive in Boston the day before CRASH-B and try my luck with the hotel scale. It says 135. The race is tomorrow, so it looks like I'm free and clear to row as a lightweight. Still, I decide to play it safe by neither drinking nor eating anything the morning before the mandatory 10 A.M. weigh-in. The plan is to hit the scale at 10 A.M. and hit the IHOP at 10:05. I should have learned by now to not make plans. Any. Ever.

In a women's locker room of Boston University's Agganis Arena, scores of young ladies strip to their skivvies and await their turn on the scale. I'm one of three women in their thirties; the other ninety-seven lightweights are in their late teens to midtwenties. After my experiences in pentathlon and team handball, I'm accustomed to being in the minority. Finally, the sea of youthful, near-naked rowers parts and I hop on the shiny metal podium and hand the two stern-looking officials my ID card, which will need their stamp of verification that I am indeed 135 pounds or less. I watch as the digital digits flicker up to 135, then flicker again, then settle on 136.1 pounds and flicker no more.

Crap.

The Weight Police look at me. I smile, because sometimes smiley people get a break. Maybe they'll stamp my card anyway. Hell, it's only a freakin' pound. Neither of the two Weight Watchers makes a move toward the inkpad and the "LWT" lightweight stamp sitting on the counter.

"Wanna try?" one official asks. What she means is do I want to try to sweat off my one pound and one ounce in one hour. Ugh. I swore to myself I wouldn't do that. I love my pounds, I don't want to lose any. Every one of them has given me strength and power, and it seems so anti-athletic to run around in sweatpants, gloves, and a hat just to sweat one pound out, only to drink it right back in.

"All the way from Tucson?" she asks, reading my ID card.

I grab my sweatpants. And hat. And jacket. And my other jacket. And my photographer's jacket. I call Steve, who is waiting for me at the IHOP near the hotel, and inform him there is no Rooty Tooty Fresh 'n' Fruity in my immediate future.

The time is 10:10 A.M. I have fifty minutes to make the lightweight qualification. For twenty minutes, I sprint around outside the arena and work up a small sweat in the freezing Boston weather. I run back into the locker room, strip down, and hop on the scale in my sweaty, stinky birthday suit. The flickering digits report 135.6 pounds.

"The scale says one-thirty-five!" I exult.

"You must be one-thirty-five *point zero*," the Weight Police say. Rowers are usually nice, peaceful people. Niceness is in the sport's history, dating back to 1928, when Olympic rower Henry Pearce stopped midrace to let some ducks cross in front of his bow and still managed to win the gold. But these ladies give me the impression they just had baby duck for lunch and loved every bite.

One thirty-five point six. Crap. (Which I've already done, by the way). I slink off the scale.

"I have very dense bones," I mumble. They look at me blankly.

"I bet my ponytail weighs about a pound," I tell them—just to provide perspective, not because I'd really sacrifice it.

"I bet it does," one of the Calorie Cops replies. "You've got twenty minutes. Weigh-in closes at 11 A.M."

Goodbye IHOP. Oh well. I did not travel three thousand miles to eat pancakes. I slither back into my slimy, sweaty Lycra rowing unitard, drenched socks, and saturated sweatsuit. Sprinting down the arena hallway, I notice a dark room filled with exercise bikes and other cardio equipment—the Boston University men's varsity hockey training room. Miraculously, the door is unlocked. I jump on an old-school exercise bike, complete with the funny handlebars that swing back and forth. Too tall. Another one has a crooked seat, and there's no time to change the settings. Finally, I find one that fits and channel my inner Lance. I wonder which is harder, climbing the Alps in one week or losing six ounces in twenty minutes. Probably the Alps, though it feels otherwise as sweaty rivers trickle out of my stifled, bundled pores and pool uncomfortably in various crevices.

At 10:57 A.M. I dismount the funky bike and sprint down the hallway and into the ladies room in hopes of peeing out an ounce or two. A girl in the stall next to me is inducing vomit. My photographer, Lucas, will later tell me that every year at CRASH-B's the janitors keep containers of kitty litter on hand to absorb the vomit and stench of purging athletes in the lightweight locker room. That is so wrong.

With a minute and a half to go, I skid into the locker room, tear off my soaked layers, trip over myself while doing so, and crash-land onto the scale. Flicker, flicker …

135.0

Oh yeaaaaah!!!! Wooohooo!" I jump off the scale and do a victorious fist pump, which is not as culturally acceptable when naked among strangers.

"Get back on!" the officers bark. "The scale needs to stay at 135.0 for three seconds."

Oh for crap's sake. I do as I'm told and hold my breath. The Scale Sergeants count to three, reach over to their inkpad and stamp "LWT" onto my ID card. 10:59 A.M. I'm in.

11:05 A.M.

With less than an hour till my event, my objective is to find the nearest feeding trough. Digestion will be an issue, as eating an hour before competing is not ideal. The only restaurant near enough to the arena is the McDonald's I was just sprinting back and forth past. After seeing *Supersize Me* in 2003, I made a vow never to eat there again. Alas, a conundrum: Do I row on an empty stomach and risk bonking, or do I fuel up with ethically forbidden McPancakes? Morals can be such a pain in the ass. Pass the syrup.

11:50 A.M.

The floor of Agganis Arena has more than sixty ergometers lined up, and every fifteen minutes a different age group or weight class begins their 2,000-meter race. The stands are filled with spectators, which is odd given rowing's less-than-mainstream popularity. The air is slightly stuffy and filled with the erg's' mechanical whirring and the participants' occasional grunts. A few minutes before noon, I take my seat at ergometer number four. My competitors warm up around me, while I, still quite warm from my weight loss adventures, sit down on the machine for the first time in a decade.

Steve is behind me, acting as a verbal coxswain. I tell him to yell encouraging things like, "Looking strong," "Keep the pace," and "Damn, baby, your ass looks hot."

Two of my old college rowing teammates whom I haven't seen for ten years, Martha and Lauren, have come to Boston from neighboring towns just to watch me erg. This is the kind of lifelong bond rowing creates. We have the pick-up-right-where-we-left-off kind of friendship, even if a decade has passed.

"What is your race strategy?" Martha asks.

"To not fall off the erg," I reply.

"What time are you expecting to pull?" asks Lauren.

"The most minimally embarrassing time possible."

Secretly, I want to do better than my best college time—seven minutes, nineteen seconds. Realistically, I should not expect that. The top ten lightweights will likely pull between 7:05 and 7:15. After ten years of not rowing, I should not expect to be one of them, but if my brain were not fond of thinking up sappy, underdog, made-for-TV movie scenarios and subjecting me to multiple viewings, I probably wouldn't be here in the first place. There are one hundred lightweights here. I should be happy if I crack the top eighty with all the nonrowing I've been doing. Here goes.

The race starts, and the rhythm of indoor rowing comes rushing back to me. The explosive push-off with the legs, the swing of the lower back, finishing the stroke with the arms and hands, then rolling up into a near-fetal position to do it again—over and over, as fast as possible. My heart rate rises rapidly and on the small ergometer computer I watch the meters count down from two thousand. Behind me, a large screen above the arena floor shows computerized boats that represent where each rower is in relation to one another. I can't see this screen, but everyone in the crowd can. The little graphic boats inch along in jerky horizontal movements, like the carnival game where you shoot water into a plastic clown's mouth to power your wooden horse toward a prize that someone else always ends up winning. At 1,500 meters left, I feel pretty good. At the halfway point, the excitement wears off and I'm starting to hurt. Badly. With five hundred meters and less than two minutes to go, my quads and hammies are burning and my Mc-Pancakes are threatening to reappear. Around me the coxswains of the other rowers are screaming, even cursing, anything to get their rower riled up to pull faster. "Come on you, @#$5!*^, PULL, Is that all you #$%*^@ got?!"

"Well done!" Steve whispers. "Go, hon!" Steve seems shyer than usual in this crowd.

"Move your @#%^# skinny ass!" screams a veteran coxswain to my left.

"Yes!" Steve concurs.

"How bad do you want it? How #$#% bad do you WANT IT?!"

"Pull!" he recommends.

Unfortunately, I have to tune him out. Steve's commands don't make me want to row faster; they make me want to eat scones. He's never been around rowers before, so I can't fault him for his neophyte coxing skills. Besides, he's *there*. Not just for me, but to try his hand in the men's race. (Where he'll whup my time by over a minute).

And then the race is done. Seven minutes, thirty-eight seconds. I place twentieth out of one hundred lightweight women. Not quite Olympic caliber but not terrible for an old woman, either. The result is somewhat surprising. Ten years off an erg and I'm only nineteen seconds off my personal best? Hmmm.

For the rest of the day, I think about the thirty-second difference between first and twentieth places. Thirty seconds. It is not an impossible feat to bring my erg score down. But losing nearly ten pounds to row at the international weight of 125—oh, did I forgot to mention that? Yeah, most international regattas enforce a 125-pound boat average for women. The Olympics is one of those events. If I were three inches shorter, maybe the choice would be easier and rowing would be my clear-cut path to athletic glory. But I've got issues with forcing an athletic body into weight loss. One pound was plenty. I still can't get the sound of Vomiting Girl out of my head. Poor kid really needed a hug. And a cheeseburger.

Body image demons are terrible. I encountered them in my teens and early twenties and do not wish to revisit their haunts. Not for all the tea in Beijing. While lightweight rowing is not to blame for starvation behaviors, the sport could take more preventive measures. Rowing could create a height-weight ratio or body mass index standards, set hydration requirements, or even better, create a middleweight division for all those stranded between light and open weights. If boxing and wrestling and weightlifting have multiple weight divisions, why not rowing? Of course, maybe I just sound bitter because I don't quite fit the lightweight mold.

Maybe this rowing experience is just one more arrow pointing me down the cycling path.

WATER BREAK

LETTER TO MYSELF AS A FIFTEEN-YEAR-OLD ATHLETE

Dear Young, Pubescent, Awkward, Generally Good-Natured Little Kate,

Eighteen years from now, you'll be sitting in a chair typing a letter to yourself. While that might not seem like much to look forward to, trust me, it'll feel good to sit down for a few hours. You're going to have a couple of whirlwind decades, but just wanted to let you know every moment will be worth it. Even the ones that knock you down harder than you ever thought moments were capable of knocking. So I wanted to tell you a few things about your upcoming life as an athlete, just so you're prepared.

You're lucky, you know. You've got something in you that won't quit. Something that keeps you driven. Some sort of weird desire to keep moving forward. At fifteen, you already understand you can't stop this motivation, even if you wanted to. Some people will respect this. Some people won't. Hell, even you won't always understand it. All you know is that you're supposed to do something with all that energy. So keep going. Keep doing. And remove yourself from the company of anyone who tries to drag you down or questions your dedication. If they try to make you feel bad, don't be angry or frustrated. Just feel sorry for them. They're really wrestling with their own doubt, not yours.

Right now, you are strong and able and confident. Your love of sport is pure. Follow your instincts. The high school cross country coach will want you to run track in the spring, even though you want to play softball. Play softball. You will get plenty of running in later. You will continue to figure skate in college, and you'll improve. You'll pick up new sports and love them. You'll meet good people and great teammates and love them, too.

LUCAS J. GILMAN

What does it take to get to the Olympics? For some, a lifetime of commitment. For others, a camera. These are the rings of glory at the Olympic Training Center in Colorado Springs.

My host for the equestrian portion of the modern pentathlon was Breezie. That's not a smile I'm wearing, but a grimace of fear.

LUCAS J. GILMAN

The easiest part of fencing was putting on the uniform. And even that kicked my butt.

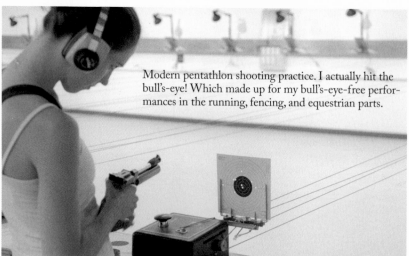

Modern pentathlon shooting practice. I actually hit the bull's-eye! Which made up for my bull's-eye-free performances in the running, fencing, and equestrian parts.

When you find corporate sponsorship, hold on tight! Jelly Belly provided stipends and free Sport Beans during my pro triathlon days and my foray into road cycling.

Two important lessons learned during this project: 1) Never, ever call a sport "easy" until you've tried it; and 2) Don't mess with USA Luge.

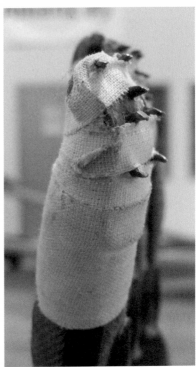

The nail-studded finger of my luge glove alone suggests the true badassness of luge.

I gave my all at national team tryouts at SUNY Cortland, but team handball is the hardest sport you've never heard of, featuring some of the most talented athletes you've never seen.

LUCAS J. GILMAN

Bring it on, bloody big freakin' jellyfish! I'm on the shores of the eleven-kilometer Bloody Big Swim, outside of Melbourne, Australia. Guts required. Swimmies optional.

LUCAS J. GILMAN

Row, row, row your ergometer, gently down the rink. At the 2007 CRASH-B World Indoor Rowing Championships at Boston University's Agganis Arena, that's me on the end, ten years past my college rowing prime.

As I find my way through the professional women's field at the Tour of the Gila stage race in Silver City, New Mexico, I am flanked by Olympic gold medalist Kristin Armstrong (second from right) and U.S. national champion Alison Powers (left).

How exactly does a cyclist go from Category Four to UCI races in the span of a year? That's pretty much what I'm wondering in this picture.
I put my trust in teammates Sinead Fitzgibbon (left) and Jenn Magur (right) as we race the criterium at China's Tour of Chongming Island. I'm not even totally sure what a criterium is at this point.

On the time trial course in Chongming Island, China. Spectators lined the course—a wonderful and rare sight at women's cycling events.

All hail the WonderMinion, Amanda Chavez, posing here with the infamous Devil fan of pro cycling. Without her help, I'd be in a ditch right now somewhere in the middle of South America.

The winner of the Tour de France gets about €450,000. The thirteenth-place finisher at the Race for the Life of Jesus in Venezuela—that would be me—gets $20 and no Olympic qualification points.

After a week of racing in ninety-plus-degree heat in the middle of El Salvador, I'm pretty sure the mascot for Yes Man yogurt was a hallucination. In any case, I've always wanted a Yes Man.

Winston Crooke, president of the St. Kitts and Nevis Cycling Federation, gives moral support while I warm up for the 2008 Road Cycling World Championships time trial in Varese, Italy.

Giving back to St. Kitts and Nevis proved to be better than any gold medal. In 2009, Nevis was able to hold its first national championships. Below, members of the Nevis Cycle and Triathlon Club celebrate their victories, wearing kits donated by Champion Systems and the Tucson cycling community.

A few years from now when you turn nineteen, your life as an athlete will change dramatically. Mom is going to have an aneurysm erupt in her brain. She'll spend three months in the ICU, suffer multiple strokes, and be given a 10 percent chance to live. Against all odds, she will. You will never look at life the same way again. You will come to understand its fragility, its fleeting nature, its incredible worth. Your sense of what is difficult, of what is hard, and of what is possible and impossible for the human body to endure will forever be skewed for the better. You will become mentally stronger. You will flourish as an athlete.

But you will stumble now and then. In your early twenties, you will question the merit of your muscles. You will wonder if they are a good thing. People in your life will try to tell you that women should be thin, that femininity and athleticism don't mix. Though your soul will see these lies for what they are, your brain will get confused. That's okay. You're still young. Just don't be so hard on yourself. If a sport makes you feel bad about your body, you need a new sport. If a coach tells you to lose weight because you'll look better, you need a new coach. If a friend makes you feel bad about your body, you need a new friend. If a parent makes you feel this way, you need a new role model. Remember one thing: The minute you starve yourself or put wiggly fingers down your throat, you are not an athlete anymore. Stand up for the strength you believe in. You will struggle for a few years, but hang in there. You will emerge twice as strong, not only physically but emotionally. You will be proud of every muscle, ripple, and indentation that your sports carve into you. These are the marks of an athlete, the tattoos of dedication. You will love your body. And it will show. Anyone who ever makes a negative comment about a woman's body while in your presence will be lucky to escape with less than a black eye. Atta girl. Welcome back.

In your mid and late twenties, you will morph from a skater to a triathlete and you will live in Arizona and Colorado. You will love it. You will be a writer and an athlete. You will thrive. You will have a wealth of health and knowledge. You will be poor as dirt. You will understand the value of doing what you love. You will follow your dream of racing triathlon at the highest level. It will kick your ass. You will love it still.

Love, however, is something you need to get a better handle on. Love, young Kate, is not always like sports. It is not a game, though many will tell you it is and many will treat it so. As an athlete, you never quit and you never give up. This is good. But these particular athletic strategies should not always apply to people and relationships. I need you to know it is okay to quit, to stop, to end, to walk away from an unfair game or an unsportsmanlike opponent. You only get one shot at this life, so seek training partners and loving partners who understand the two greatest elements that love and sport *do* share: fairness and respect.

In your early thirties, you will finally turn professional in triathlon. You will not be one of the best in the world, but not for lack of trying. You will soon understand your one true gift in life probably *is* trying. And in this field, you will become unstoppable. A professional tryer. ESPN is even going to hire you for this skill, so grab the chance, hold fast, and see what happens. That is as much as I can tell you at this point. You have eighteen years to get to here, and I'm excited to watch you grow. If you ever have any doubts along the way, listen to the voice inside you. She's an athlete. She can't possibly steer you too much off course.

Love,
Big Kathryn

10

SWITCHING GEARS

February 2007

My forays into pentathlon, team handball, track cycling, Ironman Hawaii, open water swimming, and rowing have already taken up five months of my two-year quest. Each sport was very well worth the effort and not one of those adventures was a waste of time; in fact, one sport led to another and had I not gone to the track cycling camp and met Colby Pearce, I never would have understood my potential as a road cyclist. So, no regrets. But now it's time to get on the bike. And stay there.

Only one sport on my list of things to try—race walking—has a development camp much later in the year. Maybe I'll try it, but the opportunity is months away and race walking would have to come second to my cycling schedule.

Luckily, I've been on the bike for the past eight years as a triathlete. Being on a bicycle is hardly new to me. I understand the physical demands of six-hour rides, the intensity of anaerobic intervals, the general feelings of pain and pleasure associated with the sport. I love everything about cycling, except the occasional hassle of the details it requires. Unlike running and swimming, where one hops out the door with some sneakers or into a pool with some goggles, cycling comes with a lot of gear and preparation. Even going for a short ride requires hunting down the right clothing, pumping up tires, carrying spare tubes, replacing worn items, cleaning and lubing the chain, preparing water bottles, slathering sunscreen, and lots more. None of this is particularly difficult—just time-consuming. And expensive. When something breaks or wears out on a bike, the cyclist has to take it into the shop and fork over the money for parts and labor, which is one more reason why sponsorships are so vital for elite athletes.

The rewards far outweigh the annoyances, however, which is why cycling has developed such an incredible following. Emotionally, I love cycling because of a most simple concept: Being on a bike enables me to move forward and feel the wind on my face. Physically, I love cycling because it was instantly familiar the moment I got on my first triathlon bike in 1999. The motion of pedaling—the "push down" with the ball of the foot, which immediately engages the muscles in the quads and knee, followed by the immediate "lift up" of the opposite hamstring and knee—was the exact same motion I used to jump as a figure skater. A motion completely ingrained in me for nearly fifteen years. All I needed to do was sew a few sequins on the rump of my cycling kit and I'd feel completely at home.

What I didn't realize was just how different road racing was going to be from triathlon. As far as I was concerned, the only difference was that drafting was allowed in road racing, and cyclists didn't feel the need to wear dripping wet Speedos when they rode. Yet I suspected there were more details that might benefit me. So I put in a call to one of Tucson's cycling and triathlon greats, Jimmy Riccitello, who had coached me as a beginner triathlete when I was in graduate school at the University of Arizona. Not only was he a stellar coach, but as a

Tucson native, Jimmy knew the ins and outs of local races and how to go about moving up in the sport. Despite eight years of being on a bike, I was a newbie road cyclist and had only eighteen months to make it to the top. I needed a coach with honesty, patience, attentiveness, seriousness, and a good deal of humor to help offset my intensity.

While my ESPN articles can be lighthearted, I take my training and my Olympic efforts very seriously. I have the ability to laugh at my shortcomings and faults, but I also have the ability to continuously beat myself over the head with the sledgehammer of perfection. I knew nothing about road cycling other than the one thing I needed to know: These next eighteen months were not going to be easy. I hoped Jimmy knew the rest.

Married, forty-three, and with two young children, Jimmy is a rather unique individual. He is the only person I've met who can weave the topics of George Bush, breast implants, Katie Couric, and diaper rash into one coherent monologue. The man says exactly what is on his mind, and that is both amusing and refreshing. Cycling with Jimmy is informative, technical, and physically strenuous, but not for the politically correct. For example, here are some of Jimmy's comments during our first training ride.

CULTURALLY ACCEPTABLE: "I know a woman who—"

JIMMYISM: "There's this chick ... do you mind if I call women chicks? ... So, there's this chick ..."

CULTURALLY ACCEPTABLE: "I prefer a woman with a natural anatomy."

JIMMYISM: "Dude, I hate fake tits. They don't look right, man. "

CULTURALLY ACCEPTABLE: "Some cyclists have more body hair than others."

JIMMYISM: "That guy has the ass of a Sasquatch."

CULTURALLY ACCEPTABLE: "You are sure to experience some good competition at the national time trial championships, Kathryn, so we must prepare accordingly."

JIMMYISM: "We gotta stomp on it, man, some a' them bitches can throw it down."

I've entrusted my growth as a cyclist to this man. Before setting up my training and racing schedule, Jimmy and I needed to have a firm understanding of my main objective: How exactly does one get to the Olympic trials in cycling? We sat down and checked out the extremely dry, twenty-six-page manifesto of USA Cycling's rules and regulations on Olympic eligibility. They are confusing and disheartening at best, so I was glad to have Jimmy to interpret them for me.

"Dude," Jimmy told me, "says here that USA Cycling picks their Olympic chicks from their Olympic long team, which is a group of eight #%$^ strong chicks that are like previous #$%*^# champions and stuff. Then, after they choose the eight women, they narrow it down to three just before the Games."

"Okay, so how do I get onto the eight-person Olympic long team?"

"Two ways," he says, "but the first way you don't have a chance. Like, five of the eight long team slots go to the top five USA pro cyclists who have the most UCI points … which are gained when cyclists race in specific, internationally sanctioned events. Dude, being new to cycling and as an amateur, you don't have any #$%^ points. So, since you don't have any UCI points, the only way you can get one of the three remaining long team spots is if you place top three at the world championships in Germany, in the fall of 2007."

"Well then, Coach Jimmy, how do I get to the world championships?"

"By winning the national championships in Pennsylvania in July. Of 2007. Like, a few @#%$# months from now."

"How do I get to the national championships?" I ask, sensing a rather difficult pattern.

"By qualifying as a Category Two cyclist."

"How do I get to be Category Two cyclist? I'm only a Category Four, a beginner."

"Well, you're gonna have to race every freaking weekend, win enough points as a Cat Four to move to up to Cat Three, then do the same thing to move up to Cat Two … and that takes a long @#$*time, man. Years, usually. And you gotta do it in the next five months."

Dude. Despite the slim chance and the narrow margins of becoming a national and world champion cyclist in less than half a year, I feel compelled to give it a shot. After all, maybe Bob Dylan is right: When you got nothing, you got nothing to lose. Not like I have a choice, anyway. In the back of my head, the dropped salmon calls out from the linoleum, *Play it where it lies.*

Back home in Tucson, Jimmy and I go to work on my training schedule. Through December and January I ride six days a week, alone or in a group, up mountains, through valleys and deserts. I lift weights every other day, and practice a very inflexible version of yoga ... with a full-impact sports bra, just in case I fall over. Jimmy teaches me how to calculate wattage and power output, how to sprint, draft, attack, and be patient (by far the most difficult race strategy). I go to bed early, eat well, hydrate well, and do everything Jimmy tells me it will take to stay strong, healthy, and focused. Not to mention physically and mentally exhausted.

My daily schedule goes something like this:

5:30 A.M. Wake up. Eat cereal.

6:30 A.M. Ride. Fifty to sixty miles with hills and intervals. Some days this is a five-to-six hour ride. Some days shorter and faster.

10:15 A.M. Feeling great! Big breakfast! Adrenaline rush! Ready to take on the world!

11 A.M. Passed out cold in the Beverly.

12 P.M. Check e-mail, work on articles, snack (preferably with caffeine).

1 P.M. Hit the gym for 1.5 hours weightlifting or yoga (alternating days).

2:30 P.M. Lunch.

3:30 P.M. Errands or time to work on articles.

5 P.M. to 7 P.M. Down time!

7:30 P.M. Dinner.

8:30 P.M. Talk to friends, family, boyfriend on phone.

9:00 P.M. Watch TV.

9:01 P.M. Remember that I don't have a TV.

9:02 P.M. Read (or go to two-dollar cinema on weekends).

10 P.M. Fast asleep.

Pretty typical stuff for anyone who takes their training seriously. This cycling schedule is incredibly similar to the demands of my triathlon career, and my skating days, and rowing for a Division One college team. Show up, train smart, improve, repeat. I love this schedule. As a little kid in a cold ice rink, my athleticism unknowingly signed me up for the best course in life: Intro to Striving, Seeking, Finding, and Not Yielding. At the time, I didn't know I was taking any classes. But here I am, two decades later, still enrolled in sport, still studying the craft, and hoping to graduate with honors in the summer of 2008. Or maybe even go for a doctorate in 2012.

While becoming a cyclist was a new adventure, I made a few discoveries about my long-term growth as an athlete. Remember that proverbial goody-two-shoes girl in high school who got good grades, didn't smoke, didn't drink, didn't party, didn't you-know-what, and didn't quite fit in? I remember her a little too well. All that teenage repression was manifesting itself in the strangest way in my early thirties. All of a sudden, I like speed. Not that kind. I like to go really, really fast. At least by bicycle standards. I find this utter peace and euphoria when screaming downhill over forty miles per hour on a bike, knowing that my life hangs in the balance of an unseen pavement crack. I get a rush knowing a rogue acorn could end my existence. I have also discovered I have something of an anger problem. Sometimes I just ride along, cursing. Tourette's on wheels. I'm not sure why. I have a great job, a big dream, a nice boyfriend, a roof over my head, and life is a-okay. But here I am, pedaling along with my good friend the F-bomb. Clearly I have some deep-seated issues. Yet I hope never to solve them. I *like* the F-bomb!

Not only that, but speed/adrenaline makes me utterly, albeit temporarily, brilliant. I have invented life-changing gadgets and written amendments to the Constitution while out on a six-hour ride. For example, all members of the cabinet, congress, and the president of the United States should be required to get on a treadmill or stationary bike for thirty minutes before passing any new law or declaring war. Let that pesky testosterone settle down a bit. They should have this exercise equipment lined up right there in their wood-paneled chambers. I've also invented a new reality TV show called *Turn It Off,* in which ten reality TV show producers are placed on a floating iceberg with a female polar bear and her awfully curious cub. And in an effort to find a fuel-efficient, ozone-friendly method of public transportation, I am working on a secret machine that is part ski chairlift and part Black Hawk helicopter. It's called the Chair Hawk and it runs on ethanol derived from junk mail and ... BAM!

I crash into my training partner's wheel at a stop sign and fall over. A few F-bombs and I'm okay. Better than the time I was hit by a car and went all Starsky and Hutch over the hood. That hurt for a few days. Clearly, I'm ready to race.

Little did I know how ready. February in Arizona is the start of the competitive cycling season, and I entered the Usery Pass time trial as a Category Four beginner. Within a ten-mile race, I did four stupid rookie things: brought an empty water bottle to the start line, pinned my race number upside down, didn't tighten my aerobars properly, and got yelled at by an official for blocking the finish line. Yet something strange happened. I won. By two minutes. Which is not a small margin in cycling. Of course, these were all fellow neophytes like me; it wasn't like I was pitted against Lance. I then raced Valley of the Sun, a three-day stage race in Phoenix, consisting of a time trial, a road race, and a criterium, which is kind of like a near-death cycling experience (a short loop consisting of lots of speed, lots of corners, lots of women who have no problem throwing elbows). Somehow, I won again. Weird!

Then came the Copper Valley stage race. After winning the time trial, I got to wear the leader's jersey, which I thought would feel like an honor and a privilege. Not so. Wearing that damn shirt is more like being dunked in soda and shoved in a beehive. Everyone's out to get you, and if you don't have any teammates to help with drafting, chasing, and setting the pace, then the leader's jersey means you're in for a world of hurt. The other women will do whatever it takes to wear you out, cut you off, and steer you toward potholes.

See, cycling likes to give the impression it is an individual sport. It isn't. I didn't really get that when I told ESPN I would pursue cycling toward the Beijing Games. I asked ESPN to buy me a bicycle. I should have asked them to buy me six teammates—preferably large-thighed women with triple-digit VO2 maxes. Instead, I got bees. And lots of them. Not only that, but cycling calls for intelligence. While I never considered cycling to be physically easy, I did think it was, at its most basic, a simple concept. Sit on a bike and pedal. Train hard, pedal faster. Pedal faster, win races. Win the right races, go to the Olympics. I didn't think there would be so very much to learn. And learning is especially hard when you're constantly in the mind-numbing stupor of athleticoma, where exhaustion settles so far into the brain that the most basic tasks (like speaking and eating and remembering your own name) become major obstacles.

Patience was a major issue for me. In my first road race, I panicked every time another rider got more than three feet ahead of me. I turned to my more seasoned cycling friend in the peloton and whispered, "Teri, she's getting away! She's gonna make a break, what do I do? How do I do it? You gotta help me." Teri assured me the rider was not going to get away, that I was strong enough to catch anyone three feet ahead of me, and that this particular rider—wearing a camelback water backpack and sunglasses with a clip-on rearview mirror—was probably not the cyclist I should worry about.

As it turns out, the race isn't always won by the fastest, but by the smartest, which obviously leaves me at a disadvantage. In triathlon, the biking theory was simple: Go as hard as you can at all times. In cycling, there are tactics. There are teams as well as individuals. You have to know when to sprint, attack, hold back, lead, or follow, and one miscalculation can end any hopes of a win. Cycling is like a sweaty version of chess. I was never good at chess. Small figurines creep me out, especially the pawn. What the hell *is* a pawn and why is it shaped like an earplug? I digress. Deceptive sport, cycling. Yet by the end of March, some key lessons began to sink in.

In addition to winning a nifty trophy at Copper Valley, I won thirty dollars in prize money. (That's three large pizzas!) Even better, I had scored enough points to move up to Category Three. Then came the Tumacacori Road Race and the Tucson Bicycle Classic. Could it be? No way. But yes—two wins. Somehow, I gained enough points in ten weeks to get my Category Two license—which meant I qualified for the national championship in July. To prepare properly, I found myself consuming entire grocery stores at some of the hardest races in the country. Specifically, the Tour of the Gila in Silver City, New Mexico, a five-day stage race of more than 250 miles where, in three and a half days, I consumed the following foods without any outside assistance:

2 large Domino's pizzas (Hawaiian)

4 Belgian waffles with syrup

3 bowls of oatmeal

5 bananas

3 oranges

1 Sara Lee banana nut muffin

4 Trader Joe's Thai peanut noodle bowls

2 La Salsa burritos

2 giant squares of lasagna

1 bowl of the pasta that looks like little seashells and are difficult to stab with a fork

½ jar chunky peanut butter

27 peanut butter-filled pretzel nubbins

1 Caesar salad with Brutus-size croutons

1 giant slice of garlic bread slabbed with butter

1 buffalo burger

1 plate of fries cooked in duck fat

4 Clif bars

15 Carb BOOM energy gels

8 packets Sport Beans

8 salt tablets

1 Coca-Cola

12 bottles Cytomax performance drink

4 gallons water

Two days into the race, I was officially one carbohydrate away from a mental institution. I was actually tired of eating. The sight of a noodle would likely push me over the edge of sanity. I'd heard the Tour of the Gila was tough, but somehow the pink entry form and the cute little cartoonish logos lead me to believe otherwise. But five days' worth of climbing 15,000 feet at a 5 percent gradient quickly revealed the truth. Not only did I consume nearly five thousand calories a day to replenish the ones burned after each of the near eighty-mile stages, but I lost three pounds while stuffing my face. I also discovered that the prerequisite for glory days is Skippy nights. Not a night went by when I wasn't woken up by hunger at 3 A.M. and had to swallow spoonfuls of peanut butter to get me through till breakfast. And hydration? That's a whole other game.

To stay hydrated during a four-day race in desert climates is not easy, and I was relieved (pun intended) to discover there's a mass pee break during one of the four-hour stages of the race. The entire peloton simply pulled over and peed fifty miles into the seventy-eight-mile stage, a great mass of bright spandex and white buttocks dotting the scenery of the Silver City outskirts. While male cyclists can simply whip out their anatomy and pee while riding, women can't pull this off. Even the most hardcore female athletes who are willing to pee in their bike shorts face the risk of infection and chafing, which would not fare well over a multiday stage race. If the cheaters/dopers were successfully able to manufacture the Whizzinator, I have hopes the cycling industry can develop something to help alleviate the bladders of endurance-based female riders. But I won't hold my breath.

I am still learning the intricacies of racing, and every day brings a new lesson. I notice many of the women in the race know one another. They exchange quick conversations during mellower parts of the race, asking each other how their season is going or how their family is doing. No one asks me much. New, unknown riders are not welcomed until they prove to be safe and stable. But I maim no one at the Tour of the Gila, so I'm not completely shunned by the women. A few are curious about my cycling kit. I'm sporting the Jelly Belly/Sport Beans team colors: black and neon green with a giant red jellybean plastered across my chest. When I switched from triathlon to road cycling, Jelly Belly kindly agreed to finish out my year-long sponsor contract, sending me cycling clothes to replace my triathlon suits.

"Jelly Belly has a women's team?" some of my competitors ask. "You're looking at it," I answer, groping in my pocket for samples. Carrying a few extra packs of Sport Beans in my jersey pockets has helped me make some friends in this tight-knit community.

While there is so much to learn in cycling, from strategies to alliances to handling skills to mental toughness, there is one familiar comfort of this new sport that I understand completely—the effort. Even when it feels like death. During a race, when I taste the blood in the back of my throat, I know everything is going to be okay. The blood in the back of my throat is a physical indication that I am actually going as hard and as fast as I'm capable.[5] The metallic taste occurs only when I'm at the end of my anaerobic rope, in those few seconds where I begin to see stars and just before my body shuts down the intensity, whether I want it to or not. The strange throaty aftertaste of metal is similar to sucking on a zinc lozenge. Or maybe the tailpipe of a car. For an athlete, this metallic blood taste is the body's resounding *yes* to the mind's question, *Is that all you've got?* Luckily, I get to *feel* like I'm dying without actually doing so. The upside of this blood-tasting phenomenon is that it makes me feel more alive than anything I've ever known. The downside? It also makes me dumb as a brick.

Somewhere over the continental divide, about seventy miles into my third day of the Tour of the Gila, climbing past a sign that reads "Elevation 8,234," shifting into my granny gear, gnawing on another clumpy energy bar, and trying to stay upwind from my own armpits, a thought occurred to me. Mind you, I have no idea what that thought was. I haven't had a thought cross my mind for months. While endorphins initially create a sense of inspiration and brilliance in the beginning of a race or a workout, the opposite effect settles in after prolonged bouts of energy depletion. Usually, while training, I live in the mental fog of athleticoma. Thoughts, ideas, epiphanies, opinions, and other forms of higher mental functioning defer to taxing decisions about whether to go for thin crust or deep dish. It once took me five minutes to figure out my hotel room door was simply not going to open, no matter how many times I aimed the "unlock" sensor from my car keys at it. But for a moment, on the summit of a New Mexican rocky mountain, I come out of my athleticoma and feel the pulse of a very deep, theoretical question cross my tired, vacant mind. It asked, *What the hot damn hell are you doing here, woman?*

5 While not every athlete experiences this, Nick White, exercise physiologist with Carmichael Training Systems, explains that tasting blood could be one of the following things: a change in the body's or the saliva's pH due to higher rate of carbohydrate oxidation, or the still-unproven phenomenon of EIPH (exercise induced pulmonary hemorrhage). That's lung trauma, basically, where blood vessels burst and are exhaled as an aerosol. "It's been studied in horses but not humans," Nick explains.

Three days later, I had the answer. Surviving a five-day road race among some of the best Category One and Two riders in the world was ... doable. I finished thirty-ninth in the GC (general classification). I wasn't the best, but I wasn't last. In fact, it was downright respectable for someone who had been racing only four months. The Gila was a real eye-opener for me, and I understood immediately that the sport of cycling has an abundance of talented women at the professional level and that I'll encounter them all at the U.S. nationals, a mere two months away.

WATER BREAK

THE OLYMPICS
ACCORDING TO PHLEGON

While researching the history of sports and seeking out those available to female athletes, I came across the ancient event of bull leaping. Unfortunately, I was a few millennia too late to qualify. In 1400 B.C.E., Minoan women were just starting to drive chariots and run foot races between their experiences of bearing the offspring of demigods and being turned into constellations by a cantankerous Zeus. One of the most popular events in the female athletic repertoire was bull leaping, where a woman would face a charging, rampaging bull, then proceed to grab the horns, vault over the bull, and land in a standing position on the bull's butt. I, for one, am very happy this event never made it on the modern Olympic roster, as I'm quite sure it wouldn't be the *bull's* ass I'd be landing on. However, painted vases and hieroglyphic-ish pottery survive that suggest such events took place.

While our modern Olympic Games have been around for 112 years, a second-century historian named Phlegon claims the first Olympiad took place in 1065 B.C.E. I don't know what happened there, but I'm guessing there was a rift between gods and mortals, because the inaugural games were immediately followed by a 181-year Olympic hiatus. The games were restored in 884 B.C.E. and apparently only humans took part in the festivities.

Still, some people claim that the true inventor of the Olympics was Hercules, who gathered a multitude of his otherworldly brothers to play some sports every few years—a tradition that supposedly inspired the Olympics. I like to think Herc's little sister, Jennifercules, was invited to play too. But probably not.

Female athletes were eventually given their own Olympic-ish event in ancient Greece. The Heraean Games were set up to honor Zeus' wife, Hera, and were open to women athletes throughout the country. Contestants were classified by age and virginity (or lack thereof). "Good evening gods and goddesses, prudes and sluts. Welcome to the Heraean Games at Madison Square Parthenon. Tonight's events begin with the forty-year-old virgin hurdlers, immediately followed by the preteen prostitute pole vault. Winners, don't forget to pick up your olive branch on the way out. Losers, please enjoy this nice cold glass of hemlock. Thank you for your participation!"

Apparently, the first women to compete in the Heraean Games also acted as peacekeepers between rival Greek cities. The Greeks were definitely on to something, letting female athletes hold office and negotiate peace terms. The United States and the United Nations should follow suit. Almost every professional female athlete I've encountered is educated, motivated, and just plain rational. Put a female athlete in the White House and their morning routine would be as follows:

6 A.M. Ten-kilometer run

7 A.M. Pancakes

8 A.M. Withdraw troops from Iraq

8:15 A.M. Protein smoothie

9 A.M. End world hunger

10 A.M. : Send aid to Darfur

11 A.M. Eight-minute abs

11:09 A.M. Sign bill doubling art, gym, and music budgets for every public, private, and charter school

11:10 A.M. Sign bill that NBC must televise *all 309* Olympic events, no commercial interruptions, and 50 percent less cheese in all athlete personal stories

12 P.M. Lunch

Alas, it would be eras and eras until women were allowed to compete in the Olympics alongside men. One of the first women to do so was an athlete named Melpomene, the first female winner (and only female participant) of the marathon in 1896. Melpomene was a fully mortal Greek woman, despite the goddessy sound of her name, and the Olympic committee refused to grant her an official entry. Melpomene ran anyway, starting a few minutes behind the men. When the officials wouldn't let her into the stadium to cross the finish line, she simply ran around the structure and called it a day ... but not before passing a good number of her male competitors and clocking an impressive five and a half hours in this pre-running-shoe century. Despite the achievement, history mostly forgot about Melpomene until she was later reincarnated as Kathrine Switzer, who stormed the all-male Boston Marathon in 1967 and finally brought women's distance running into the spotlight.

When the modern Olympics were created in 1896 after a thousand-year hiatus, there were no women's events. But by 1900, pressure from activists introduced the world to tough, spunky female athletes in a variety of winter and summer sports. Later in the century came the female athletes no one will ever forget: Nadia Comaneci, Katerina Witt, Picabo Street, Bonnie Blair. But perhaps none will ever be as tough as the lesser known U.S. track and field athlete Elizabeth Robinson, who was nearly killed in plane crash in 1931. Her seemingly lifeless body was taken from the crash site directly to the mortuary—where she eventually woke up. After five years of healing her multiple fractures, she got back to training and won the Olympic gold medal in the 4-by-100-meter relay in the 1936 Berlin Games. That's a tough woman. I believe she would have made a very good team handball player.

My favorite Olympic story, however, is not of a female athlete but the rather egocentric Roman emperor Nero. In 67 c.e., Nero demanded that five thousand fans fill his stadium to watch him race the Olympic chariot events, in which he decreed himself eligible to take part. Halfway around the track, he fell out of his chariot. The officials, fearing Nero's wrath, stopped the race, dusted him off, and put him back in the chariot. Nero was declared the "winner" of all the events he entered. Unfortunately, Nero was reincarnated two millennia later as George W. Bush.

THE OLYMPICS ACCORDING TO ME-GON

One of the greatest aspects of the Olympics—both ancient and modern—is the steady inclusion of new sports, thus marking the progression, adaptation, and growth of athletics worldwide. Even if we never see a third of these sports broadcast on NBC, at least they are out there. Phlegon would be proud of how far we've come since bull leaping.

With the growth of sport comes the growth of athletes. Records fall, benchmarks are shattered, and bars are raised. The only negative aspect of such progression is the attempt to skew it. Cheaters, dopers, druggies, mad scientists, hypocritical doctors, insecure coaches—as long as there is sport, there will be those who try to cheat. That's the reality. And here's the solution. Instead of spending millions of dollars and hours of precious time trying to catch the cheaters, I have an idea that will save time, energy, money, and restore sport to its rightful, clean participants. Let's give the cheaters their own Olympiad: the Doperlympics. Every four years, disgraced athletes can finally get exactly what they've been striving for—fame, misfortune, cerebral hemorrhaging, and the chance to duke it out against others of the same moral fiber. Here are some of the events to be included in the inaugural games.

Football

Regular NFL rules apply, but supplemental points are awarded to the team that inflicts the most bodily harm.

Permanently maiming tackle: 7 points

Temporary paralysis: 6 points

Internal hemorrhaging: 2 points

Witty yet grammatically correct insult of opposing player's mother: 1 point

Baseball

Regular MLB rules apply, but instead of three outs per team per inning, innings are over when any given batter spontaneously combusts en route to first base. Games may run longer, but probably not as long as cricket.

Track and Field

Races will be conducted on a win-at-all-costs basis. For example, a 100-meter event will consist of six competitors. The winner will win a years' supply of EPO. The five losers are injected with more steroids and forced to race again, every thirty minutes, until they surpass the winner's time or explode while trying.

Cycling

Time trial, road, track, cyclocross, and mountain bike disciplines will follow regular UCI regulations. However, all Doperlympic cycling events will be held in the Serengeti. In August. Racers will receive one water bottle filled with cold, refreshing liquid steroids. Also receiving individual bottles of steroids will be a pride of emaciated cheetahs. Prior to the start, all dopercyclists will be rolled in hyena manure. Cheetahs will be dressed in chafing yellow jerseys. All's fair in the Doperlympics. May the best cheetah win.

In all seriousness, there really is a way to curb steroid use in professional sports. It's called playing hardball. Not every sports federation has the guts to enforce the rules, especially where multi-million-dollar endorsements are on the line. But, should the powers-that-be choose to nut up and just do it, here's the four-step penalty we should impose on cheaters: Step 1—lifetime ban for the first offense; Step 2—forfeiture of all titles/medals won during the previous year; Step 3—all earnings during the current calendar year donated to charity; Step 4—five hundred hours of community service at a local oncology ward, where the dopers/cheaters can come face to face with the people for whom EPO and steroids are truly intended: cancer patients and the terminally ill.

U.S. NATIONAL U-TURN CHAMPIONSHIPS

June and July 2007

Between February and July of 2007, I successfully "catted up" to cycling's Category Two, which qualified me for the U.S. national championships. All of my efforts are centered on preparing for this race, which will be held at the Seven Springs resort area in Champion, Pennsylvania, just outside of Pittsburgh. I will have no teammates, no ranking, no laurels, and no fame to take with me into the race. Just the same things I started with at the beginning of my cycling career: a bike, a coach, a plan, and a pocketful of jellybeans. I have to win nationals—against a field of the best professional riders in the United States—to qualify me for worlds, in which I then have to medal to be considered as a solid "maybe" for Olympic contention. Needless to say, these possibilities are long shots. These possibilities do not favor me.

These possibilities induce doubt. Yet these possibilities motivate me.

While I understand the process of qualifying for the Olympic team in cycling is complicated, multitiered, and ultimately subjective, there is comfort and confidence knowing I have earned the right to race among the best. These longtime pros and seasoned veterans are sure to have more experience, skill, and savvy. But I know that when we all roll up to the starting line in July, I get to have the very same thing as everyone else: a chance.

Part of my training regimen requires a lot of time spent alone on the bike, but at least twice a week I ride with Jimmy or head out on group rides with some of Tucson's best cyclists. Four mornings a week, there are group rides that leave from Cafe Paraiso, just west of the University of Arizona. For thirty-three years, Ralph Phillips, owner of Fair Wheel Bikes, has lead a bunch of local cyclists through the outskirts of Tucson, where the roads open into the most breathtaking desert views anyone has ever seen. Most of us don't see the views, as scenery comes second to intensity and safety on these rides. Cacti are wonderful to marvel at, but not when your bike is traveling two centimeters away from another guy's wheel and the entire group is averaging nearly thirty miles per hour. On Tuesdays and Saturdays, I wake up while it is still dark and ride the five and a half miles it takes me to get from my home on Second and Wilmot down to Cafe Paraiso on University Boulevard. I leave my house a little bit late, so that I have to ride fast to make it before the group departs. This is the only way I can warm up enough to stay with the faster men.

There are a handful of other women on the rides, but the men outnumber us in droves. During the winter, professional cyclists and triathletes flood Tucson for its climate-friendly training, and the group rides see anywhere from sixty to two hundred participants. Everyone is welcome, but the serious riders move immediately to the front of the pack to dictate the pace and stay away from the jittery beginners and their unpredictable movements. When the pros head out of town for the season, the locals keep the pace just as fast. After a few months of showing up on these group rides, the men tolerate my presence and have come to view my bike-handling skills as mostly safe and trustworthy. Still, I have to fight to stay in the front. None of these guys wants to get dropped from the group once the pace picks up, and I have to prove myself on every ride. Prove that I belong here, that I want to be the best. And not just prove it to them but to myself. Thinking I belong here and knowing I do are two different things, and while I've been on a bike for almost a decade, I'm still new to the dynamics of road cycling. Feeling comfortable in the middle of a peloton of strong, experienced men does not happen overnight.

I love the guys I ride with, though I don't know all their names yet. During the warmups and cool downs as we head into and out of town, the wind carries snippets of conversation through the peloton, underlining some of the discrepancies between how men and women think.

"That's Jay in the GST Team jersey," some guy tells me.

"Oh, you mean the tall guy in the black, white, and blue jersey with the nice smile?" Men see print and text. I see color and shape.

Perhaps I don't notice the text and team names on jerseys because I am often dangerously anaerobic and on the verge of spontaneous combustion just trying to keep up with these dudes. My brain grunts, *Stay on wheel of fast man wearing red shirt with monkey emblem* or *Man with strawberry logo, good climber* or *Guy with pretty jersey the colors of sunset throws down a wicked sprint.* Maybe someday I will be able to read the bold text and sponsor logos, but not just yet.

No one talks in the middle of the ride—the effort is too intense. Between the sprints and climbs, the attacks and bridges, sometimes there are short salutations and a quick "How's it going?" If I'm riding well and climbing strong, these men will sometimes tell me. The compliment is quick and genuine: "You're riding well." I like these men because they have accepted me as a cyclist, not a female cyclist. I have grown up trying to excel in sports, my radar finely tuned to the vibes and energy that come from training or competing with men. On these rides, when the effort increases the peloton narrows, and we all jockey for a good position, I know when I'm being passed because I'm a cyclist and when I'm being passed because I'm a woman. On a legitimate pass the man will come from behind, create a smooth slipstream of speed and power, and slide easily into an opening that is safe and calculated. On a ponytail pass, as I've come to call it, a man (typically one I've passed earlier) will rev up his speed, fly by me with the frantic quality of a hamster in an exercise wheel, cut right in front of me, and immediately stop pedaling, a dangerous way of communicating his disrespect. Amid the pack of clean-shaven man calves, pontytail passers are usually hairy leggers with logo-less jerseys. I have, on more than one occasion, heard one man whisper to another as I ride by, "You gonna let that happen?" (I love testosterone! I have my share of it too.) I do not take these comments personally anymore. It used to bother me a lot when I first started riding, until a friend quipped about the ponytail passers, "I don't think their mothers loved them enough." Now I smile sweetly when I pass them back and offer a very cheery, fully oxygenated, "How's it going?"

These Tucson group rides are primarily named for the day of the week on which they take place. The Tuesday ride, the Wednesday ride, and so forth. The one day that gets its own distinct nomenclature is Saturday. Saturday is the Shootout. Staying with the group for the entire sixty-mile hammerfest takes every bullet I have, and when I first started riding the Shootout, I got dropped faster than the first cocky cowboy in a Clint Eastwood western. But after months of learning how to draft, when to move up, who to follow, and who to avoid, I've gotten strong enough to stay with the lead pack of men. You would think my only motivation for not getting dropped is that I need to be in the best shape possible for my Olympic hopefulness. Sometimes this is true. Most of the time, my motivation to go as hard as I can and hang onto the pack is much simpler: I don't want to ride alone. I already go home alone, sit down at my computer alone, eat alone, sleep alone. Occasionally, after an early ride, the group will stop for coffee. I look forward to this coffee stop as much as Christmas. I don't even like coffee. I just want to sit there for a little while among the coffee-drinking cyclists, not being alone.

Athletics and creativity—my twin passions—have united in a job, a lifestyle, and an Olympic dream. Bike rides consume my mornings, while afternoons are spent working on new chapters. Surviving off lunch shift tips no longer dogs my existence. I have a paycheck these days. And because the Walt Disney Company owns ESPN, there's a

Mickey Mouse on it. I have training partners who motivate me, friends and family who love me, a boyfriend who cares for me, and strangers who believe in me. I have a roof over my head, food in the fridge, and clothes in my closet. I'm fortunate and grateful. Sometimes, though, being alone gets to me.

My boyfriend, Steve, works and lives in New York City. We see each other roughly every five to six weeks. There have been promises of more permanent togetherness, but uncertainty reigns. Issues revolving around finances are the ones we admit to, but I suspect there's a lot more. It can't be easy to love a woman who says things like, "Hey hon, can you pick up some eggs at the store and, by the way, for the next two years I'm going to try to go to the Olympics."

"Move to New York," friends tell me. "Be with him." But I believe love is much like real estate—a large part of success is the right location. Cities hurt my soul if I'm there for too long. While the people are wonderful and the culture vibrant, I am simply in need of open spaces right now. Big skies. Mountain views. Big roads with wide bike lanes that trickle down to unnamed dirt trails. Much like determination and inner drive, preference for certain places of comfort usually comes hardwired in our psyche. The Southwest feels like home right now, so here I am. I like being in Arizona for the unmatched training and year-long race calendar. I like the people I ride with; they are kind, encouraging, and merciless. People here have a saying that the desert is healing. New Age as that sounds, it is true. Cyclists thrive here. I'm thriving here.

Well, most of the time. Despite my love of Arizona, living alone doesn't always come easy. On certain days, I feel very far away from everything. Loneliness visits, uninvited. Working from home has its benefits, but human interaction isn't one of them. Sometimes I go all day, even two or three, without hearing or seeing another person. I try not to let that happen, even if it means a trip to Trader Joe's or the gym just so I can be around live human beings. I do not think we humans were meant to be alone for long stretches of time. "Try to get out more," friends say. But loneliness is not a synonym for boredom. I have plenty to keep me busy. My days are packed with effort and progression, athletics and literature. My Olympic quest is thrilling and exciting and vigorous and I love it. But sometimes when I slow down for a moment, come up for air, and catch my breath, I notice how tired and alone I am.

Except for Beverly, my beloved recliner, my house is empty. I really need to lean on more than a cell phone, a new book, or an old DVD. I need a warm body to tell me I'm doing okay. Even if I don't ask. For chrissake, I need a freaking hug. More than once I've come home from a great group ride with my cycling friends, only to start sobbing because I am tired of coming home to just Beverly. Usually, tears are an indicator that I need a nap. But sometimes they are more. The bottom line is that despite all the encouragement and friendship I get from outside sources, cycling toward the Olympics is an individual effort. I'm alone on this quest. Sometimes that's hard. The reality of it is laughable but true: I can pedal a bicycle uphill for hours at a time, pushing almost three hundred watts of power, and then I can do it again the next day and the day after that and physically nothing can faze me, nothing can break me. But if I can't get a hug, I'm on my couch whimpering like a baby. I'm not sure how that works. Are we all this fragile, or am I just lucky?

Yet much like the opposites of athleticoma and endorphin brilliance are products of the same effort, I find much happiness and joy in my quest, despite the periodic bouts of loneliness. The funny thing about joy is that not everyone can handle it. The catch-22 of being a motivated, joyous, life-celebrating woman is that I tend to scare the bejeezus out of some guys. They have absolutely no idea what to do with me. At first, I make these guys feel great because I'm so happy and fun to be around and I smile a lot and have lots of energy. Kind of like a puppy. But if the guy happens to be a less-than-happy type deep down (a condition that rarely reveals itself on the first date—or the tenth), the balance shifts and he begins to loathe my inner Happy.
Which is no fun.

I've already learned the lesson about trying to fix other people's broken happy buttons, and I'm starting to think my boyfriend's Happy is coming undone. In a long-distance relationship, it isn't always easy to tell. The phone is a lifeline in the lonely times, and I find myself avoiding major relationship discussions, settling instead for reports on how my training is going and what the weather is doing. I'll see how it plays out. We're new, Steve and I. It's too early to make a Happy call just yet. Besides, we all have flaws. One of mine seems to be knowing exactly what I want and not settling for anything less than this: a Happy guy. Who also happens to be goal-oriented, motivated, passionate, funny, taller than me, heavier than me, polysyllabic, likes to travel, enjoys athletic endeavors, mountains, reading, intimacy, sex, comes free of strange diseases and addictions, has some form of employment, and thinks I'm the coolest thing ever. Basically, I want a mantopia. The upside of such a request? I get a mantopia. The downside? I'm probably still searching for him at age eighty-six.

Alas, while we joyful women sometimes get criticized for putting our dreams and goals ahead of our significant others, the way I see it, if our dreams and goals are what make us happy then our Other should be significantly proud. Truth is, we all *should* put ourselves first. If we don't do what makes us happy, how can we bring happiness into a relationship? That's a whole other book. Likely not published by ESPN.

Yet, while I struggle with just how much of the personal element I should weave into my quest, the deciding factor for relationship inclusion is this: Chasing a dream means putting every aspect of your life into the journey. My journey includes a boyfriend. Relationships of all kinds affect the person on the quest. After all, a body will only do what the mind tells it to, and the mind is ultimately run by the heart, so the heart better be one sound, strong, supported, happy little beater. If an athlete chooses to let someone near the heart, then the quest will take certain paths. Sometimes those paths are clear. Sometimes, like this very moment, they're a little harder to see.

Right now, I can see well enough to get by. My Olympic dream is stronger than sadness and tougher than the tough days and I know to the only thing to do with the loneliness is embrace it, observe it, understand it. And then, when the time is right, kick its ass out the door and invite Happy to come on over. Which is what I really need to do right now. I've got nationals to focus on. When that race is over, I will gladly take my loneliness out for a coffee, a chat, and a big hug. In the meantime, I'm going to Colorado, where it is scientifically proven that loneliness cannot survive at 8,600 feet.

ʖ ʖ ʖ

The month before my road race and time trial nationals, I head to Nederland, Colorado, a tiny mountain town just west of Boulder, more than a mile and a half above sea level in the Indian Peaks National Forest. I am quite familiar with Nederland, having lived and worked there for two years while training as a triathlete. The town is exactly what I want in a Colorado lifestyle: small, rustic, community-oriented, and only forty-five minutes from Costco.

Nederland is also haunted, at least for me. Every day, I ride past the house where I once lived with my ex-fiancé, a man who didn't think much of my athletic dreams. A man who was wonderful when sober, but when under the influence called me every name in the book and a few creatively slurred new ones. A man who questioned my strength and confidence, and worse, caused me to question them too. At the time, I couldn't see that my strongest virtue—endurance—was also my weakest. I took too much of his emotional toxicity, not because I wanted to but because I could. Because nothing could break me. *Go ahead and try.* I mean, if physical pain was something I could endure, why not endure the emotional variety? I simply didn't understand that *pain* isn't supposed to be endured. It's supposed to be stopped. Pain—physical and emotional—is a screaming beacon that tries its best to say, *Hey, jackass, wake up! Something isn't right. Do something about it. Preferably today.*

On this trip, Nederland proves healing. As I ride past the old house each day, I think up a few creative names of my own but usually settle on whispering something better to myself: *Hell yeah.* As in, *Hell yeah, look where my life is eighteen months later. Hell yeah, I really did make the right choice. Hell yeah, I'm trying to be an Olympian. Hell yeah, Nederland is beautiful. Hell yeah, cycling is a powerful exorcist.*

My training in Colorado averages 300 to 350 miles a week during the month before nationals. My daily routine is simple and focused:

ride, eat, sleep, eat, nap, eat, doze, sleep. Funky little muscles begin to protrude on my quadriceps, while my upper body slightly narrows. "Yeah, you'll get bigger on the bottom and smaller on top," Coach Jimmy explains. "All cyclists do."

Yay. Big hips and small boobs—just what every woman in her thirties wants! But I feel strong and proud of what my legs can do. Twice weekly I ride with cycling's infamous Bustop Ride. This large group of fast men congregates in the parking lot of the Bustop, a strip club on Boulder's north side, before heading out for a forty-mile slugfest. An odd feeling it is, being the lone female among a herd of Lycra-clad men cycling around in front of a nudie bar. We average speeds between twenty-four and thirty miles an hour, and it takes every ounce of my strength not to get dropped from the pack. During one ride, a fellow Bustopper asks me if I am training for nationals. *Yes, I am!* He then advises me to take this year's race as a learning experience and not put too much pressure on myself. "Learn the course and the tactics this year, and kick butt next year," he counsels.

Okay, I'll do that. Right after I ask the IOC to move the Olympics to 2009. Regardless, the Bustop rides improve my sprinting and pack riding skills. When not training with a group, I find peace training alone. Sometimes I ride one hour, other days I take five-hour jaunts through the Peak to Peak Highway, where I keep myself occupied the way a writer-athlete does: composing poems and song lyrics, and envisioning my future conversations with Oprah. I also work on my List of Crap and List of Pain, a ongoing tally of everything I have seen discarded into bike lanes over the course of my national and international training and racing, and everything that has been thrown at me or unexpectedly struck me along the way. On the scenic highways through national forests in Colorado, there isn't much to add other than the occasional hippie hitchhiker, but over the past year or so the lists have grown long.

LIST OF CRAP

Beanie Baby, a teal manta ray named Ray
Happy Meal toys
Two-by-fours

Rubber dildo
Handcuffs
Nails
Bananas
Shoes (never a pair, always individuals)
Gloves (ditto)
Mardi gras beads
The left hand of a mannequin
Prickly pear cactus
Hypodermic needles
Razor blades
Sleeping bags
Compact discs
Carcasses (gophers, birds, coyotes, deer, cats, rabbits, raccoons, skunks, snakes, javelina)
Live animals (all of the above plus bears, foxes, and a hiker who looked like Bigfoot)
Pornographic trading cards

LIST OF PAIN
Car hood
Car side mirrors
Dust devil
Tumbleweed
Hands of passengers (teenagers)
Slurpee cup (mostly empty)
Beer bottle (empty)
Small bag of garbage (full)
Compact discs
Cigarettes
Partially eaten McDonald's hamburger
Other cyclists

When I'm not working on my lists or my Oprah dialogue, I race local hill climbs and road race events, mostly on the weekends, and often end up passing women who beat me earlier in the season. On Wednesday nights, I compete in the Boulder time trial series. On my last Wednesday, I broke the course record. So did one other woman, Anne Samplonius of Canada. She finished twenty-four seconds ahead of me. Two weeks later she went on to win the Canadian national time trial championships. The second place rider was thirty-five seconds back from Anne. Third place, 1:05. What, exactly, did this mean? I was strong. Better. Faster. Better and faster than I'd ever been. Six months of training and it was starting to become clearer to me: I was good at cycling. Maybe even better than good. The question now, though, was if I was good enough.

🚲　🚲　🚲

On July 11, I fly to Pittsburgh and drive a couple of hours to the U.S. national championships race venue at Seven Springs in rural Somerset County's town of Champion. The start list for the elite women's time trial and road race events is impressive. Kristin Armstrong (no relation to another famous cyclist named Armstrong, though I think they should double-check the DNA) is back to defend her national title. Joining Kristin and my unranked, nonmedal-winning self are seventy-two other professional, semi-pro, and top-ranked amateur cyclists. To race as an elite woman, a rider must be a Category One or Two competitor, which is what I spent the last six months trying to become. Most of these elite women have spent the last six *years* at this level, so perhaps I should be intimidated. But a deer in headlights hardly has time for such an emotion.

THE TIME TRIAL

Any race that takes place on Friday the thirteenth has to have some kind of story. However, I probably would have been more successful fending off a machete-wielding hockey-masked monster than I was at maneuvering U-turns on the rather funky time trial course. The most logistically simple of all cycling events, the time trial is usually an out-and-back or point-to-point race where riders go off individually and race the clock. No team, no pack, no drafting, no tactics, just an all-out effort. Whoever has the fastest time wins.

A couple weeks before nationals, competitors were informed that the time trial course had been moved and shortened (from thirty kilometers to twenty-four) due to some road closures. Rats. I like the endurance side of things; more is usually better for me. I've found a niche in outlasting other people—a surprisingly positive side-effect of once walking an Ironman marathon. Slightly more troubling was that the time trial course was no longer an out-and-back with a nice, wide turnaround point. Nosiree. Now the stretch of road was only six kilometers long, so the course was set up as out-back-out-back in a zigzag pattern that required four sharp little U-turns. Or, as Steve would correctly summarize, the course had "too many twisty bits." My stomach did a quick flip ... U-turns. Crap. I'd spent much of the last six months learning how to go as fast as possible. I practiced sprinting and climbing, descending and drafting. But sharp, tight U-turns? Not a lot of expertise there. How exactly does one do a U-turn in the space of a road's shoulder at twenty-seven miles an hour? Correct answer: practice. Wrong answer: prayer. With clumsy braking and wobbly cornering, I avoid disaster but achieve mediocrity.

In the time trial, riders go off individually, with about a minute between racers. On the seventy-two-person entry list, my start time is 4:28 P.M., about halfway through the field of competitors. The pre-race ritual includes having my bike weighed and measured to ensure it is within regulation standards. I then warm up on the trainer for an hour, get my heart rate high, my muscles ready 'n' sweaty. In the warmup area I run into two fellow cyclists from track cycling camp, Katharine Carroll and Lara Kroepsch. Their familiar, friendly faces calm me. At 4:27 I take my place on the start line, at 4:28 I roll down the ramp. Not a lot goes through my head during the actual race. The familiar mantras of *go, go, go* and *push, push, push* are crosschecked with general data from flight control: check for overexertion, underexertion, proper aerodynamics, and relaxed breathing. Other than that, there are two emotional sentiments battling it out for mind control: *You should be proud just to be here,* is one. *That's not good enough,* screams the other. When I cross the line thirty-five minutes and twenty-five seconds later, I am in eighth place. When the entire field finishes, my time is only good enough for thirty-fifth. Right smack dab in the middle of the results. Actual, numerical mediocrity. Despite my average speed of 25.2 miles per hour, the women in the top ten average around 27 miles per hour and produce times in the thirty-three-minute range. Kristin blows us all away with a 30:47, a full four and a half minutes faster than me. At least she's the world champion. That helps lessen the sting. Man, my U-turn skills really bit me in the ass. Thirty-fifth? That is such an awkward number. *Hi! I'm Kathryn Bertine and I'm thirty-fifth best in the country! Will you be my friend?* Yeah, that's weird. Then again, so am I.

THE ROAD RACE

Luckily, there is little time to wallow in un-Olympic disappointment. Monday brings my second shot at redemption with the 92-kilometer (57.2-mile) road race. My father has driven seven hours to come watch me race, and Steve has flown down from New York. ESPN has sent a camera crew to film the races. Some competitors feel pressure when loved ones come to watch them compete, but I've always gotten an extra rush of adrenaline from personal support. Besides, I'm such an unknown underdog at this event that nothing could compare to the pressure I feel within. I have one year and one month to try to make the Olympic team. Winning this race would secure an appointment to the Olympic development team, but places second through seventy-second would not. Yet it does no good to think about the odds; all I can do is control my own race and hope the wheels don't come off, so to speak.

The opposite of the time trial, the road race is a mass start where all the competitors roll out together. At the start line, teams of women congregate, discussing strategies and adjusting their earpieces (which link to a radio communication system enabling them talk to one another while riding). Ooooh. Earpieces. I feel a quick sizzle of envy. I want to be good enough to wear an earpiece. I wonder if anyone other than David Hasselhoff would think I was cool if I spoke into my watch and asked my imaginary team car to pull around? Probably not.

My only tactic as an individual rider with no teammates: Don't get dropped. How do I do this? Draft. Stay right on the wheel of the woman in front of me. Don't attack, that's stupid. The big teams will send their sprinter goons to hunt me down and reel me back into the pack. Be smart. Be aware. Be excited but not afraid. Be confident. Eat. Drink. Drink more. If there is an appropriate opportunity to move up or break away, take it, take it, take it. In cycling, hesitation is the devil. The devil, I tell you. Even the briefest pause of uncertainty—say, the decision to coast for one second instead of pedaling at full pressure—can destroy a rider's chances of staying in the main peloton. Above all else, my main strategy was this: patience. Learn from these women, absorb everything, don't be The Beginner Who Thinks She Knows Everything. No one likes her, especially the karma monster. And above all else, note the direction of the wind. I've learned the hard way that one cyclist's snot rocket can indeed fly right into the mouth of another. With those thoughts in my head, the race begins.

The goal of every cyclist is to stay in the pack for as long as possible, so they can save energy by drafting. It is not uncommon for a field of seventy-two riders to stay in a large group until the last few hundred meters of a race, where an all-out sprint ultimately decides the winner. But the road race course at nationals is extremely hilly, with only four miles of flat ground. Within twenty miles of the start, the amoeba-shaped peloton thins into a dribble of riders and I lose visual contact with the leaders. Not only lose contact, but at one point I am likely last in the entire group. Not being on a team, I find it difficult to stay in the front of the pack where all the uniformed jerseys cluster tightly together. Individual newbie stragglers like me spend lots of energy jockeying for position. To make my way back to the peloton, all I can do is time-trial as fast as possible and hope to pick off people along the way. Slowly, this begins to happen. And the last shall be … seventy-second, seventy-first, seventieth. For a while I ride in a small group of fellow stragglers. At one point, a view of another small group looms ahead of us … fifty-sixth, fifty-fifth, fifty-fourth …

"Come on," I urge the woman next to me, "let's work together [rotate leading and drafting] and catch them."

One woman, on a professional team no less, laughs sarcastically. "Not like it matters," she scoffs, referring to the fact that we'll likely not catch the leaders in time.

"It fucking matters to me," I roar. *Welcome F-bomb! So glad you could make it!* The beauty of cycling is that so much can change in such a short period of time. Crashes happen. Tires pop. Roadkill obstructs. Traffic congests. Furry little animals run into the road and cause slowing and chaos. In a matter of minutes—even seconds—the first can be last and the last really can be first. While no decent competitor would wish detrimental events on another, these are the very reasons to push through, to keep going when all hope seems lost, to chase an unseen leader. Strong riders can have a weak day and weaker riders can have a strong day. No one is unbeatable, no one knows what will happen over the course of one mile, let alone 57.2. The Unknown can be used as fear or inspiration, but I've found it is a lot more helpful as the latter. Speed, strength, smarts, and mental fortitude are vital to cycling success. But so is luck. Sometimes the race goes to the swiftest, sometimes to the smartest, sometimes to the luckiest—so damn straight it matters to keep going. If I've learned one thing in the past six months of cycling, it is this: The only way to avoid the What Ifs after a race is to answer them during the event.

But if none of it *matters*? Then get the hell off the course. (Readers, Angry Kathryn; Angry Kathryn, readers. I'm not sure you have met yet.)

"I'll go with you," another, more determined competitor offers. "Let's try to catch that pack," she says, introducing herself as Jenny. We don't talk much after that. And so she and I go, for thirty-odd miles pushing ourselves and slowly picking off the other stragglers ... forty-third, forty-second, forty-first ...

After 57.2 miles, I cross the line in thirty-fifth place, out of breath, out of energy, having left everything I had out on the course. My new friend and impromptu teammate, Jenny, finishes with me. I later find out she too is an ex-triathlete, hardwired to always keep going, to never give up, to make sure every race matters, even if the win is out of reach. Dad and Steve are at the finish, cheering and offering supportive hugs and asking how the race went. I have no breath to respond, which is in fact the only acceptable answer.

Icameinthirty-fifthinthetimetrialandthirty-fifthintheroadraceatcyclingnationals. No matter how quickly I say it, the result still stings. I've come to the USA Cycling national championships with the hopes of making the podium, with the hopes of turning the heads of the coaches at USA Cycling, with the hopes of gaining a spot on the developmental Olympic long team. For those who believe in failure, I failed. Or so it feels right now, on the dreaded Day After, when an athlete mentally replays her race over and over again and finds numerous Could Haves and If Onlies and What The Hell Was I Thinkings. There's the third U-turn on the time trial course, so slow and tentative I easily lost fifteen seconds of acceleration. There's the hill at mile fifteen on the road race course, where I dutifully focused on the wheel in front of me, only to look up and see that the pack had split and I was too far back. I should have moved into a better climbing position, I should have turtled my-self into a more aerodynamic crouch, I should have known better after six months of preparation.

For a moment the What Ifs are so intense, I feel the unsportsman-like desire to blame someone or something. Let's see, how about Coach Jimmy? No, he's done nothing but help me prepare. How about the race course selection committee? That zigzag time trial pattern was terrible! No wait, it was challenging. Unfortunately, there's a difference. Who else can I blame? My parents! No. My dad drove seven hours to Champion, Pennsylvania, to watch me render the town's name ironic. But he looked so proud despite my middle-of-the-pack finish. He even passed out Sport Beans to the spectators. Maybe I could blame Steve? No, he flew to Pittsburgh to support me and voluntarily hugged my sweaty, spitty, snot-covered self at the finish line. How about ESPN? They sent a documentary cameraman to nationals who gave me quite a complex when he played back the footage confirming that yes, indeed, I really do look and sound *like that*. This blame thing is not looking good. Seems I have only myself to deal with.

So there we are—thirty-fifth and thirty-fifth place. I am, at least, consistent. Or perhaps it is a sign that when I turn thirty-five, I'll kick everyone's ass. But in the meantime, is it possible to be simultaneously proud of and disappointed in oneself? Proud to be at this level yet disappointed not to have done better? It is an odd, dual sensation.

When it comes time to write the article for the ESPN web site, transcribing the events of nationals is a lot harder than any of the other pieces I've written. Handball, pentathlon, track cycling ... I tried each of those sports for a week. I was a guest on their playing fields. I had little emotional connection to wielding an épée or throwing a sticky ball into a goal. Or not into a goal. Whatever. But cycling? Six months of everyday effort came down to this race, this chance, this glimmer of possibility, this how-good-can-you-get-and-how-quick-can-you-get-there opportunity. When I first got on my bike as a fledgling road cyclist, I did it because it was my job. But over the miles, a silent yet drastic change took place. Between training groups and solo races, between podium finishes and flat tires, I remembered that I'm not riding for ESPN. I'm doing all of this for myself. The Olympics were—and still remain—my dream. I don't believe in failure. I never have. As sappy and self-helpy as that sounds, the only true failure in life is missing out on it. I have no problem coming in thirty-fifth or dead last. I've done it many times. It doesn't hurt. But not even trying? That's the only failure I know.

"But, technically, you did fail to make the USA's Olympic long team in cycling," my frank but kindly ESPN.com editors, Chris, Kevin, and Jay, point out during our post-nationals meeting. "What are your intentions now?"

In all honesty, it breaks my heart to think of giving up cycling. I've improved so much and accomplished a lot in six months. I don't want to do a new sport. It seemed I didn't have much choice, though.

"Well, there are still a few other summer Olympic sports I could try," I say. Archery, race walking—I begin to name a few possibilities but Chris, Kevin and Jay shake their heads.

"No, you've already done that try-and-fail thing. If you keep trying and failing, we're going to lose readers. They'll get bored with you."

"But my readers apparently like watching me flounder," I protest. "We can't let them down now!"

"No, it isn't good for the project, all this failure."

"Well, if I can't try new sports and I no longer have a shot at the U.S. cycling team, what do you want me to do? Find another country to cycle for?" I laugh.

Silence.

More silence.

"Well, we never said you had to get to the Olympics as an American."

What? *What?!*

"But I am a U.S. citizen."

"Well, see what you can do."

WATER BREAK

FAILURE, REJECTION, SACRIFICE, EQUALITY, AND YODA

There are two things in life I do not believe in: failure and rejection. I'm not annoyingly optimistic, I just do not believe in their existence. Failure is illogical. Who exactly came up with this concept? Some bored, old, cranky philosopher who got picked last for bull leaping? The entire idea of failure is completely inaccurate. Any dictionary will argue failure is synonymous with let down, catastrophe, disappointment, and other such cheery hype. But it doesn't make sense. To "fail" (or succeed or fall anywhere in the middle of those socially bedraggled concepts), one first has to *do* something, or at least attempt to *do* something. Is there anything catastrophic or disappointing about attempt itself? When a team loses, do we say they failed? When a major league ball player strikes out, do we say he failed? Please. Failure is nothing but a glass-half-empty overflowing with melodrama. As long as there is attempt, there is no failure.

The two people in history who understood the myth of failure best? Yoda and Theodore Roosevelt. Yoda said, "Do or do not, there is no try." There is no "try" because trying *is* doing … to do is to *do*. Yoda's not saying "do" means *win* and "do not" means *lose*. He means get off your butt, take a chance, and do something. Even if the force isn't necessarily with you. And Theodore Roosevelt, the forefather of doable, really nailed the paradox of failure in his most famous speech, "Citizen in a Republic": "It is not the critic who counts, not the man who points out how the strong man stumbled, or where the doer of deeds could have done better. The credit belongs to the man who is actually in the arena, whose face is marred by dust and sweat and blood; who strives valiantly; who errs and comes short again and again … who at best, knows the triumph of high achievement; and who, at the worst, if he fails, at least fails while daring greatly, so that his place shall never be with those cold and timid souls who know neither victory nor defeat."

Like failure, rejection doesn't actually exist either. We fear "no" because we think it closes doors, ends possibility, and leads to nothing. But here's the funny thing about "no": It doesn't do any of those things. In fact, "no" doesn't *do* anything at all. It just sits there, doing nothing, leading nowhere. Yet it often trips us up because we don't understand "no." Why don't we understand "no"? Because there is nothing to understand about it! We should think of "no" not as rejection, but as an acronym for "not open." Go elsewhere. "No" cannot open doors or bring change or alter the course of life. Only "yes" can do that. As in, "Yes, ESPN, thank you, I *would* like to try to be an Olympian. Yes, I *would* like my soul to be neither cold nor timid!" Only the acceptance of opportunity will bring change.

My quest did not end with USA Cycling saying no; it simply showed me some new doors to knock on. Life is a really long hotel-like hallway with hundreds of closed doors. We start at one end of the hall and walk toward the other. Along the way, we're supposed to knock at each door. (Or you can just keep walking and not knocking, but that's pretty boring. You're in a hotel, man, have a little fun! Knock! Knock and wait, knock and wonder, knock and run away, whatever … just knock.) The doors that don't open just leave us right there in the same place, middle of the hallway. We aren't any farther back or farther ahead. Neither victory nor defeat. So we knock elsewhere. Nothing to lose, nothing to fail. And the doors that do open? Well now, those are the rooms to go into. At the very best, there will be more rooms to explore off that room. At the very worst, a room will simply lead you right back to the hallway. But the doors that don't open? That isn't rejection. They're just not supposed to open. Like fire doors. And there's no fire, so leave them alone already. March forward and knock loudly. That is all we have to do. There is no such thing as rejection. Or failure. And sacrifice? Nothing but hype.

Sacrifice. The word reminds me of three things: virgins, goats, and baseball. The term does not belong in sports (even baseball), nor should it ever be used in conjunction with an athlete. The media loves the sacrifice cliché, painting pictures of hard-working athletes toiling in obscurity, pushing all physical boundaries, leading lonely, focused existences—O the sacrifice!—while chasing their dreams of Olympic or professional glory. What a load of crap. Hard work? Perseverance? Risk? That's not sacrifice. That's choice. And there's a hell of a difference between the two.

Sacrifice plays no part in a true athlete's existence. Take the sacrifice bunt in baseball. Sacrifice? I don't think so. The goal of baseball is for a *team* to win, not an individual player. So technically, a player can't sacrifice himself for his team. It's his job to do whatever it takes for his team to win. And if being on a team is your job and you choose your job, sorry pal—that ain't sacrifice. I hereby make a motion to rename the sacrifice bunt the volunteer bunt.

Growing up, I was head over heels in love with figure skating. Beginning at age eleven, I begged my dad to take me to the rink so I could skate for two hours before school. I went to bed at 8:30 P.M., I did my homework immediately after school, and I didn't try to be socially accepted in high school (mission accomplished). No one forced me to do these things. I loved my sport and my early morning rink existence. These were my choices. My father's decision to get up at 4:45 A.M. and drive me to the rink? Okay, that's a sacrifice. He lovingly sacrificed his time and his sleep for his daughter. But what did I sacrifice of myself to be an athlete? Nothing. It was my choice. Life is so much better than pillows and blankets.

As a struggling professional triathlete and Olympic hopeful cyclist, I willingly committed myself to a twenty-five-hour training week. To earn money, I needed a job that I could work around those hours. Waitressing, substitute teaching, pet-sitting ... were these ideal? Were these my life goals? No. Did they allow me to do what I loved, to follow my passions, to entertain the possibility of athletic glory, to live in the moment, to better myself? Yes. Well then, that was an easy choice. Had income, sleep, or mediocrity been more important to me than freedom, aliveness, and the glory of possibility then yes, trying to be a professional athlete would have been a sacrifice. But renunciation in the service of one's own dreams? I have sacrificed nothing. Not even a goat.

When athletes love their sport, honor their bodies, and thrive on competition, they make only choices, not sacrifices. And if their instincts are pure and positive and honest, then so too will be their effort. On certain days that effort will be enough, on other days that effort will fall short, but an athlete is not made in one day. True athletes are shaped by time and perseverance. True athletes are shaped by the synonyms of loss and victory, both of which build and reveal an athlete's character.

As for equality in modern-day sports, we've got a bit of work to do. On a plane ride en route to one of my cycling races, I sat next to an elderly couple. They asked me what I did for a living and I told them I raced bikes against other women. The gentleman leaned over to his hearing-impaired wife and relayed the information. She looked at him, crinkled her crinkly brow, and said, "They have that?"

Indeed. We exist. The world has female cyclists, but our

existence is still lost on the greater American population. This could so easily be changed. Awareness is not all that difficult to create, but our media have not caught up to the reality.

· For five straight weekdays before the Beijing Olympics, I read the sports sections of the *New York Times* and *USA Today*. Here's the breakdown of articles devoted to men's and to women's sports.

Before Olympics (five-day tally)
New York Times: 101 articles on men's sports (20.2 average per day), 9 on women's (1.8 per day)
USA Today: 84 articles on men's sports (16.8 average per day), 14 on women's (2.8 per day)
During Olympics (daily average, which combines Olympics articles and regular-season professional sports articles)
New York Times: 31 articles on men's sports, 5 on women's
USA Today: 23 articles on men's sports, 4 on women's

We can do better than that. There must be awareness before there is interest. In the United States, home to the biggest media conglomerates in the world, how is it possible women are still virtual unknowns in sport?

Maybe it has to start much smaller. Much earlier. During the run of my ESPN column, I received a bunch of e-mails from devoted male ESPN readers who told me they would print out my columns and give them to their daughter(s) to read. I was touched. But why not give columns about women athletes to their sons as well? I believe the beauty of athletics knows no gender boundaries, as stories of loss, triumph, underdogs, and superstars all ring true to male and female athletes alike. Even better, giving boys articles on female athletes will have an incredible if subtle impact on gender equality.

Straight from the womb, many girls, like boys, have innate athletic drive and ambition. Imagine what strides could be made—what female athletes of all ages and abilities could achieve—if women's sports were given equal coverage and attention to men's. If the mass media wants to play dumb and cry, "We didn't know the public wanted to read about women's sports!" then let's tell them. Write the editors and owners of local, national, and global newspapers and magazines and web sites. Ask, nicely, for more coverage of female athletes. Give them some names and sports and events, from familiar stars to people they have never heard of. Asking is a powerful weapon.

Better yet, cook up a few story ideas and offer yourself as a reporter covering the sport you love. Try it. Let's see what happens. Maybe a few years from now, I'll be on a plane and an elderly woman will note my funky cyclist's tan and ask, "Mountain, track, or road, dear?"

HIPS ON FIRE

August 2007

Three weeks after my cycling nationals, while I'm feeling a little bummed about my race performance and wondering if ESPN was serious about me trying to race for another country, an e-mail appears in my inbox from USA Race Walking. It is the first week of August 2007, and Vince Peters, the director of the race walking development program, has finally responded to my February inquiry about the sport. He has attached a file that I quickly download. It reads "USA Race Walking: Your Passport to the Olympic Games."

Oooh, *my passport!* Now we're talking.

Here I am running around like a crazy person, trying to get to the Olympics, when an undeniable omen falls in my lap and tells me to walk. It's all coming together now—first, the *Go for the Gold* banner in the "free stuff" box at the Olympic Training Center, and now my very own passport to Beijing. Someone clearly wants me to keep my Olympic dream alive. Will it be cycling or race walking? Someone is trying to show me the way. As of this very minute, I'm going to let go and let Zeus.

"We're having a talent ID camp the weekend of August 11. Can you make it?" Vince asks me over the phone.

"My schedule's pretty free, Vince," I admit, sadly. Besides, what better way to heal my broken cycling heart than to make out with a new sport for a weekend? How bad can I be at the sport of walking? (That's rhetorical, thank you). I am either too big or too small for rowing, too unsprinty for track cycling, too old for pentathlon, too inept for team handball, too summery for luge, too middle-of-the-pack for pro triathlon, too slow for elite open water swimming, and apparently too American for road cycling. What, in the good name of sport, is left to try for a thirty-two-year-old with twelve months left to make an Olympic team?

I still haven't been to the Olympic Training Center in Chula Vista, California, where rumor has it that most race walkers train. "Are you training in Chula Vista?" I ask Vince.

"No," he says, "we'll be staying at the Best Western in Teaneck, New Jersey."

I have a sudden feeling that race walking is about to replace team handball as the most underfunded U.S. Olympic sport.

As with all the other camps and clinics, I figure the baptism-by-fire approach will be the same for race walking and that I'll be thrown into the sport during the first practice, only to emerge sore, disheveled, and dejected. Possibly rodeled. So before arriving at the camp, I have a couple of private race walk lessons with fourteen-time national title holder, forty-six-year-old Ray Sharp. Ray informs me that there are two rules to the sport of race walking: One leg must be in contact with the ground at all times (otherwise it's called "running"), and the knee of the front leg must remain locked/straight/unbent until it passes the vertical point of the body. In other words, I have to walk like a mummy. A mummy in a hurry. Ray says that referees are stationed along the course with red cards, looking for infractions. Red cards are posted on a scoreboard that resembles some sort of Price Is Right game. Three red cards, you're out.

Two rules. How hard can that be?

On a deserted cul-de-sac in Tucson, I ask Ray to hit full stride, to show me what it looks like when a race walker revs up to a sub-six-minute-mile pace. Ray obliges, and the result is a gait so frenzied and funky that it borders on convulsive. His hips swivel ferociously back and forth while his right leg sweeps around in a half-limp, half-skip movement. The stride is simultaneously fluid and jarring. He looks something like a ninja with hamstring issues. I can see his heel strike the ground, but his legs are moving so quickly that I wonder how an official can ever discern if an athlete's foot is firmly on the ground.

"Sometimes they can't," Ray informs me. Which is why there are multiple judges, and why it takes three red cards from three different judges to disqualify a race walker. For the next hour, Ray goes over some drills with me so that I get the feeling of slamming my heels into the ground and locking my knees.

"You know when you're a kid and you're at the local pool, running around, and the lifeguard blows his whistle and screams for you to walk? And you immediately go as fast as you can without technically running? *That* is race walking." The lightbulb goes on. I get it! But not for very long. Apparently, there is a method to the technique that enables the race walker to move at the speed of a runner. "It is called the Flow," Ray explains.

Which, after the first workout, is apparent I don't have.

"It takes time to get the Flow," Ray says, encouragingly.

"How much time?" I demand.

"Sometimes weeks, sometimes months. Even years."

"It can take a *year* to learn how to legally walk fast?"

"Yes."

"A calendar year?"

"Yes."

"Why, Ray? Why? This is not what I want to hear. A freaking year. Dude, you're killing me. Why are you telling me this?"

"Because ... you asked."

"Oh. Did I?" I'm not sure whether this oversight is due to my Olympic quest time constraints or just congenital, but lately I find myself forgetting to run all thoughts through my Don't Say That Out Loud filter.

The Best Western in Teaneck, New Jersey, sits between a mall and a highway. I arrive on a Thursday evening and meet the rest of the talent identification camp invitees. My prediction, that everyone else at the camp will be younger than me, proves true. A gaggle of twelve high school girls from New York City and three boys from Ohio have come to Teaneck to receive a weekend of coaching, knowledge, and guidance on all that race walking has to offer. All fifteen of them have been practicing the sport for a year or longer, making me once again the oldest rookie. At the culmination of our camp, we will all drive two hours to Long Island and compete in a legitimate 3-mile race walk event.

On our first morning, I awake to rain, exhaustion, and a wicked case of bed head from the pillows sandwiching my ears to keep the turnpike noise out. My high school roommate, whom I shall refer to as Textaholic, has been up all night clickity-clicking on her phone with the boys down the hall. Muffled giggles, beeps, and cell phone illumination have emanated from her bed like an all-night miniature amusement park. Textaholic and I part the curtains to reveal pouring rain, so our day begins not on the track but in the Best Western conference room, which reeks of cigarettes and damp shoes. Vince and his assistant coach, Olympic hopeful Erin Taylor, show us videos of race walking technique and pass out booklets on stretching and nutrition. A few hours later, the rain has not subsided and the natives begin to get restless. Vince and Erin decide to hold afternoon practice in an enclosed, rain-free venue. This turns out to be not a local gym or indoor track, but the third level of the parking garage for the Bergenfield Mall. The concrete is dry, the lot is nearly empty, the breeze is warm, the pigeons are tolerable, and we begin to walk to the beat of the Muzak filtering in from the elevators at the far end of the lot. For twenty minutes, Vince and Erin work on my arm swing, my elbow position, my hip rotation, and my toe elevation. Before a half-hour's time, the backs of my knees are on fire and my hips hate me. I look like a cross between Shakira and Frankenstein as I waddle full-throttle around the mall's parking lot. Vince and Erin yell things I've never heard coaches yell before, like "Nice hyperextension!" and "Legal, legal, legal … illegal! … legal, legal …" and my all-time favorite athletic critique, "Kathryn, the good news is your left leg is race walking. The bad news is your right leg isn't."

Just as I'm certain my knee tendons are about to rupture, I am saved by the most unlikely source—mall security, Jersey style. Two potbellied men in a white Jeep Liberty make a five-mile-per-hour beeline for Vince and Erin, the yellow flashing lights on their roof rotating with bland authority.

"Watchoo doin?" one security guard asks Vince.

"We're just trying to stay out of the rain," Vince explains. "The kids are learning to race walk."

"You gotta permit?"

I stifle a snicker. I hate it when I leave my *free to walk through a mall parking lot* permit at home. The Liberty men take away our walking freedom and within ten minutes, we're back at the Best Western conference room taking notes on the history of race walking.

Often incorrectly referred to as speed walking or power walking, race walking became an Olympic event in 1908, and thus will be celebrating its centennial anniversary at the Summer Games in Beijing. A couple of hundred years before red cards and straight-knee rules were part of the sport, race walking was known as pedestrianism and it was a big hit in Europe and North America. While the sport isn't regarded as mainstream in today's society, race walking was one of the most popular and lucrative athletic sensations of the mid-eighteenth to early nineteenth centuries, an era when people began to gamble on sports and athletes. Walking was an easy contest with easy regulations: "I bet I can walk farther and faster than you." Before long, walking contests were held for both time and distance, and in 1762 a man named John

Hogue broke the hundred-miles-in-a-day barrier, winning enough glory, riches, and fame to ensure a life of leisure.

By the late nineteenth century, running became the focal point of endurance competitions and pedestrianism struggled to maintain its golden reputation as the most demanding athletic endeavor. When it came to covering ground on foot, speed gave way to distance as the public's choice of entertainment. Still, the sport of race walking remains wildly competitive at international elite levels, despite the poor publicity and pitiful funding it receives within the United States. With Ecuador, Poland, Russia, and Mexico leading the field, neither the American media nor the Olympic committee pay enough attention to it.

Surely race walking was not helped by Bob Costas' commentary during the 2000 Sydney Olympics when he jabbed, "What's up with the race walkers? I mean, I respect them as athletes but come on … a contest to see who can walk the fastest is like having a contest to see who can whisper the loudest." Yikes! A senior national sportscaster just ripped on a sport with United States citizens competing for gold. An on-air jab at clean-cut, hard-working, scandal-free athletes by an overpaid, unsportsmanlike, nonathlete TV anchor? Not so cool, Bob. I think someone needs to be sent down the luge track.

🚲 🚲 🚲

The next day in Teaneck, the rain subsides and we hit the local high school running track for some proper outdoor training. The total mileage we will be putting in is … one mile. One mile? Are you kidding me? The Olympic race walking distance for women is twelve miles, and if I'm going to be a race walker I've got to get a bit more mileage in.

"You'll race three miles tomorrow, so this is enough for today," Vince explains.

Sure enough, after one flowless, unbendable mile, my legs are screaming with stiffness, though my cardiovascular system barely ekes out a sweat. Bizarre. I clock eleven minutes. To get to the Olympic trials, I'd need to do 12.4 miles at a pace averaging roughly 7:53 minutes per mile. And to do this, I would need the Flow. At the moment, all I possess is the Dam.

The next day our race walking camp heads to Long Island, where the race is held in the large, looping driveway of a corporate office building. I line up for the 5-kilometer race with a few experienced race walkers my age and a few older folks and a few people with a bit of bulge to their bodies. The gun goes off and *bam*—the older and larger participants not only pass me but eventually lap me. They have the Flow! I don't. I come in last. But the truth is, I started in last. Mentally, anyway. Usually a race situation—in any sport—makes my entire body tingle with electricity, with determination, with amped-up endorphins. Usually, when that gun goes off, I'm transported into some euphoric state of physical movement that it sometimes takes days to come down from. But the starter's gun at the race walk event brought nothing but noise, tendonitis, and three miles of wishing I was elsewhere. That isn't a bad thing, necessarily, as wishing I was elsewhere usually helps me figure out where my true elsewhere lies. Here's the conundrum of race walking: I love to race. I love to walk. I hate to race walk. While I respect and appreciate the sport for what it is (incredibly difficult, extremely athletic, and under-appreciated), race walking just doesn't feel good to me. This is amplified by the fact that after three days, the Flow continues to elude me.

Something is telling me to walk as fast as I can … back to my bike. All I want—and all my body wants—is to get back to my bike, to go for a hundred-mile ride, to feel the burn in my muscles from making myself better, faster, stronger in a sport that I adore. Somewhere in that three-mile stretch of race walk temptation, I recalled more than just my love for cycling and my desire to be an Olympian. I knew, with renewed love, passion, and vision, that I was going to fight for it.

WATER BREAK

WRITING, SPORTS, AND MY GREAT, GREAT PIERRE

My armpits sweat when I write. This is either because my body thinks I'm a bad writer or because I've got well-developed lat muscles from years of swimming, which rub against my upper arms when I type and don't allow much airflow to my pits. This is important information, as readers can now enlarge their stereotype of the anguished writer. Ernest Hemingway had alcoholism issues, Percy Shelley had his opium problem, Kurt Vonnegut was a chain smoker. I have sweaty pits. It's a vice that puts me, I like to think, almost in their league.

Which makes me wonder what they might have written had they been in *my* league. If Hemingway was a professional athlete,[6] *The Sun Also Rises* might have been about young figure skaters and the parents who drive them to predawn practice sessions. If George Orwell was an athlete, *1984* might have been about the Los Angeles Olympics. Jane Austen would have centered *Pride and Prejudice* around the emergence of minority athletes in the 1960 Olympics. If Charles Dickens had been more athletically inclined, *Oliver Twist* might have concerned an aspiring gymnast sent away to the poor house by the British Gymnastic Federation after breaking his ankle on a vault. Dickens' famous gruel scene would have read much differently.

"Please sir, may I have some more? I've been turning the grist mill for sixteen hours straight and this bowl of gruel only has 145 calories. That shan't do at all, sir. I appreciate the carbohydrates, sir, but I need at least 5,400 calories per day if I'm to work here, and 40 percent of that should come from protein. Have we any oxtail, sir?"

Last but not least, perhaps my beloved Vonnegut could have put my Olympic quest at the centerpiece of his final work,

---

6 He was, in fact, an amateur boxer.

A [Wo]Man Without a Country. I've been searching through my family history for clues of international heritage and dual-citizenship possibilities in hopes that my Olympic dream can move forward.

While looking into my ancestry recently, I discovered that my twin interests in both writing and Olympic athletics have genealogical roots. While the ancient Olympic Games were said to have begun back when mortals and gods mingled in Greece, the modern Olympic Games were founded in 1904 by Frenchman Baron Pierre de Coubertin. My father, Peter Bertine, comes from a long line of French "Bertin" folk. After an extended genealogy search, it turns out that the founding father of the Olympic Games is quite possibly my great, great something. Perhaps uncle. Maybe cousin. The math gets fuzzy after the first few genealogy branches on the free heritage web sites. However, in a foreword by Olivier Margot in the book *The Olympics: Athens to Athens 1896-2004,* Margot writes about my possible ancestor Baron Pierre, describing Pierre's writing as "… the kind that would raise a smile yet was often riddled with ridiculousness." I rest my case. We're *totally* related. Not to mention, he played rugby and I was a figure skater … we both fell down a lot. Pierre preached equality in sport, which in his day and age (1863 to 1937) meant equality of nationality and race, not gender. While some sites claim he was fond of seeing women compete in sport, I did find one quote of Pierre's that suggested he thought otherwise: "I oppose female Olympiads, they are uninteresting, unaesthetic, and incorrect." Oh well. That's okay. The family tree indicates that Pierre had an older sister. Perhaps she kicked his butt in sports, causing him to become bitter and compelling him to one-up her by starting the Olympics. That's a genealogy I can live with.

(13)

1-800-POLANDS

September 2007

When ESPN posted the column about my "failure" at the U.S. cycling nationals and my editors suggested I look for a new country to adopt me, the e-mails poured in. Half were from folks who thought ESPN was joking. The other half of my readers—who correctly took ESPN at its word—suggested where I might begin looking.

- Number of e-mails asking if I'm Jewish and could represent Israel: 43
- Number of e-mails asking if I'm Catholic and could represent Vatican City: 34
- Number of e-mails asking if I'm willing to convert to Islam and race in a burqa: 6
- Number of e-mails asking if I could race for Lichtenstein, the world's smallest nation: 13

- Number of e-mails suggesting I race for Bermuda, Bahamas, come on pretty mamas: 10
- Number of e-mails suggesting that Steve marry me so I can race for Great Britain: 52
- Number of e-mail marriage proposals from Serbia: 1
- Number of e-mails from Mormons asking that I write "fudge" instead of the F-bomb: 1

The last e-mail was the only one over which I had any control. As for marriage, Steve was off the hook, at least for now, seeing as Britain requires a waiting period of two years after marriage before a spouse gains the right to apply for dual citizenship. The twenty-one-year-old Serbian suitor, who assured me the older woman-boy toy relationship works well for Demi and Ashton, is also off the hook. For now. As for the religious-Olympic affiliation, I'm out of luck there. I'm neither Muslim, Jewish, Catholic, nor Mormon. I currently attend the church of Saint Cyclius the Divine. Anyone can join. Here are the Four Commandments:

1. Find something in this world to believe in.
2. Make sure it doesn't hurt anyone.
3. Don't try to convert anyone.
4. Worship the hell out of it.

My only options in regard to obtaining dual citizenship in another country, and thus attempting to represent that country at the 2008 Olympics—which is now less than a year away—are as follows:

1. Ask my parents if they're actually retired foreign spies posing as Westchester residents, and if so, may I use one of their many passports?
2. Find out if my late Grandpa Vic was born in Poland or New Jersey.
3. Petition Arizona, or even just Tucson, to secede from the Union and become an independent nation. By August.
4. Cross the Canadian or Mexican borders and beg asylum from the Bush regime.

Option two seems the most likely, as some countries offer citizenship to those who can prove a solid family lineage. I call my father. Unfortunately, his French and British ancestors have been hanging around New York since the Mayflower days. That rules out getting citizenship from France or Britain, which usually require parents or grandparents of that nationality. Some countries don't allow dual citizenship at all, and some silly countries actually require a person to have been born there to be considered a citizen! Picky, picky. Where's the love? Aren't we all children of the earth? Couldn't I just represent the Planet? That would be groovy. But unlikely. A call to dad should help. Dads know lots of things.

"Hi, dad. Hey, quick question: Are you an international spy?"

"I don't think so."

"Any chance I was switched at birth or perhaps an illegitimate love child?"

"Your little pink wristband definitely said *Bertine*."

"Damn. Any chance that you or mom were the product of sketchy, foreign conception?"

"Probably not. Birth-switched illegitimates weren't too common in the 1930s and '40s."

"Jeez, dad, work with me here. What's mom's heritage?"

"She's got German and Polish ancestry. Sweetheart, are you all right?"

"Loaded question, dad."

I quickly rule out Germany. They've got tons of world-class female cyclists who could kick the weinerschnitzel out of me and therefore have no reason to go around adopting foreign cyclists. But Poland, known for a slew of talented male cyclists, boasts a women's national team that, while talented, might not be of quite the same caliber. In the last Olympics, their riders finished twenty-seventh and forty-second out of the sixty-two person field—a bit removed from the main peloton. On line, I find a very encouraging paragraph saying that Poland not only allows dual citizenship but has no immediate restrictions on how far back one's Polish bloodline goes.

"Dad, was mom's father was born in Poland?"

"I think he was born in Newark."

"Crap."

"But *his* parents were definitely born in Poland."

And there it is. My Olympic dream is hanging by a thread.

If only I knew how to get in touch with the Polish Cycling Federation.

"Just call Poland," Steve suggests when I visit him in New York City on my way back from race walking in Teaneck.

"What, like 1-800-Poland?" I say, shooting him a gee-you're-so-helpful look. Yet in the spirit of leaving no stone unturned, I try the number anyway. Nothing. Not enough digits. Okay, then … 1-800-Polands. A busy signal! For a split paranoid second, I'm afraid the line is tied up by another American cyclist asking if she can race for Poland. On the second call, I get through. It is a recording asking if I'd like to chat with "live lonely women."

I hand Steve the phone. "Here. It's for you."

Online, I find the number and e-mail address for the Polish Cycling Federation. I draft an e-mail and send it through a web site that does free translations. I decide to keep it short and simple.

Dear Polish Cycling Assoc. President,

My name is Kathryn Bertine, I'm an elite U.S. cyclist. I am writing to inquire about the possibility of racing for and representing Poland in the 2008 Olympics. I have Polish ancestry and I would like to speak to you about dual citizenship procedures and Polish cycling regulations.

Please let me know if this e-mail has reached you, and if I may follow up with a phone call in the coming week.

Thank you for your time and consideration,

Kathryn Bertine

Just before hitting send, I decide to run my translation backward—from Polish to English—just to make sure the text came across as somewhat coherent. Or not.

Dear Polish Brilliance Ass Cycling,

It named Kathryn Bertine, It elite AMERICAN bicycle.

It about capability to take participation quota in races. Write enquire for and introducing presents in 2008 Olympic Polish Poland. It beguiles Polish origin and would like to say about double procedures of citizenship and Polish Poland brilliance cycling regulations.

It asks allow if this e-mail reaches Polish Brilliance and if It can chase you with call of phone in arrival of one week.

It thanks you for your time and consideration,

Kathryn Bertine

I might as well have signed it "Borat." The only thing left to do is find a native Polish speaker who can call Poland on my behalf and act as my translator. While calling and e-mailing friends to see if they know any Polish people and researching ways to contact the Polish Embassy in the United States, I begin to get a taste of how difficult and tedious this process will be. Questions swarm. If I can barely get through to Poland, what are the chances I can become a citizen and race for them at the Olympic level, all within the next eleven months? Communication, paperwork, potentially living abroad … could all this be done in addition to carrying a full-time training schedule and making journalism deadlines? And what about the moral component? I've been so focused on the task of finding citizenship, but in all honesty, the thought of switching nationalities raises some issues about my self-centeredness. *I* want citizenship so *I* can race because it's *my* dream to go to the Olympics. *Me me me.* Yikes. I know that some people will consider what I'm doing despicable. They will chastise me for putting my quest above my own country. Others might add that if I'm not good enough to make the U.S. team, why should I bother trying to get to the Olympics, where I will surely get slaughtered on an international level? Have I no shame, have I no respect for my country or for the Olympics?

Actually, I've got nothing *but* respect for the Olympics. Every couple of years a bunch of international athletes gather around the Olympic campfire and sing *Kumbaya* for two weeks, kicking each other's happy asses. And for what? The chance to win an olive branch halo and a glorified coaster tied to a piece of ribbon? No. For the chance to be a part of something good. Something worthwhile. Something bigger than ourselves. Something that celebrates the body rather than trying to demolish it. That's what I respect. That is what the Olympics mean to me.

So does it really matter what country I try to represent? Some will say yes, that patriotism comes first. But America cherishes the principle of providing a haven for the needy—"Give me your tired, your poor"—so why would anyone object to another country welcoming me in the same spirit? As an elite female athlete in an obscure endurance sport, I too am tired and poor. And hungry. Plus determined. If I can find foreign shores to welcome my bicycle and me, then I'm going to do it. If, through my job with ESPN and through another country, I can bring more exposure to women's cycling, I'm going to do that too. If I just really want to see how good I can be as an athlete, can I let anything hold me back? I can't answer for everyone else, but my answer is no. Fudge no. I'm not going to break any rules. I'm not going to disgrace myself or my country—or countries. I'm not going intrude on anyone else's dream or take away their Olympic opportunity. I'll find the right way to do this. I anticipate people standing in my path and trying to block my efforts. That's okay. Bring it on. I've gotten really good at U-turns.

🚴 🚴 🚴

After a week of trying to find a Polish interpreter, my body was sulking, my mind was spinning, and my spirits were sinking. I needed a break. Actually, what I really needed was a sign. *Are you there, Zeus? It's me, Kathryn. If I'm supposed to keep hiking toward Mt. Olympus, could you throw me a benevolent thunderbolt?*

Later that day, the phone rings. It's my brother, Pete, who darts in and out of my life, as older brothers tend to do.

"Hey K, long time since we've talked. Whatcha been up to?"

"Not much. Trying to go to the Olympics. Emigrate to Europe. You know."

"Yeah. Hey, I've got this awesome new girlfriend."

"Oh? What's she like?"

"She really great. She's Polish."

A few days later, I meet my brother's new girlfriend in New York City. Kasia is a lovely woman who has lived in the United States for fifteen years, works in Manhattan, and spends her free time running, cycling, and being active.

"I'm happy to help," Kasia says, "What can I do?" She's actually been reading my articles on ESPN.com, so she is familiar with the quest so far. I tell her of my plan and ask if she would be willing to do a proper translation of my e-mail and then call Pawel Meszko, the head of the Polish Cycling Federation. Kasia agrees. After she's sent an e-mail in both Polish and English, we gather in her office to call Poland. I bring the two telephone numbers that I've tracked down through the Union Cycliste Internationale (UCI) web site. The first one rings and rings. As Kasia dials the second number, I feel my stomach muscles tighten and my pulse quicken just a bit, more so with each unanswered ring. I'm calling a person I don't know in a country I've never set foot in to ask if I can become a citizen of their nation and join their Olympic team. And to top it all off, I want this absurd request more than I've ever wanted anything in my life. I wonder how long it will take for Mr. Meszko to hang up on me. The best I can hope for is that my request is amusing enough to intrigue him. I can work with intrigue. Intrigue is doable.

After the fifth ring, a voice answers—a live, human voice—and offers a salutation in Polish. Kasia engages in conversation. I sit there, listening. The receptionist has put us through to Mr. Meszko, and I try to interpret the intonation of the dialogue. I find myself with a hoard of butterflies in my stomach. I can't decipher the chatter, so I listen to the inflections. Are there happy intonations? Angry? Annoyed? Will the conversation end in five seconds or five minutes? Their tone is neither cheery nor discouraging, but flat and businesslike. I listen for hopeful lilts or gruff syllables. So far, the phone call is devoid of emotion, but I also sense it is not going poorly, for Mr. Meszko has answered Kasia's questions with full sentences. For what seems like hours (but ends up being roughly five minutes), I listen to my dream being discussed while I sit on the sidelines. The outcome of this phone call could change my future, and all I can do is sit there quietly and listen and keep tabs on my breathing pattern so I don't sound like a crank caller.

When Kasia wraps up the call, my heartbeat quickens. She relays the details, and the findings are, well, not terribly optimistic. The good news is that yes, dual citizenship is allowed in Poland but not very common and can take a good deal of time to procure. The clincher is that the Polish Cycling Federation would not take steps to personally sponsor me. In other words, if I wanted citizenship, I'd have to find it on my own and *then* go talk to the Polish Cycling Federation. A tough path to navigate at this point in the game. But, if I were able to get citizenship, I could get in touch with Mr. Meszko again. Of course, he added, there's no certainty I'd make the Olympics because I'd need to gain roughly a hundred UCI points and even if I did, there are still other Polish team members who are veteran cyclists and likely get the Olympic spots.

I'm uncertain about the hundred points, though. What are UCI points and where do I get them? All I know is that points usually have to do with games and that I like games very much. Games and points! Oh boy! But how do I play? I know of one person who just might know the rules. A few months ago, while making sure I understood the criteria to get myself qualified for U.S. nationals, I called Andy Lee in the public relations department of USA Cycling. If anyone knows how to navigate the Olympic qualification procedures, it's Andy. Of course, he would have no obligation to help me find a new country to race for, and might even completely disagree with my efforts to find citizenship elsewhere. I expect the call to go nowhere, to be the final chapter, to have an officially informed person tell me that there is nothing else I could try. I expect Andy to tell me I've reached the end of the road in my Olympic quest. But for over an hour this kindhearted man talks me through the rules and regulations of international racing, downloads documents and procedures, and metaphorically holds my hand as I try to navigate the UCI web site. And there, at the end of the road, just off the paved shoulder and barely noticeable to the mainstream traffic whizzing by, Andy and I find a path—albeit, overgrown with What Ifs and Probably Nots—but a gnarly little footpath nonetheless.

"This is where the UCI points come in," Andy says. If I were to be named to a country's national team, it does *not* automatically ensure me an Olympic berth. I'd still have to go through the process of qualifying, just like every other Olympic hopeful cyclist. "You'd have to look at the international calendar of 2008 UCI races and go to the ones where you are allowed to race as a member of a national team. Some races you can simply enter, others you have to be invited to. If you do well in those races, you win points. If you have enough points (usually around a hundred) to put you in the top one hundred ranked women in the world by May 31, 2008, your country gets one spot in the Olympics." Points, levels, qualifications—feels almost like a video game. Frogger, perhaps. But with only one life, no reset button, and extremely real traffic.

"So if I'm the only one on my adoptive national team and I win one hundred points throughout the season, I would get the Olympic spot?"

"Yes, if you earned the one hundred points and there were no other women racing for your new country, yes, you'd automatically get the spot," Andy tells me.

Well, hot damn.

From Brazil to Belgium, Luxembourg to the Netherlands, and patches of Europe between, there are twenty-seven races in which I could compete. I can pronounce three of them. Tour of New Zealand,

Tour of Belgium, and the Mt. Hood Cycling Classic give me comfort. The Omloop van Borsele, Majowy Wyscig Klasyczny, and Drentse van Dwingeloo kind of freak me out. Dwingeloos and Omloops sound like things cyclists should avoid. Then again, so does tiramisu and baklava, so I decide not to be afraid.

Just how feasible is it for me to get these elusive one hundred points? The international race calendar starts on January 6, 2008, and the deadline for collecting Olympic points is May 31. Roughly five months. There are two kinds of races on the international circuit: 1.1 and 2.1. At the higher 1.1 races, the winner gets eighty points, with fifty-six, thirty-two, twenty-four, twenty, sixteen, twelve, eight, seven, six, five, and three points going to the second through eleventh place finishers. In the 2.2 series, the points go only eight places deep, ranging from forty points for a win to just three points for eighth place. Andy tells me that one downside is that some races require an invitation. I can't just show up to any one that strikes my fancy.

In a perfect world, I'd win a couple of races and pack my bags for China. In reality, the hardcore European ass-kicking women will show up in droves. But despite the numbers, the odds, the chance of all this falling into place, my mind clings to one image: the path. Small as it is, I see it. After my conversation with Andy, I now understand the nature of the path and the bottom line of my dream: new citizenship. Twenty-seven races. Four and a half months. No teammates. One hundred points. Beijing.

Andy and I circle back to the issue of my citizenship. Poland is now out, seeing as the cycling federation is not going to personally help me get citizenship, and with such a short time frame, I will need all the help I can get. I will have to find a new country from scratch. But aside from the daunting task of reaching out to unknown people in unfamiliar countries with my unbelievable request, there was a whole other issue at stake. Morals. My inner athlete was ready to do whatever it took to get to the Olympics, but my ethics control center was sending out some warnings. Namely, that it was not okay to barge into some underfunded, third-world country with a legitimate but struggling cycling team and try to take an Olympic dream/opportunity/spot away from a bonafide national citizen. That's about as Unolympic and Ugly American as it gets. But What If there was another way … a way in which my Olympic dreams could actually be of mutual benefit to a country?

An idea comes to me. Which is exciting, seeing as this means athleticoma has not yet killed all my brain cells. I ask Andy about the possibility of finding a country with a legitimate cycling federation but no active women's team. Because cycling is still a male-dominated sport, many countries have male-only cycling federations simply because women haven't been exposed to the sport.

What If I were the *entire* national women's team? Racing solo. Of course, we know how well that's worked for me so far. Teammates make a huge difference in race strategy. Teammates are usually the reason a cyclist can win a race at all. But if I am the entire team, I'd be racing against other countries, not teammates, to gain points. Bingo! I can't take an Olympic spot away from someone who doesn't exist. Oh happy day, oh glorious path!

As I spoke with Andy and we navigated paths and rules and points, it also occurred to me that my crazy dreams might actually benefit another country. What If I, by cycling for them, could help that nation establish their own legitimate national women's cycling team? Maybe I could help their federation with coaching and recruiting local women. Maybe I could help them navigate their own future Olympic paths. Maybe not for 2008, but surely in time. What a consolation prize that would be, even if my Olympic dreams come to an end. This project doesn't actually have to be all about me. There is a "we" in sight. I can chase my dream *and* offer something in return.

So instead of trying to find my way into a country with an established cycling team, I will contact every small nation without a women's cycling team and see if they want to start one. With three months left till the start of the 2008 race calendar, only faith, hope, and cycling can help me now. That afternoon, I sit down at my computer for a six-hour marathon of composing and sending over a hundred e-mails around the world. Some months ago, on a Post-it above my desk, I had scrawled the Olympic creed: *Citius, Altheus, Fortius*—swifter, higher, faster. Now, after *fortius* I add a fourth command: Googleius.

14

HOPE HIDES IN THE STRANGEST OF PLACES

Fall 2007

On the Union Cycliste International web site there are 163 nations, from the Antilles to Zimbabwe, with registered cycling federations. (Only registered federations can compete toward Olympic points.) There is also a list of current rankings, from which I can figure out what teams are not even a blip on the radar screen of international competition. Chances are that most of the nations that don't show up on the women's ranking list probably don't have women's teams. I scoot my mouse randomly over to Cyprus and click. The address, e-mail, phone number, and names of the cycling federation's president and secretary pop up. More information than I expected. This is good. Daunting, but good.

I print out the list of nations, grab four pens, and begin color coding my possibilities: red to rule out countries completely because their women's teams are so strong they don't need to adopt other cyclists; black for countries that, for political and/or religious reasons, probably won't favor a female cyclist; green for countries I know nothing about and would struggle to find on a map; and blue for the long shots that are mostly island nations that I imagine as happy places with happy people who might look favorably upon adopting a happy thirty-two-year-old.

There are forty-five red-circled nations that won't need me: Australia, Austria, Belarus, Belgium, Brazil, Canada, Chile, China, Chinese Taipei, Colombia, Croatia, Cuba, Czech Republic, Denmark, El Salvador, Estonia, France, Germany, Great Britain, Hong Kong, Indonesia, Ireland, Italy, Japan, Kazakhstan, Lithuania, Luxembourg, Mauritius, Mexico, Namibia, Netherlands, New Zealand, Norway, Poland, Russian Federation, South Africa, South Korea, Spain, Sweden, Switzerland, Thailand, Ukraine, United States of America, Venezuela, and Zimbabwe.

There are thirty black-circled nations that are either busy with war, unlikely to warm up to the idea of an unreligious white chick from the United States asking to cycle for their nonexistent female national team, or require that I cycle in a burqa: Bahrain, Brunei Darussalam, Congo, Egypt, Georgia, Iran, Iraq, Israel, Ivory Coast, Jordan, Kuwait, Kyrgyzstan, Lebanon, Libya, Morocco, Myanmar, Oman, Pakistan, Qatar[7], Saudi Arabia, Sierra Leone, Sudan, Syria, Timor, Turkmenistan, Uganda, United Arab Emirates, Uzbekistan, Vietnam[8], and Yemen.

There are sixty-five green-circled countries that I have no idea how to categorize (they may or may not have women's cycling teams and I may or may not be able to find them on a map) and which I've labeled Maybe Just Maybe #1: Albania, Algeria, Andorra, Angola, Antilles, Armenia, Azerbaijan, Bangladesh, Benin, Bolivia, Bosnia-Herzegovina, Bulgaria, Burkina Faso, Burundi, Cameroon, Cape Verde, Comoros, Cyprus, Dubai, Eritrea, Ethiopia, Finland, Gabon, Grenada, Guatemala, Guinea, Guyana, Honduras, Hungary, India, Kenya, Laos, Latvia, Lichtenstein, Macao, Macedonia, Madagascar, Malawi,

---

7 Interestingly, Qatar might not be such a longshot. After the 1996 Atlanta Games, this desert nation paid eight Romanian weightlifters 1.5 million dollars each to move to Qatar, convert to Islam, and represent them at the 2000 Summer Olympics in Sydney. Now that's extreme. But they won a bronze medal, putting Qatar on the Olympic medal map. The thought of asking a country to pay me never entered my mind, and I was pretty certain if any money was going to change hands, it would be changing from mine to theirs.

8 I will later discover Vietnam does have a women's cycling team.

Malaysia, Mali, Moldova, Mongolia, Montenegro, Nepal, Nicaragua, Niger, Nigeria, Panama, Paraguay, Peru, Portugal, Romania, Rwanda, San Marino, Senegal, Serbia, Singapore, Slovenia, Suriname, Togo, Tunisia, Turkey, Uruguay, Zaire, and Zambia.

In the final blue-circle list of Maybe Just Maybe #2 are twenty-three countries that seem exceedingly friendly, appear to have no female cycling team, may be receptive to my idea of starting one, and probably have lots of coconuts: Antigua, Aruba, Bahamas, Barbados, Belize, Bermuda, Cayman Islands, Costa Rica, Dominican Republic, Ecuador, Fiji, Grenada, Guam, Haiti, Jamaica, Malta, Monaco, Philippines, Puerto Rico, Seychelles, St. Lucia, Saint Kitts and Nevis, and Virgin Islands.

With my color-coded list next to my laptop, I start drafting an e-mail template into which I will cut and paste the names of the countries in the last three groups and their cycling federation presidents. I begin by telling each country's cycling officials my name, my cycling status, and then explain what I'm trying to accomplish with my Olympic goal. I mention my affiliation with ESPN and what I can give back to the nation in terms of helping to build a cycling program for women, as well as garnering international publicity as a journalist. At the bottom I list my 2007 race results,[9] from my first Category Four race to my state champion title to my pair of thirty-fifth place finishes at the U.S. nationals. While my results boast no international victories or world championship races, something unexpected hits me. After all the fall-downs and mishaps and U-turns and no goods, I feel a faint pulse of something much needed: confidence. Looking at my first-year list of rookie results, I see the one thing I really need to see before I send one hundred-ish e-mails all over the world: I don't suck at cycling. If there were time to linger more in this moment, I would. But there's not. So, instead of sending each e-mail immediately, I decide to save all of them so I can proofread each one before hitting send. The chance I will likely

---

9 2007 cycling results: Valley of the Sun Stage Race (Arizona) 1st, Copper Valley Stage Race (Arizona) 1st, Usery Pass Road/Time Trial (Arizona) 1st, Tumacacori Road Race (Arizona) 4th, Tucson Bicycle Classic (Arizona) 1st, Colossal Cave Road Race (Arizona) 1st, Vuelta de Bisbee (Arizona) 8th, Tour of the Gila (New Mexico) 37th, Sunshine Canyon Hill Climb (Colorado) 9th, Hugo Road Race (Colorado) 15th, New York State Road Race Championships 5th, National Time Trial and Road Race Championships 35th, Boulder Time Trial Series (Colorado) 1st and 2nd (broke course record), Arizona State Time Trial silver medalist, Arizona State Road Race Champion.

address Angola's e-mail to Andorra's president is quite high. In the subject line I type "From USA cyclist Kathryn Bertine."

🚲 🚲 🚲

Around 8:30 A.M. on a Wednesday morning in late August 2007, as I cut and paste names and countries into my template and save each e-mail into a "Waiting to be Sent" folder, the nice, confident, race result encouragement feeling passes and the absurdity of what I'm about to do slowly dawns on me. I'm about to e-mail 118 countries in hopes that:

  a. Each e-mail makes it out of my AOL.com network and into e-mail accounts ending with .fz and .qr, among other unfamiliar suffixes
  b. The recipient of each e-mail reads English
  c. The recipient doesn't hate America
  d. The recipient tolerates females who don't wear burqas
  e. The recipient doles out citizenship like candy
  f. The recipient has a national cycling team and wants me on it
  g. The recipient has no cycling team and wants me to be it
  h. The recipient can get me a passport by 2008

In the process, I learn many interesting facts. For example, the Croatian word for cycling federation is *biciklisticki;* that, out of 163 cycling federations, 23 presidents have government e-mail accounts with Hotmail or Yahoo; that the cycling federations of Azerbaijan, Grenada, Honduras, and Lichtenstein have women presidents; that five nations have federation presidents named Mohammed. The award for Coolest Name of a Cycling Federation President is a three-way tie between Mr. Toots of Estonia, Mr. Moutouboulou of Gabon, and Mr. Win of Myanmar. The prize for countries that sound most like a rotating dessert carousel goes to Cameroon, Macao, and Malta. The countries that sound most like a rock band are St. Vincent and the Grenadines. And the country that sounds most like a superhero and her sidekick? St. Kitts and Nevis.

I develop carpal tunnel syndrome from typing just the following countries' names: the Islamic Republic of Iran, the Lao People's Democratic Republic, the Libyan Arab Jamahiriya, Brunei Darussalam, and the Former Yugoslav Republic of Macedonia. Tying for shortest country name are Fiji, Guam, Peru, Iraq, Mali, and Cuba. On the web site Chile is listed as Chilis, and I wonder if I could use this typo as a loophole and legally represent the fast food chain as its own specific nation. I'm getting goofy, and I know why. I use silly humor to deflect the truth of my situation: I want to go to the Olympics so bad it hurts. I don't want my quest to end here. I love cycling—more than I knew it was possible to love a sport. I want a chance to keep racing and because this decision is now outside of my control, all I can do is count typos and list ironies and put all my hopes and dreams into a folder marked Waiting to be Sent.

Drafting 163 e-mails is not the most pleasant task. I decide to draft all 163 nations, even though about forty-five nations probably don't need me. What-Ifs like to crawl in my brain and make me do things like this. Even with the help of a template, I still feel the need to include some sort of personal note to each country at the end of each e-mail. My once unflappable leave-no-stone-unturned mantra is beginning to feel like a rock that just landed on my head. By the time I'm in the Cs of my alphabetized country list, my hands are shaking. *What's the harm in skipping Comoros? Where is Comoros, anyway?* But I consider myself quite intimate with Murphy's Law. I know that if I don't send an e-mail to Comoros, this will likely be the one nation whose cycling federation is sitting around wondering, "Gee, I wish we had a female cyclist we could send to the Olympics." Then again, would Murphy's Law apply to nations that Mr. Murphy himself probably can't even find on a map? Hmm. Probably.

I push on. Comoros. Costa Rica. Cypress. By Fiji I'm fidgety, by Hungary I'm starving, and by Oman I'm exhausted. And I'm getting sloppy. My sincerity is slipping, and I want to cut through all the mumbo jumbo of my situation and write one e-mail that is simple and direct. "Dear Ecuador, Please let me race for you. You have cool islands. I like turtles. Thank you. Write soon, Kathryn Bertine."

Nearly five hours later, I've reached Peru and am barely halfway done with the list. Deciding this is a good place to take a break, so too does my computer. The screen freezes, and a slow, cold sweat breaks out on my body. My "Saved on AOL" folder appears anything but. With choppy breathing and elevated heart rate, I call tech support with the panic of a 911 call.

I explain the situation to the tech man in a calm and gentle fashion. "My babies are trapped in there! Save my babies! Oh god, don't let me lose my Libyan Arab Jamahiriya!" Genius Tech Man unfreezes me and for whatever reason, I lose only half my e-mails. I decide to cry half as much. Then, emboldened, I decide the Waiting to be Sent folder is for wussies. I position my finger over the Send All button and, with a bizarre surge of hope, strength, and terror, I send my Olympic dream into cyberspace. The thought of 163 rejections is an acute reality, but then again, rejections don't really exist. All I need is one acceptance. Good things come to those who knock. All I need is one door to open, just a crack, just wide enough for me to stick my giant foot into. Just one door out of 163.

Immediately, four e-mails bounce back, undeliverable (Guam, Grenada, Dubai, Eritrea). Okay then, one door out of 159. I once thought being an Olympian required nothing more than big muscles, powerful lungs, and constant drive. I know now that supple wrists, a thick skin, and saintly patience are just as important.

For the next few days, I check my e-mail with giddy trepidation. I see the little You've Got Mail flag waving and my stomach plummets. Will it be Zaire? Turkey? Bermuda? Hairclubformen.com offering to end my baldness? I feel like I'm dating online, only with entire countries. On the third day I get my first response. It's from the Virgin Islands and it's a pleasant thanks-but-no-thanks.

I then get some more no's from Puerto Rico, the Bahamas, and Costa Rica. After two weeks, no new e-mails come in ... including Qatar, which I've e-mailed five times. Feeling lost and a little dejected, I flick around the web for a while, distracting myself with sites that have nothing to do with sports or the Olympics. In the corner of my screen an icon pops up, asking if I'd like to open my spam folder. Yeah, spam—that should cheer me up. I click out the box, but miss the "x" and end up opening the spam folder by accident. There, at the top of the list of spam mail, from the sender "windsurf," I see a familiar subject line that reads, "Re: From USA cyclist Kathryn Bertine." I hit read. And read I do.

Hi Kathryn,

Very nice to hear from you, and what a request!!!

Can you tell me how you got my name and how you would plan to achieve your goal? To get citizenship is not impossible of course, but not so easy.

We in St Kitts & Nevis would of course benefit greatly from the presence of an athlete of your caliber, so I would like to hear more about how you plan to help us in exchange.

I look forward to hearing more from you. In the meanwhile I shall be Googling you ad nauseum.

Yours in sport,

Winston Crooke
St. Kitts and Nevis Cycling Federation

I don't know if there is a God. I don't know if I believe in fate or karma or chance or luck. But I now understand that the purpose of a quest is to ask questions and seek answers, no matter how outlandish the request. And when you can't find the answers to life, check your freaking spam folder. Hope hides in the strangest of places.

My Olympic dream now lies in the hands of a man named Crooke. That's not comforting. But his first name is Win. Winston Crooke and I begin an e-mail correspondence about my Olympic quest, which soon graduates to phone calls and then plans to meet in Florida, where we will both attend an upcoming race. He asks if I've ever been to St. Kitts and Nevis, and I admit I have not. *Yet!* He asks why I contacted him, and I say truthfully that I thought a smaller island nation could help me with citizenship more easily, and in turn I could help build a grassroots cycling program more easily. Winston understands. He is also extremely candid about the marketing aspect of my proposal.

"I understand completely what you are trying to achieve, Kathryn," Winston tells me on the phone, "and the spin-off for our small cycling nation could be hugely beneficial in shining a light on us. I will tell you straight up that I will be looking for optimum publicity benefits for St Kitts and Nevis. If I can make this happen, I will. A year is a short time, but one can but try. Nothing is impossible."

I like this man immediately. His willingness to try and his dismissive attitude toward impossibility are real. His belly laugh and British accent seal the deal of his jovial nature.

"You know how I know you're okay, Kathryn?"

"How, Mr. Crooke?"

"You have a British boyfriend, so you can't be all that bad!" It turns out he did Google me ad nauseum, read my ESPN articles, and already knows too much about me. I make a mental note to send Steve flowers. A few more thanks-but-no-thanks e-mails roll in from St. Lucia and the Cayman Islands, the latter of which takes a bit of delight in telling me, "Unfortunately you are not eligible to represent the Cayman Islands! Am afraid you will have to try a little harder to qualify for the GREAT OLD USA." Oh well. If that is the worst response I receive, then I'm doing okay. All I need is one country, one open door. While there are no promises, I've made it to the ranks of possibility with St. Kitts and Nevis and as far as I'm concerned, at this juncture possibility feels better than a gold medal.

Because my meeting with Winston is not for another six weeks and because nothing is set in stone, no papers filed, no citizenship certain with any country, I do the only thing that an athlete with a dream can do: prepare.

With renewed energy and a wealth of motivation, I reevaluate my training schedule, race plans, and short-term goals. If a nation does grant me citizenship, then I need to be ready to race. My dreams may be in someone else's hands, but my body is in mine. Six days a week

I'm on the bike riding around Tucson and hitting the gym getting stronger, because I know those women in Europe are doing the same thing getting ready for the 2008 Olympic season. Not a day goes by that my mind doesn't drift to St Kitts and Nevis. During training rides I'm never alone, even when I'm riding solo. I see myself among my international competitors, on the start line, in the pack, at the finish. I am there. I am trying. I am still on my quest. I am not sure what will happen, but I'm certain about one thing: We owe it to ourselves to show up to our own dreams. No matter whose hands they're in.

Every week, I e-mail Winston just to check in. I picture these people who have my dreams in their pocket, going about their day. Doing laundry, making lunch. Going into the office, where my dream sits patiently in their inbox. *Hey Mr. President of a Caribbean Nation, do you have any answers for me yet? I'm jumping out of my skin here, dude. For the love of God, give me an answer before I spontaneously combust.* Instead, at the end of each week I send a squeaky-wheel e-mail (a squeaky whee-mail?) to my hopeful countries, wishing them a nice weekend and asking whether or not there is anything I can send them.

I continue to get better as a cyclist. On group rides, I keep up with the men who once dropped me. I master tactics and skills that eluded me just months before. I can now fly around corners and sprint around cyclists and jump over potholes. Just the other day, at twenty-five miles an hour, I surprised myself by bunny-hopping over a two-by-four lying in the bike lane that, had I run into it, would have knocked me to Jupiter. I don't know how to bunny-hop but apparently my instincts did. Being on the bike daily and observing the tactics of more seasoned cyclists pays off in a multitude of ways, clearing two-by-fours included. My confidence has doubled since my experience at nationals. My U-turn skills have improved with a vengeance. Not just in training but in races. In September, I win the silver medal in the time trial event at the Category One-Two Arizona State Championship. In October, I win the state title for the road race event. *The state title?* Ten months ago I didn't even know how to pin a race number on correctly. I've always been a late bloomer, but I never would have guessed I'd be a state champion at age thirty-two. That *totally* makes up for not getting asked to the prom.

When the cycling season ends in October, I throw in a few triathlons to keep my fitness up and my training focused. Despite not having run and swam much, I grab sixth place at the Westchester Tri, second at the Mighty Montauk, and first at the Tucson Tinfoilman, where I break the bike course record for the women. (And would have placed eighth in the men's field). That was weird. But cool. Compared to the Olympics or the international races it'll take to get me there, these events are not even blips on the radar screen of greatness. But I wake up every day wanting to ride. Wanting to see where it takes me. Wanting to learn more and be better.

One day, the road led to Gord.

As much as I loved working under the tutelage of Coach Jimmy, with his talent, knowledge, and unique humor, I'd come to a coaching crossroads. Jimmy had a lot of other things going on in his life. A slew of online cycling/triathlon clients, a head referee job with the Ironman corporation, and a young family all demanded his attention. Jimmy and I both agreed I needed someone a bit more hands on, someone who would be around to observe and improve my training, technique, and racing. Especially my sprinting, which needed a lot of work. Jimmy suggested Gord Fraser. For cyclists, this is the equivalent of someone suggesting that Wayne Gretzky help you work on your hockey skills.

I'd seen Gord before, mostly flying by during group rides before disappearing into a pack of cyclists I could only dream of keeping up with. His otherworldly, badass talent inspire both love and dread in other cyclists. Trying to keep up with Gord puts everyone in the hurt locker, and we're better athletes for it. His good nature and sharp sense of humor only yield when cars come too close to cyclists or if he needs to educate a rider on peloton safety/etiquette. Gord has a quick middle finger. It is also a good idea to get his name right: It's Fraser-rhymes-with-laser, not Frasier-rhymes-with-Kelsey-Grammar.

The entire Tucson cycling community respects and reveres this man, and with good reason. The Canadian-born sprinter has been to the Olympics not once, but three times ('96, '00, '04), and rode in the 1997 Tour de France for Motorola, earning a seventh-place stage finish and four top-fifteen stage placings in the twenty-one-day event. One of his teammates in 1996 was a twenty-five-year-old kid named Lance Armstrong. As if that wasn't cool enough, Gord kept kicking ass for a total of fifteen years. In 2005, at the age of thirty-seven (ten years after most pros retire), he had such a stellar season that he was arguably the best sprinter in North America. Gord, his wife, and kids have called Tucson home for almost two decades and now, at thirty-nine, Gord coaches full time for Carmichael Training Systems, the company founded by Chris Carmichael, Lance Armstrong's coach.

Gathering up a fair amount of courage, I ask Gord if he has the time and desire to work with me. I explain my Olympic project and dreams to him. While he understands my goals, he doesn't sugarcoat his feelings about the reality of my situation. "You can't just assume you're going to get really good really fast and go to the Olympics. You have to pay your dues." He explains that he's seen a lot of athletes adopt a cocky attitude toward Olympic goals, and ultimately pay for their disrespect. "But I don't think you're that type," he adds.

"Gord, I have nothing to be cocky *about*."

"I don't know if I agree with what you're doing … trying to find another country to race for."

I can only imagine what he's thinking. *Here's this woman trying to do in eighteen months what it took me twenty years to do. What a jackass.* Still, he takes this jackass on as one of his athletes.

Over the next few months, Gord introduces me to his methods of coaching. Watt calculations, pedal cadence, heart rate monitors, and the daily downloading of my PowerTap data will be come routine for us. (Every revolution of my wheels is recorded in a little yellow computer that sits on my handlebars and contains tiny magic elves who scribble down the math and mileage. I then take the PowerTap, plug it into my laptop, and send the files to Gord, who knows how to decipher my improvement.)

Better by far are the days when Gord trains with me. Sometimes in groups, sometimes alone, Gord will ride behind me and bark orders and advice and knowledge. "Your watts are too high, back off. Hands in the drops. One gear down. Cadence up. Pedal, pedal, pedal. Good girl, Kathryn. Nice work." Sometimes I stay at his wheel, my body about to "red-line" or combust from the effort of just trying to stay in his draft. I can barely hold my head high enough to see anything but his back wheel, the stroke of his pedals dipping in and out of my peripheral vision. To look ahead, to know that the road is longer than just the twelve inches in front of me, is not a fact my brain can handle. Adrenaline and exhaustion coexist in this place, and I accept the fact that keeping my head so low and my sight so limited means I'll have no reaction time for any unseen pothole or pavement crack. I put all my trust in the rider in front of me, and thank the cycling gods that this person is Gord.

Despite the regular ass-kicking Gord bestows upon me, our relationship has moments of humor and genuine friendship. During warmups and cool downs, we argue the accuracy of Led Zeppelin lyrics, discuss the merits of mayonnaise (he is in favor, I am disgusted), trade PowerBars for Sport Beans, swap our favorite Chris Farley quotes, share stories about sports, childhood, and what we did before cycling. We have an ongoing debate about which of us is taller, the outcome depending on our daily choice of shoes.

Like Jimmy, Gord prefers a less politically correct manner of offering instructions and praise. Instead of wishing me luck among my female competitors, he decrees, "Kick 'em in the box." In lieu of encouraging me to stay strong and ride hard, he simply warns me not to "ride like a pussy." I enjoy this. He's not treating me like a woman, he's treating me like a fellow cyclist, taking me behind the iron curtain of male motivation, and I like it. With me, he's even vulnerable; sometimes Gord refers to himself as a high-school dropout. I tell him to shut up. I don't often tell Olympians to shut up, but I get angry at his self-deprecation. He knows more about real life than most multiple-degree-toting people I know. While most of us spent our late teens and early twenties (and, um, thirties) wondering what to do with our lives, Gord was doing something with his. I remind him of this, I tell him that no book or classroom can ever teach someone how to bunny-hop rattlesnakes, plow through sand washes, draft in a crosswind, or sprint to glory.

As he slaps my race number onto the back of my skinsuit at the state time trial championship in Arizona, I have an unhealthy delusion that I will gain all of Gord's talent by osmosis. Hopefully, by the summer of 2008.

🚲　🚲　🚲

In early November of 2007, I pack a suitcase for Florida. In a few days I'll travel to Clearwater to meet with Winston Crooke and see if my dream is safe. Maybe he'll be able to see in my eyes how badly I want this chance to represent St. Kitts and Nevis, how much I want to keep my Olympic quest alive. Maybe he'll be the one to believe in me, the one door to open. Before heading to Florida, I take another look at the St. Kitts and Nevis cycling web site so I can ask the right questions and be prepared to converse competently. Reading about their cycling club and race schedules, I come across a proverb Winston uses that also sums up my entire Olympic quest: "From small acorns do big oak trees grow."

🚲　🚲　🚲

Winston Crooke's hearty laugh precedes him into the restaurant of the Radisson Hotel Clearwater. All meetings should start with laughter. Winston stands just over six feet and has the build of an endurance athlete, but with a more muscular upper body than most cyclists. Chronologically, he is fifty years old, but he looks at least a decade younger. With him is Greg Phillip, the secretary general of the St. Kitts and Nevis and Triathlon Federation. Greg, who handles the publicity work, has the powerful build and all-black wardrobe of a bouncer. Like Winston, he has a good-natured smile and a jovial laugh. As we sit down to dinner, I feel a sense of ease—a feeling that, out of all the nooks and crannies in the universe, this is exactly where I'm supposed to be right now—here at a roadside Radisson restaurant in central Florida during the Tuesday night all-you-can-eat king crab special.

Winston and Greg have come to Florida to support two of their triathletes, Reggie Douglas and James Weekes, who qualified for the 2007 70.3 Triathlon Championships. This is a half-Ironman distance race consisting of a 1.2-mile swim, a 56-mile bike, and a 13.1-mile run. I've just come from the Florida panhandle, seven hours away by car, where I competed in the Ironman Florida in Panama Beach City.[10]

---

10 Why on earth would I do another Ironman if I'm trying to be a cyclist? Well, my cycling season was over and I needed to stay motivated for winter training. An Ironman features a 112-mile bike ride, so I figured that was a good thing. Having not run all year, however, the marathon was 4.5 hours of not-a-good-thing. I managed to finish in 10 hours 57 minutes—not too shameful for a cyclist—but note to self: No more Ironmans while cycling.

When Winston told me he'd be in Florida the same time I would, I coordinated my schedule to drive to Clearwater after my race. My body, unhappy with my decision spend ten hours doing a 2.4-mile swim, 112-mile bike, and 26.2-mile marathon and then get in a car for seven hours, retaliates with soreness, swelling, and ankles the size of telephone poles. Luckily, we had arranged a dinner meeting and not an athletic evaluation.

For the next couple of hours, Greg, Winston, and I discuss how best to persuade their government to grant me dual citizenship. We need all bases covered, all doubts countered, all questions answered. We talk about the pros and cons, the pros centering mostly around my relationship with ESPN and how I can help bring media coverage not only to St. Kitts and Nevis cycling, but to the tourist industry as well. Winston wants to set up cycling camps. I can help with that. Greg wants to bring a new level of coaching to the program. I can help with that, too, and mention my connection to Carmichael Training Systems. Both gentlemen want to see an athlete pursue her dreams and watch cycling gain international/mainstream publicity. That, I promise, I can do. I'll move to St. Kitts and/or Nevis, I'll help build a grassroots team, give them all my Sport Beans.

We scratch our heads trying to think of reasons why I should not be granted citizenship, but come up with very few. One, Winston and Greg speculate, is that the government might want a *guarantee* I'll make it to the Olympics. Two, they won't be interested in my personal journey, or cycling in general. Three, they just won't feel like offering me citizenship.

"What will you do if our government says no?" Greg asks, quite fairly.

After a short mental debate over whether honesty truly is the best policy, the pro side wins and I only hope it is what he and Winston want to hear.

"Well, if St. Kitts and Nevis doesn't offer citizenship, I would look elsewhere. I have to; I'm hardwired to search out all possibilities. I can't give up on my dreams till I'm sure I've tried everything. But at the same time, I don't want to race for anyone else. I want to race for you, because you believe in me. Because you answered my e-mail. Because this feels right." All of it is true, even though I sound like I'm scoring quite high on the corn-o-meter. This is the one chance I have to let them know how much I want—even need—this path to continue. Still, I shut up just before nominating myself for a daytime Emmy.

"My Olympic dream is in your hands," I finish. Then I happen to look down and see that in each of my hands is a crab leg, with which I've been gesticulating and emphasizing the importance of my dream for the past half hour. I'm glad these men are from the Caribbean. They seem nonplussed by crabversation. Somehow, they still want me to race for St. Kitts and Nevis.

Winston and Greg tell me they want to put together a presentation about my project and present it to their premier and government officials.

"You're going to *the premier*?" I say, astounded.

They laugh. "Yes, his office is right down the street."

"Down the street from what?"

"From everything. From where we live and work."

"And you can just walk in?"

"Well, you have to let him know you're coming."

Oh. Okay. Well, then. By all means, let him know I'm coming. I enjoy this daydream of chatting with the St. Kitts and Nevis prime minister for a moment, until it is interrupted by reality.

"It would be most helpful if you were there, Kathryn, so the government could meet you," Greg says. "When can you come to St. Kitts and Nevis?"

WATER BREAK

BICYCLE CONVERSATION WITH MAN ON A HARLEY DAVIDSON AT THE INTERSECTION OF SABINO CANYON AND TANQUE VERDE ROADS, TUCSON

Harley man: Hey, honey, how much you pay for that thing?

Me: My bike?

Harley man: Yeah.

Me: About four grand.

Harley man: You paid four thousand dollars for a bike you have to *pedal?*

Me: Yep.

Harley man: Damn, girl, you got ripped off.

15

FROM SMALL ACORNS DO BIG OAK TREES GROW

December 2007

Between now and my meeting with the St. Kitts and Nevis government, I have three weeks. There is very little I can do to prepare for the fate of my citizenship. My cycling results are what they are. I'm prepared for whatever questions they might ask about my goals, dreams, and commitment to St. Kitts and Nevis. Now I need to bone up on the country's history.

The truth is, I've brought up the web sites on St. Kitts and Nevis a few times, but I've been unable to read them. Part of me doesn't want to get too attached to a country that might reject me. It is scary as hell to want something so bad that the tiniest thought of getting it alters all rhythm of breath and heartbeat and nerve and fiber of your very being. But I manage to overcome my mental resistance, not so much because the government of St. Kitts and Nevis may quiz me on the names of capitols and regions, but because there is a legitimate possibility that I actually may need to know my way around them.

Out of all the nations that comprise the Americas—North, Central, South, and West Indies/Caribbean—St. Kitts and Nevis is the smallest not only in size but also in population. St. Kitts and Nevis protrude from the Caribbean Sea about one hundred miles southeast of Puerto Rico and make up part of the Leeward Islands, along with Antigua and Barbuda. Together, both islands of St. Kitts and Nevis total 101 square miles, and with a population of 43,000, the country is smaller than the undergrad enrollment of Penn State. The larger St. Kitts and smaller Nevis are separated by a two-mile stretch of shallow water that some islanders wish was wider—and deeper. In 1983, the islands broke from British rule and in 1998, they attempted to break from one another, but could not muster the two-thirds majority vote to do so. Ties remain politically strained. Nevis often feels like the ignored little sister, so Winston has reminded me to always refer to the nation as St. Kitts and Nevis, not just one or the other.

St. Kitts and Nevis may have the distinction of being the only nation legally and geographically referred to by its nickname. The island of St. Kitts is actually named St. Christopher, and was given the name by Christopher Columbus, who may or may not have had quite the raging ego. He named Nevis after Our Lady of Snows—*nieve* being Spanish for snow. However, a year-round temperature of eighty degrees suggests that our favorite egomaniac, Columbus, was either delusional from scurvy or delightfully sarcastic. The world will never know. But legend has it Columbus mistook the clouds above Nevis's highest peak for a snowcapped mountain.

For roughly 350 years, the nation's main economic industry was sugar, but in 2005 the state closed most of the sugar plants. The popularity of the Atkins diet surely didn't help. Now tourism is the primary source of revenue, along with the manufacture of lightbulbs and electronics. In 1998, Hurricane Georges caused $445 million dollars in damages, followed a year later by another storm. September 11, 2001, did little to further the country's tourism-based economy. There have been bright moments as well, like Kim Collins' world championship victory in the 100-meter dash in 2003, and the national football team, affectionately known as the Sugar Boyz, made a strong run at qualifying for the 2006 FIFA World Cup.

The nation's motto is, "Country above self," which sounds like it may bode well for my fate. As for their government, St. Kitts and Nevis has a national assembly of eleven representatives and three senators. Two of the senators are appointed by the prime minister, one by the leader of the opposition, and all serve five-year terms. Senators do not constitute a separate senate, but sit in the national assembly right there alongside the representatives and the prime minister like one big happy family. I wonder if the St. Kitts and Nevis government is proud of the Nevis connection with nineteenth-century U.S. politician Alexander Hamilton. Hamilton, the first United States treasurer and second-place finisher in the Hamilton-Burr duel, was born in Nevis and spent his childhood on the island. He likely should have stayed there. I'm not sure how dueling is looked upon in Caribbean culture. Maybe I won't bring that up at my first meeting.

Photos of the country show beautiful rainforests, sugar crops, beaches, and palm trees. There is even a fortress on a steep mountain all of five hundred feet tall, and I wonder if this is where I will do hill repeats. I also wonder about road surfaces and cycling shops and what the airport will charge for bike box travel. I can almost feel the breeze, humidity, and salt air. I am overwhelmed with wonder and—for a few moments—grant myself the permission to revel in the Maybes.

Then, before I know it, I am flying into Nevis. In early December 2007, three weeks after my crab dinner in Florida with Winston and Greg, I'm on a plane to St. Kitts and Nevis. With me is my ESPN entourage—my photographer Lucas, my documentary filmmaker Jim, and Coach Gord. Vance Amory Airport in Newcastle, Nevis, is that island's only airport and it has only one runway. On the approach, I see from our turboprop a handpainted wooden sign next to the landing strip advertising pizza. Behind it is the ocean. Next to it is a herd of brown goats I will later learn are sheep. I see no restaurant, but any country that welcomes its visitors with the promise of pizza is my kind of country.

It all feels slightly hallucinogenic. A year ago exactly, I was panting through pentathlon, whirling around a velodrome, and throwing handballs into what seemed to be an Olympic dead end. Now I'm aiming for a spot on the St. Kitts and Nevis Olympic road cycling team. The reality of it blows me away.

After we clear customs, Winston, the head of the St. Kitts and Nevis Triathlon Federation, wrestles my mammoth bike box and the entire ESPNtourage into his fifteen-year-old crimson Vanagon, which creaks and moans and heehaws under our shifting weight. Two miles later, we pull into the driveway of the Oualie Beach Resort, a collection of gorgeous pastel bungalows situated a mere twenty yards off the Caribbean Sea in the St. James Parish of Nevis. Behind us is the mountain Columbus saw from the sea, and sure enough a blanket of white, billowy clouds enshrouds the top of the peak. Winston has arranged with Alastair Yearwood, the gracious owner of Oualie, to comp my hotel for the week. The Oualie Beach Resort really puts the Econo Lodge in its place. Hammocks sway between palm trees. Old surfboards have been planted vertically and turned into showers for sunbathers to rinse beneath. A string of small white buoys bobs in the current offshore, marking a 100-meter swim course where the local triathletes put in their laps. An outdoor restaurant with tables is set up among a garden of local flora and fauna, next to the walk-up bar where a steel drum band is tapping out mellow rhythms for people drinking frothy, fruity things.

Adjacent to the hotel is Wheel World, Winston's cycling and windsurfing business, housed in a little white and turquoise building. Winston's cell phone number is scribbled on an outdoor chalkboard. Welcome to Caribbean time; sometimes Winston's at work, sometimes he isn't. Call, though, if you need something. I am grateful that my citizenship quest has brought me to Nevis and not, say, Iran.

The next three days in Nevis are a whirlwind of training, sightseeing, meeting the premier, and paperwork. Winston, Greg, and I set to work outlining my quest for citizenship. We produce a one-page list of bullet points for the premier, whose support is essential and who alone has access to the prime minister. Our meeting with the Honorable Premier Mr. Joseph Parry is set for Thursday, two days away.

This time of year would normally be my training and racing off-season. As if moving from Category Four to Category One in one year wasn't physically stressful enough, I need to be ready to race immediately if citizenship comes through. In all honesty, I'm tired. And a little cranky. I could use some rest. But the Olympics are now just eight and a half months away. Luckily, the eighty-degree Nevis weather isn't such a bad motivator for getting on the bike

Gord and I head out on a two-hour ride with Winston, Greg, and Reggie Douglas, the St. Kitts and Nevis national champion in triathlon and cycling. With dreads poking though his helmet, red-yellow-green-black beaded necklaces, and the chiseled physique that is a combination of his daily training and a strict vegan diet, Reggie stand six feet tall and weighs no more than 155 pounds. A full-fledged Rastafarian, he is kind, soft-spoken, and has an easy laugh that surfaces at least once every sixty seconds. As we make our way down the thirty-mile road that encircles the island of Nevis, Reggie points out Nevisian hotspots and shares snippets of his country's history. Cycling along, we pass a woman who waves and calls out, "Hey, Reggie." Reggie heys back. *Aww,* I think, *how nice to pass by a friend!* But soon I realize that everyone—literally everyone—within a twenty-mile radius knows Reggie Douglas. As we pass through town, an old man standing in a doorway calls out to him. "Reggie!" In the countryside, a girl holding her infant sibling calls from the open upstairs window of her home. "Reggie, Reggie!" As cars drive past, hands sticking out the window, horns beeping, calls of "Reggieeee" are carried on the wind. A sense of community, belonging, and safety comes over me. I could train here. I could live here. Assuming, of course, I adapt to riding on the left and stopping for the herds of sheep that randomly skadoodle across the road.

"Watch for monkeys," Reggie warns as we climb the rolling hills on the east side of the island. "They run out faster than sheep." Ah, yes. Monkeys. Okay. In New York State I watch for squirrels and deer, in Boulder I watch for prairie dogs and lighting storms, in Tucson I watch for coyotes and snakes, and in Nevis I watch for monkeys and sheep. Got it. No problem. As long as I remember where I am. Which has become increasingly challenging this year.

On our second day, we take the ferry from Nevis to the island of St. Kitts. The forty-five-minute ferry crossing drops us in Basseterre, the capital of St. Kitts and Nevis, and from there we spend the day riding the roads of the larger island. Lucas and Jim, my ESPNtourage, pile into a cab so they can shoot footage as we train. About half an hour into our ride, their cab pulls ahead of us and stops in front of a slightly ramshackle building. Our cycling group continues on, but the cab driver screams after us "Lunch!" The old building is a restaurant belonging to the cabbie's sister. We are instructed to eat. Gord and I look at one another, neither of us accustomed to stopping for lunch in the middle of our workout.

"When in Rome," Gord says with a smile. We de-bike and head into the restaurant, which comprises one table, six chairs, and a pool table. Given the choice of cheeseburger or fish soup, I decide the latter will be easier to ride on. Turns out to be one of the best meals I've ever had. While we wait, we play a heated game of pool. Reggie and I form Team Americarribean and Gord and Kristina Stoney, a fellow Nevisian cyclist originally from Alberta, team up as the Canadian Expatriates. We tie. But overall, I'm on a winning streak: pool, fish soup, and Rastafarians. Strange are the ingredients of an Olympic dream.

Later that day, the ESPNtourage asks how exactly we got here, to St. Kitts and Nevis. I tell them the abbreviated story—how Winston appeared in my spam folder and now we are on the shores of the Caribbean. "Crazy," they say. I agree, and change the subject. I'm still unable to express how much I want this dream to continue. I've learned something about myself this year: my desire scares me. When I want something, I want it badly. I'm a put-every-freaking-egg-in-the-basket type, and it'll either leave me with a giant leaking mess or one hell of an omelet. All I can do is carry a fork and hope for the latter.

Our meeting with the premier is scheduled for 10 A.M. on the third day of my St. Kitts and Nevis visit. "Kathryn, you owe me for this," Winston says with his signature laugh. "I have to wear a *tie* today!" Before we all head to the meeting, Gord sends me out on an early morning training ride. I am supposed to do hill repeats on one of the steep inclines a few miles from our hotel. My PowerTap records the data, and when I return Gord clicks on the buttons and reads my average watts for each interval.

"Kathryn, what's with the sudden drop in watts on your third hill repeat?" Gord asks.

"A herd of sheep cut in front of me."

"Oh. Okay. And the watts on the last climb?"

"I was distracted by a broken donkey." On the side of the very steep road, intermingled with the lawn-mowing sheep and an occasional bleating goat, I saw a donkey with a broken knee. An actual lame ass. He was eating shrubbery with his bizarrely twisted limb dangling at a terrible angle. I was dripping with sweat and standing on my pedals in full exertion. Startled, we both looked at each other and I know we were thinking the exact same thought: *That is the weirdest thing I have ever seen.*

I shower, put on some nice clothes for my meeting with the premier, and meet the gang for breakfast at our hotel. Winston and Greg have asked Gord and me to be on Nevis' sports radio broadcast before we head to the premier's office. We happily oblige, discussing topics such as sponsorship, sports journalism, and professional race experiences. Most of the callers want to talk to Gord, having heard that he is a three-time Olympian and Tour de France rider. Gord has thoroughly enjoyed the pronunciation of his name in the eastern Caribbean dialect, an accent that silences the "r" and renders Gord a "God." Gaahd Fraysah. When people call in, Greg is able to personally identify each caller by the sound of his or her voice.

"Hello caller, you're on the air with Sportsrap."

"Hello, Greg."

"Ah! Ga' maahning, John …

"Yes, this question is for Mr. Gaahd …"

After an hour, I go with "God" to the premier's office. Waiting in the lobby, I keep my nerves calm by reading a *Good Housekeeping* from 2001, which features happily married Kim Basinger and Alec Baldwin on the cover. The plastic Christmas trees seem even more out of season in the premier's un-air-conditioned foyer. I'm feeling as limp as the tinsel. Also nervous. I have an uncanny ability to become tongue-tied and say stupid things in high-stakes situations. Gord has been no help, joking about the consequences should I make the mistake of saying "St. Nitts and Kevis." Winston impresses upon me the importance of addressing the Honorable Mr. Joseph Parry as "Mr. Premier."

After five minutes, we're led into a conference room where the Honorable Mr. Joseph Parry, a relaxed and kind-looking man in his fifties, shakes our hands and asks us to sit down at the U-shaped table. Parry has already been briefed about our request, and he seems to be intrigued by my Olympic citizenship mission. Better still, Mr. Premier appears to be enjoying the presence of Lucas and Jim, who are clicking and shooting the whole time. The meeting is lighthearted, ranging from our delight at being in St. Kitts and Nevis to Mr. Premier's past as a 400-meter runner. When the premier mentions his enjoyment in watching the Tour de France, we tell him of Gord's participation in the 1997 tour and his three Olympic experiences. Smiles all around. The premier asks us about my training and about the upcoming Olympics, and I assure him I'm ready to give it everything I have. He nods softly and tells us, diplomatically, he hopes it will all work out. He will take the matter up with the prime minister.

Yessss! Another hurdle cleared! He's going to the prime minister, woohoo! We politely thank him for his time and begin to file out of the office.

I am pleased but disappointed. Everyone agrees the meeting went extremely well. But in my mental movie, the premier was supposed to shake my hand and say, "Kathryn, I don't need to go to the prime minister. I'm going to issue you citizenship right here and now. We'll get the passport fairies to materialize all your documents momentarily. Would you like a glass of mango juice while you wait? Oh, and here is a newly laminated UCI elite racing license for all your 2008 cycling needs. Is there anything else I can do for you?"

Little do I know I'm in for at least ten days of mental anguish. There is no set date for the premier to go to the prime minister, although he knows we would need to formally register my name with the UCI by December 20. That is the deadline for those who wish to chase Olympic points. It is now December 8. And so my Olympic dream is out of my hands yet again.

After saying an anxious goodbye to Winston and Greg, I leave the beautiful islands of St. Kitts and Nevis, wondering if I'll ever set foot on these magical shores again. A couple of days later, I'm back in Tucson, pacing, pedaling, fidgeting, and waiting.

As I wait for St. Kitts and Nevis to deliver the verdict, Winston e-mails me that it could take up to two weeks to arrange a meeting with the prime minister. This is cutting it dangerously close to the cycling regulations that require all countries to submit a roster of international athletes to the UCI by December 20. The minutes trickle by and I check my e-mail every few hours to find out when, where, and how the meeting will take place. I picture the premier, with my dreams in his pocket, going about his daily routine, drinking coffee, running a nation. I ask Winston if I should e-mail or call or write a letter to the prime minister. "Noooo," he says, "we just have to be patient." I'm not good at patience. I'd rather eat dung than be patient. I'm bordering on desperate, but Winston is right. What would I say, anyway? "Hurry up, Mr. Premier?" Slowly, the value of patience becomes clearer to me.

Back home in Tucson, I've become so consumed by the waiting that all I can do to keep from jumping out of my skin is bike 350 miles a week and mentally prepare for the deciding moment. A No will give me lots of free time, but a Yes will change my life dramatically. A Yes will mean I get to keep racing, even if it won't magically transport me to the start lines of foreign races. To the contrary, a Yes is only the beginning. The UCI race calendar starts in six weeks and there is so much to prepare for—entries, travel, training. I'll need to have Winston contact each race director and ask how and if I can enter. Yes, *if.* Some races are invitation only. Most of these race directors have no idea St. Kitts and Nevis has a cycling federation. They might not even know where St. Kitts and Nevis is.

Before asking these race directors for an entry, the logistics loom large. Find the web site for each race. Translate the language of the web site (only four out of twenty-eight races are in English-speaking countries). Find the race directors' e-mail and hope s/he reads a bit of English. And before doing any of these steps comes the biggest gamble of the game: With a fair bit of the race schedule comprised of overlapping events, which races do I go to? Which do I skip? Where will the best riders be? Which events will offer the most points? Do I go to the big races and take on the big guns but risk placing lower and gaining fewer points, or stick to the smaller races that offer fewer points but better chances of placing higher and therefore winning more points? What? Huh? Beg pardon? Exactly.

My mind spinning, I plunk myself down next to Gord's desk at Carmichael Training Systems and we begin sifting through Yes strategies. We look at the daunting UCI race calendar and Gord comes up with the brilliant idea that I should focus on the races that are directly after World Cup events. "The best girls will be at the major World Cup events," Gord explains. "So you need to go to any race that is scheduled on the same day as a World Cup. I think that's the best way for you to score points." Sounds wise. Also sounds like I'm a weenie, looking for the less competitive races.

"No," Gord says, "you're forgetting: This UCI calendar means you're racing against the best elites in the world at every race. There are no easy races. I'm just trying to find the ones where you might, um, get less slaughtered." He laughs. While Gord believes in me, there's no sugar coating the truth about these events—these are the hardest races and toughest competitors on the circuit. Women race for years before making it to this level. I'd be lucky to have the chance to be among them, let alone to represent St. Kitts and Nevis.

After an hour, Gord and I look at the calendar we've printed off the UCI web site. We've crossed out the ineligible races, underlined first choices, starred second choices, drawn arrows between different race locations, circled rest days, and into the margin we have tattooed several different dates for several different countries. "El Salvador early March, Poland late March, Belgium for one race early April then immediately to Holland, Spain for a two-day race, then a night flight to Italy for a one-day event, then take a night flight back to Spain for another, United States has the last two races in May before the Olympic cut-off ... but let's keep Brazil, New Zealand, and Luxembourg as maybes." I look at this page of scribble and fact, this weird blueprint of hope. The process exhausts me. Sometimes dreams can be quite heavy to carry.

December 20, the official date to register me as a cyclist with the UCI, comes and goes without word from the premier and the prime minister. What we do know is that the premier did meet with the prime minister, and that the Honorable Dr. Denzil Douglas seemed intrigued. With this flutter of hope, Winston put in a request for a UCI registration extension. Despite three attempts, the UCI does not answer us at all. "Perhaps they are still thinking," Winston says optimistically.

I can't bear the thought of being granted citizenship but just missing the deadline to race internationally.

December 20 is gone. December 25 brings holiday closings to government offices. The first week of January passes without a call or e-mail from Winston, other than a sympathetic salutation for a Happy New Year and a brief acknowledgement of my predicament: "I still have hope." *Okay, then. If you do, I do, buddy.* But the days come and go.

January 10: No word.

January 12: Nothing

January 14: Nada

January 15: Nooo Caribbean love

January 16: Zip

January 17: Zilch

January 18: Still no word. What's going on? .

January 19: Six weeks since our meeting with the premier

January 20: One month past the UCI deadline for team registration

January 21: Five months since I began my quest for citizenship

January 22: Five months and one day

January 23: Let's take this three at a time, shall we?

January 26: Guess that doesn't make a difference

January 29: How many days are in January again?

February 1: Shoot me now

February 3: UCI races start in less than a month

February 6-10: Eat, sleep, train, check e-mail, cry, repeat

February 11: I'll be thirty-three in three months—old enough to be the mom of an Olympic gymnast

February 12-28: See February 6-10

February 29: Great! Leap year. One more day of agony.

March 1: That's enough. I can't take this anymore. I e-mail Winston, as I've done every day for the past three months, thanking him for all he's done for me. Winston always writes back within the day, but this time I hear nothing from him. For three days. I guess neither of us can bring ourselves to say goodbye, to face the facts, to accept that we did our best but that we have to move on.

March 4: Descending Tucson's beloved Mt. Lemmon on my bike at 12:57 P.M., my cycling jersey pocket starts to vibrate. I pull over. I don't know why. I never answer my phone while riding. Just like I never check my spam box.

"Kathryn," Winston bellows, "the prime minister and his cabinet approved it! You're a citizen of Saint Kitts and Nevis!"

I vaguely remember whoops of exhilaration followed by a breathless silence of disbelief. I vaguely remember telling Winston that I love him. I vaguely remember riding my bike back from Mt. Lemmon. I vaguely remember calling my parents. What I do remember distinctly is March 4, though I didn't catch the symbolism at first. All I could see was the three months of waiting, the eight months of citizenship hunting, the unending wondering and questioning. But the answer came on the one day of the year that is an answer in itself—*march forth!* It is the one day that honors anyone on a quest, anyone who has ever doubted themselves and wondered if they should keep going.

March forth.

I will.

16

ALL HAIL THE WONDERMINION

March–April 2008

If March 4 was one of the best days of my life, March 5 was one of the most hectic. I had less than three months to qualify for the Olympics in cycling, and there was the slight glitch that I might not even be allowed to race.

After diving into the sixty-eight-page rulebook of UCI regulations for Olympic qualification, I discovered that although UCI national *teams* needed to be registered by December 20, *individuals* of national teams could still compete in the races if they were asked to be on an established professional team. (It doesn't matter what country a cyclist represents, as all Olympic points are determined individually, not by team finish.) Since St. Kitts and Nevis does not have any professional cycling teams, the only way I could get to UCI races would be as a guest rider on another UCI-licensed team. Guest riders aren't common, but occasionally a team with a sick or injured cyclist will bring in a reserve. That was my only chance. Made slimmer by the fact no one in international cycling even knew I existed. Vampires have the undead and cycling has me—the unreserved.

Between March 4 and May 31—the cutoff date for acquiring Olympic points—there are twenty-seven races, some of which overlap. Some are single-day events. Some are multi-day stage races. Most of them are in Europe, Asia, and South and Central America. My mission is to e-mail every race director and ask for a list of competing teams, then write every competing team to see if they need a spare rider, then contact a local hospital and schedule me for carpal tunnel surgery.

The task of e-mailing and calling twenty-seven race directors and far more team directors (and doing it over and over again) makes my previous task of e-mailing 163 countries look like child's play. But that's just the beginning. What if some teams actually need me or some races let me attend individually? Looking at this list of foreign races, it hits me like a freight train that I need help not only to get into races, but to get me *to* them as well. I don't think I can do this alone. To book travel, fly to all these cities, find accommodations, drag two bikes to each event, then disassemble and assemble them, get myself to the start line, and find food in my usual athleticoma, all the while surrounded by people speaking a foreign language … for the first time in my quest, the reality of trying to do this on my own overwhelms me. If I am allowed to race, who will spoonfeed me carbohydrates (and other forms of encouragement) when I'm too tired to feed myself? Who will scrape me off the pavement, emotionally and maybe literally, if I crash? Do teams look after their guest riders or do we pinch hitters just freelance for ourselves on the periphery of greatness? I understand now that training for the Olympics and trying to get to the Olympics are two very different things. It is time to ask for help.

A few days into sending out my first batch of "Please let me be your reserve" e-mails, help arrives in the form of Amanda Chavez, a twenty-two-year-old Tucson cyclist and recent University of Arizona graduate. I know Amanda from local races and from her part-time job at Fair Wheel

Bikes. Her kind, easygoing, helpful demeanor distinguish her as much as the fact that she is a blonde, blue-eyed Mexican. One night at the dinner table of a mutual friend, the topic of my ESPN quest came up.

"Hey, Kathryn, do you need a minion?" Amanda joked. "Can I help carry your crap to races?" She may have thought she was kidding. I thought she was brilliant. A WonderMinion! I immediately hire Amanda to track down as many race directors/teams as possible and e-mail and call them morning, noon, teatime, and night. Amanda readily agrees, and begins drafting e-mails to cycling teams in every European, Hispanic, and Asian language. "Make sure you double-check them through the translation web site," I warn, telling her of my Borat-quality e-mail to Poland. Despite my attempt to keep it lighthearted, Amanda understands how much this quest means to me and how important her role is. My last chance at racing for Olympic points depends on her ability to contact these teams, while I train as hard as I can each day, in the hope that someone actually responds.

Sadly, as with my attempt to contact adoptive countries, responses aren't coming. To say my heart sank would be an understatement of titanic proportions. There simply isn't time to wait. Every day that goes by without racing is another day of Olympic qualification slipping away. After two years, all of this effort, all of this training, the incredible journey of citizenship would end here, with the ability to race but no team to compete with. So close. Too close. I can barely stomach the disappointment. I call Winston, my superhero of St. Kitts and Nevis.

"Winston, I think we're too late. No cycling teams are responding."

"Kathryn, I have an idea," Winston says. "There is still another option."

"You and Greg are going to dress up as women, form a composite team for me, and we'll quietly infiltrate the UCI calendar?"

"No. Sorry. But, there might be another way. Remember, I'm not just the head of the Nevis Cycling Club. I'm head of the triathlon federation as well. You could race on the ITU [International Triathlon Union] calendar and try to get Olympic points in triathlon."

"Winston. Let me get this straight. Two years ago I gave up triathlon to try to get to the Olympics as a cyclist and now my only chance to get to the Olympics might be as a triathlete?"

"Yes," he says.

"That's not funny, Winston."

"Well, you can try."

The problem is, I *did* try. For three years (and that was just counting the years as an elite competitor). I wasn't fast enough to pull off Olympic qualifying times for the United States. Then again, I'm not sure exactly what the competition among the Caribbean and South American races is like. Maybe there's a chance. I could try. I *am* a professional tryer.

"Okay Winston. When is the first ITU race?"

"Oh, you've missed the first three races."

"Right. Of course I have. When is the next race?"

"Twelve days. In Nevis. And the next one is in Peru."

What Winston is suggesting—that I switch sports yet again—is both inspiring and absurd. Inspiring because he's keeping my Olympic dream alive by offering me a shot at racing international triathlons. Absurd because I've been cycling my brains out for a year and a half. I'm a cyclist now, not a triathlete. Triathlon points (should I even win any) are not transferable to cycling. It is a whole separate sport, and so I'm at a crossroads: return to triathlon and see what happens, or sit home and await the fate of the unreserved? I push any cycling disappointment out of my head, as I'm simply unwilling to believe it is the end of the road just yet. I'm not sure if I'm being completely rational or I'm knee deep in denial or I'm just an optimistic idiot, but there are too many What Ifs, too many e-mails Amanda has sent out, and too many unanswered Maybes to throw in the cycling towel. Sometimes the best thing to do with a lingering What If is to morph it into a What Now?, as in *Okay, I've been given an opportunity to race some triathlons ... So, what now? Gonna do it or not?* Maybe I could have the best of both opportunities. I tell Winston I'll see him in Nevis and I'll try my luck in Peru, but if I get a call from any cycling teams that need me, that'll be my first priority. Winston agrees and wishes me luck with training. Oh god, training ...

Twelve *days*? Nevis? Peru? To be competitive, I'll need to swim 1,500 meters in under twenty minutes and run six miles in under thirty-nine minutes to place high enough to win any ITU points. Those are fast,

fast times—especially for someone who's been cycling exclusively and hasn't seen a sneaker or a pool for nearly two years. Oh, just for some added stress, if I don't finish within 8 percent of the winner's time, I won't get *any* points. But, if I'm able to bike my way up to the leaders, hmmm ... I call Coach Gord.

"Gord, I have an ITU triathlon in twelve days. What am I gonna do?"

"Better start running."

"Good idea, Sherlock. Thanks."

Despite my lack of swimming and running and the high risk factor of coming in last (and the fun of getting to write all about coming in last on a major sports web site), I decide to try the triathlons in Nevis and Peru. Worst case scenario: I come in last and get nary an Olympic point. Best case scenario: I discover cycling as been a good cross-trainer for swimming and running, manage to pick up a few Olympic points, and realize that maybe I really can get to the Olympics in triathlon. Besides, what else am I going to do? Sit around and wait for cycling teams to not call me? No. No way. I took this assignment—to do whatever it takes to qualify for the Olympics—not only for myself but for every athlete scraping by on talent and pocket change and big dreams. Three years ago, I was working crappy jobs and living paycheck to paycheck as a substitute teacher, pet-sitter, and lunch-shift waitress, saving every penny I had while training up the wazoo to be competitive enough to make the world circuit as a professional triathlete. To have this opportunity and to *not* try? Not an option. Even though my heart is in cycling, maybe my body still has a few triathlons left in it.

On March 16 I head down to Nevis, my beloved new homeland. (With citizenship paperwork still in the making, it will be months before I relocate to, and train, in Nevis.) Winston and Greg do what they can to fend off my incessant hugs. Reggie and James greet me warmly, welcoming me as a citizen of their country.

"Reggie, can you believe this crazy journey?" I ask him.

"Kathryn," he says, "if it's not crazy, it's not a journey."

As predicted, twelve days of triathlon training isn't going to get anyone to the Olympics. I come in tenth out of the ten elite women.

Between the ninety-degree heat and the complete shock to my body of being asked to use rotator cuffs and running shoes, I put up a pretty amateur result. Even my bike split is slow because my body is so drained from the sprint-paced swim. No Olympic points here in Nevis.

"Kathryn, you're just getting warmed up," Winston consoles me. "Try one more race."

Later that day I call Amanda to see if any cycling teams have gotten in touch with her since I've been in the Caribbean. None have. Okay, then. One more go at triathlon. Got to keeping moving forward. I head to Lima, Peru, to try again. This time, the race is much better. I come in ninth out of ten. Better still, I have the fastest bike split and my time of 2:14 is only about five minutes off my personal best, when I was training as a full-time triathlete. Not too shabby, but still no points. Now it is April 9. Only fifty-two days left on the Olympic points cycling calendar. My cycling hopes fading, I am convinced there is not enough time for cycling teams to pick me up as a guest rider. Yet, at the same time, fifty-two days still seems like too much time to give up hope. I can't figure out if my dream is giving up on me or I'm preparing to give up on it. Maybe I needed to see a dream counselor. I can't find one in Lima, so I decide to take a quick side trip to Machu Picchu to see the Inca ruins to take my mind off racing, dreaming, and Olympic attempting for a couple of days. Sometimes just breathing is the best training one can do.

At the base of Machu Picchu, the 550-year-old Lost City of the Incas, I find an Internet cafe sandwiched between the llama-wool shops and Inca boutiques. I log on and read my e-mail. Lo and behold, there's one from the WonderMinion, informing me that two cycling teams (from Trinidad-Tobago and El Salvador) have asked me to be a guest rider in five UCI races being held throughout Venezuela and El Salvador.

"Kathryn," Amanda writes, "these races are before the Olympic points cut-off date. You still have a chance. Get home quick."

If I have learned one lesson on this quest, it is to ask the universe for what you want. Ask out loud, until somebody hears you. There is no harm in asking. The loudest No will always sound better than the quietest What If? Ask, ask, ask. Yell when necessary. Who knew an echo could carry from Arizona to Nevis to South America? Sometimes echoes even make it to the other side of the world.

In addition to Amanda's news, I receive an out-of-the-blue e-mail from Sarah Tillotson, one of the talented riders I met last year at track cycling camp.

"Kathryn, I'm a guest rider on a New York-based cycling team heading to a five-day stage race in China. They need an extra cyclist. Can you make it?"

Can I make it? To China? To the very country I've been attempting to get to for two years? Um, lemme think about that for a nanosecond ...

And just like that, the dream is revived. The dates are set. From April 24 to 29, I will race in China. I will then fly directly to Caracas, Venezuela, for races on May 4 and 5. From there, WonderMinion and I will hit the capital of El Salvador for nine days of racing. That'll bring me to the end of May and the end of my Olympic points quest. Or maybe it'll be a whole new beginning.

March forth.

To China.

17

THE GREAT WALL OF CHINESE CYCLISTS

April 2007

Sometimes reality can be a real bummer. For example, when I found out I'd be racing in China, I deluded myself with the idea that the typical female Asian cyclist would probably be a small, gentle, peaceful woman. The reality? Yao Ming has twenty-seven sisters and they're all on the Chinese National Cycling Team.

On April 19, I leave Tucson for China. After missed connections and a fourteen-hour layover at LAX, I arrive in Hong Kong on April 20 and am picked up by Louis Shih, the owner of Champion System clothing and the sponsor of the first team on which I will be a guest rider. After wrestling the Beast (my obnoxiously large bike box) into the back of his Porsche Cayenne, it takes only moments to discover that Louis is one of the most generous sponsors in the sport of cycling.

As I tell him about my Olympic quest and St. Kitts and Nevis citizenship, I mention that the St. Kitts and Nevis cycling program has had an incredibly difficult time raising the $2,000 it costs to make national team uniforms.

"Tell Winston to send me the artwork," Louis says without the slightest hesitation. "I'll make the kits for you. No charge. I'd be happy to help." It's a reminder of how incredible this journey has been all along, how the generosity of total strangers has become the cornerstone of my Olympic dreams.

Louis drops me off in Sian Kang, a small town outside of Hong Kong, where I meet the four other women on Team Champion System: Sarah Tillotson (my Boise-based friend from track cycling camp), Sinead Fitzgibbon, Jenn Magur, and Lucretia Cavan (all three New Yorkers). Immediately, there is a friendly vibe and good dynamics. Over the next ten days these women will morph from teammates to friends, which is rare in a competitive environment like elite cycling. We spend countless hours hanging out in our hotel rooms discussing the three most crucial elements of female cycling: rest, race tactics, and relationships. I find most of my wisdom lies in the first category, so I do a lot of listening. With my feet up on a leather pillow.

What's more, my newfound teammates offer to work for me during the race—to strategize, to block, to let me draft, to help get me up to the line where I can sprint for points. Without points, I won't be able to get St. Kitts and Nevis a slot in the Olympics. "We think what you're trying to achieve is really cool, Kathryn," Sinead tells me.

I don't think these women will ever understand what such an offer means to me. A month ago I had no idea I'd be in a foreign country, racing for UCI points with an actual team. And my teammates want to *help* me get to Olympics? The only thing this picture seems to be missing is a little dog and some ruby slippers.

Sarah, Jenn, Sinead, Lucretia, and I soon learn that there will be fifteen teams in the Tour of Chongming Island, with a total of about seventy-five competitors. Eight of the teams will be Chinese and the other seven will represent the Ukraine, Poland, South Africa, New Zealand, Vietnam, Thailand, and the USA (with one St. Kittian and

Nevisian guest rider!). What we haven't figured out just yet is that all of the Chinese teams will be working together to keep the foreigners from winning Olympic points. If China does well at this race, they will earn a third spot for their country in the Olympic Games, so they're pretty motivated. Trying to break through the Great Wall of Chinese cyclists will become the strategy of every foreign team, Team Champion System included.

For three days, we train on the beautiful hilly roads of Sian Kang, Hong Kong, before hopping on the two-hour flight to Shanghai and the one-hour ferry to Shanghai's Chongming Island, the site of our five-day race. "We wanted to keep you ladies out of the pollution in Shanghai until the race," our team manager, Andrew Kozak, reasons. It proves a good decision. For our entire time in Shanghai, a yellowish haze hangs in the sky and we see the sun only through a filter of dingy clouds. Yet it is hardly a distraction, as the culture of Chongming engrosses us all. Bicycles and pedicabs are everywhere. Vendors selling foods, from exotic fruit to barbequed chicken feet, line the streets, and there is a cell phone store on every corner.

At the hotel in Chongming, where Sarah and I room together, it's obvious that the Chinese prefer hard mattresses and leather pillows, but what takes the most getting used to is the constant smell of cigarettes. Smoking is permitted everywhere—restaurants, hotels, bathrooms—and there are one billion smokers in China. Thankfully, everyone on our hotel floor is a nonsmoking cyclist, so we're able to breathe a little easier.

A huge highlight for me is a visit from my little cousin, Noah, who lives and works in Shanghai as a manufacturing business owner. He has taken the day off to come see me in Chongming. There's nothing like family when you're far away from home. After not seeing Noah for a decade, I decide it's time to stop calling him "little cousin," seeing as he is only a year younger than me and about to be a father. Noah and I take a pedicab around the city and visit some local temples. I have always wanted to see a giant Buddha, as Buddhas remind me of my favorite childhood bath toy, the wobbly Weeble. All fat and smiley and indestructible. Who wouldn't want to worship one? For the going rate of six dollars an hour, the nice pedicab cyclist carts us around Chongming, and I feel terribly guilty about sitting in/on a bicycle that I'm not personally pedaling. Noah and I likely add up to three hundred pounds, and we're just sitting there watching our poor driver sweat it out on his single-gear cyclewagon. I stave off the guilt knowing that in less than a day, I'll be the one sweating it out.

The first day of our five-day stage race is a 20-kilometer time trial on the pancake flat roads of Chongming Island. At last year's Tour of Chongming Island, teams were told to leave their aerodynamic time trial bikes at home due to a storage space shortage at the hotel. This year, time trial bikes are allowed. Unfortunately, our manager didn't get the memo. Almost every team has brought time trial bikes, complete with disc wheels and aerodynamic helmets. Without one time trial bike among the five of us, and yet another miscommunication as to whether or not our sponsor would be providing aero helmets, we try to make ourselves as sleek and wind resistant as possible. Sarah shows me how to tape over all the vents in my regular helmet, and she removes the spacers under my handlebars so that I can drop my shoulders lower into the wind. The gloves come off, my braid gets tucked into my skinsuit, and I even take off my stud earrings, flimsy hairclips, and plastic sports watch.

Just before heading to the start line, I grab my tube of Chamois Butt'r (try explaining that one to Chinese airport security). While I discreetly put my hand down my pants and slather my private parts with anti-friction cream, I'm suddenly aware of the most amazing site I've ever seen at a women's cycling race: spectators. And I don't mean a smattering of family members and coaches and the otherwise obligated. I mean strangers. Hordes of them. Young, old, newborns, men, women, all lining the streets of our race, for miles on end. Three rows deep. Craning their necks, they peer into our open-sided tents, smiling and wondering. Children reach out for water bottles and souvenirs that the riders toss into the crowd. A woman has decided that the delicate row of bushes separating the spectators from the racers will work just fine as a bench, and she plops herself down into the thin branches, undeterred by disapproving race organizers and policemen. I turn away to Butt'r myself, only to confront still more spectators peering into our tent from the crosswalks, side streets, and medians surrounding the coned-off athlete area. I feel like most of China's 1.3 billion people are trying to get an eyeful of me smearing blister lubricant goop onto my private parts. Sarah and Jenn do their best to provide cover, but I still hear a gaggle of giggling women in the crowd. The men simply look confused, but not exactly displeased.

Lubed, taped, and aerodynamically correct, I finally roll up to the starting ramp.

Unfortunately, while the roads are perfect for a fast time, the wind isn't. Chongming may be flat, but the hardest part of island racing is almost always wind. The invisible resistance feels like a hand around my tires, clamping the brake pads together. The key is to keep a high cadence, not to slog it out in an exhaustingly high gear.

Five minutes into the ride, and I begin to taste the metallic flavor of blood in the back of my throat, telling me I am going as hard as I can. *Mmm. Blood.* My body is trying to convince my mind that it is in pain, but my mind knows better, and battles back. *You know what real pain is? Sitting around your whole life and wondering what pain tastes like. Your legs are fine. Kick it up a notch, Speedracer.*

Despite the fact that neither mind nor body has any desire to sightsee while time trialing, two memorable impressions will stand out from the blur of Chongming as I fly by. During a particularly tough section of wind and pavement, a school of young Chinese children comes out to cheer the cyclists, chanting, *"Jia you! Jia you!"*—which my cousin Noah tells me literally means "Add oil!" but figuratively (and luckily) turns out to be the equivalent of yelling, "More power!" The rhythmic words of encouragement are exhilarating. Then, at the fifteen-kilometer mark, an assemblage of ethnic drummers dressed in flowing robes beats a triple rhythm—bohm, bohm, bohm ... bohm, bohm, bohm—which hauntingly grows and fades as I near, then pass, their location. Other than those two fleeting memories, I see nothing of the twenty-kilometer time trial course on Chongming Island. When fatigue sets in, I think only of each pedal stroke. When exhaustion roars, I think of points, St. Kitts and Nevis, and how lucky I am to be here, seeing nothing and everything all at once.

Between the thirty-mile-per-hour tailwind and the twenty-mile-per-hour headwind, I average around twenty-six miles an hour on the rectangular race course. Out of the sixty-four cyclists, I finish thirty-second with a 33:28. It's the exact middle of the pack, just where I was at the U.S. nationals a little less than a year ago. Only now I am midpack in an international field of elite competitors, many of whom are Olympic-bound. But despite being the top finisher for Team Champion System, I haven't cracked the top eight overall, where I can gain coveted Olympic points. When the results are posted it becomes abundantly clear that the Yao Ming sisters do not need to "add oil." They are already incredibly powerful. China dominates the top twenty spots in the results. Most of the women are track cycling specialists and many of them are close to six feet tall with thighs like train pistons. Not to mention, they have no problem with aggressive riding. A few of the English-speaking competitors in the race have written Chinese words on their wrist, lest they need to communicate with the Chinese women in the peloton. The most helpful phrase seems to be *gun chu*, which means "get out of my way."

The next four days of racing are broken down as follows: a seventy-two-kilometer criterium (a short circuit race consisting of laps, kind of like NASCAR), a seventy-eight-kilometer road race, a hundred-kilometer road race, and finally another seventy-two-kilometer race. For each race, the peloton averages twenty-six miles an hour and the last twenty kilometers of every day will be an all-out hammerfest of sprinting and attacking. The quality of the competition and the speed and aggression of the Chinese (and other international women) is top-notch. Alas, with aggression comes physical contact and with physical contact comes crashes. While I manage to avoid any carnage, I endure my fair share of shoulder bumps and near-entanglement with others' handlebars.

My teammate Jenn isn't so lucky. During the criterium, she ensnares her bike with four other riders (one of whom got rightfully spooked by a spectator leaning out to snap a photo) and goes down. Hard. Road rash covers Jenn's shins, knees, and elbows and her back is snaked with long, thin bruises from where our competitors' tires have ridden into her. You can almost see the indentation of Maxxis and Continental tread on her skin. Despite it all, Jenn gets back on her undamaged bike and finishes the course. (To not finish this stage of the race would mean she'd have to drop out of the entire event.) When she returns from getting her wounds dressed at the hospital, Sarah, Sinead, Lucretia, and I heap rock-star admiration on our teammate.

"It's nothing," she shrugs. We later find out Jenn lives not only with the stress of being an ER nurse, but is in remission from thyroid cancer and is going through a painful divorce. Road rash isn't even a blip on her pain radar. And I thought trying to get to the Olympics was hard.

Between races, we do what most professional cyclists do on tour: nothing. We sit around the hotel room, feet elevated. Someone mentions a craving for pizza. Probably me. Ah, pizza. My favorite recovery food has not quite made its way to Chongming Island. While we're fed three square meals a day by the Chinese cycling federation and are very grateful for free sustenance, breakfasting on Kung Pao beef and barbequed chicken feet does not come naturally. In the afternoons, we wash our cycling kits in the sink and hang them out the fifteenth-floor window to dry, pinning our socks, shorts, and jerseys to the curtains just in case a breeze picks up. Before dinner, some of us venture out to get our leg muscles worked on at the local Massage School for the Blind. For less than nine dollars an hour, visually impaired Chinese students practice their healing technique on our lactic-acid-filled bodies.

After five days, at the end of the stage race, Team Champion System hasn't been able to make a dent in the Great Wall of Chinese cyclists. Despite finishing with the main pack each day and within mere seconds of the winner, none of us gains any points. This is cycling. One can be so close and so far, all at the same time. While I did my best, it wasn't good enough here. But I still have thirteen more races in South America where Olympic points are offered. I say good-bye to my Champion teammates in Shanghai, as well as the chicken feet and smog, and make my way to Venezuela for the next chapter of dream chasing.

18

POTHOLES AND JESUS IN SOUTH AMERICA

May 2007

Amanda has been able to take the entire month off work at Fair Wheel Bikes to assist me as a translator and Sherpa throughout South America. Unfortunately, there are no direct flights from China to Venezuela, so I meet the WonderMinion in Houston, where we board a red-eye to Caracas. As soon as we land, I realize that hiring her was the smartest decision I've made in the past two years. Fluent in Spanish, Amanda will be in charge of helping me negotiate airports, decipher race rules, start times, transportation issues, and everything else that comes our way as I spend the next month racing thirteen events in Venezuela, Uruguay, and El Salvador. But I also need her as a friend and psychologist.

In addition to her minion duties, Amanda will become insanely popular among the South American coaches, managers, and race directors, who adore the fact this blond, blue-eyed, fair-skinned white girl is named Chavez—which also happens to be the name of the president of Venezuela, Hugo Chavez. In fact, Amanda will become so adored that people will call out *her* name when I pass by on the bike. *"Vamos, Chavez! Vamos Chavez, Chavez, Chavez!"* By the end of our month together, she will have racked up nearly a hundred phone numbers, e-mails, and web sites of doting male cyclists.

Shortly after arriving in Caracas, Amanda and I find Francisco and Julio, the officials who have come to take us to the race venue. My immediate concern is that two men are attempting to stack my enormous bike box and the semi-enormous bike box of a Mexican cyclist onto the roof of the Venezuelan equivalent of a Geo Tracker, tying the boxes together with a ball of fraying twine.

"WonderMinion, quick, tell them that strap on the bike box is not a handle!"

"Cuidado, este cintron no es un—"

Rrrrrrip. Or in Spanish, *reeeeeeeep.*

We settle into the car for what I assume is a quick trip to the local race venue somewhere near Caracas. In the back of my mind, it registers that I am a young foreign female getting into a car with two older men who are complete strangers. My cell phone has no reception, I don't know exactly where we are going, ESPN has no idea exactly where we are going, and my abundance of faith in the goodness of humankind is really not based on anything concrete. The possibility of human trafficking enters my head. Nonetheless, my immediate emotion is one of gratefulness. Amanda's presence calms me, especially when the car trip reaches the half-hour mark.

Three and a half hours later, we are in the town of Valencia, site of the first race. Although I am jet-lagged and newly graying, Amanda helps me assemble my bike so I can get in a quick ride. After twenty-four hours of flying from China, my legs aren't exactly pleased with me. They would like to stretch out in slumber, but that would be a big mistake. A nap would completely throw off my fourteen-hour time change acclimation. Besides, I'm here to race. Gotta wake up the muscles.

Guiseppina, the Mexican cyclist in our carpool, and I take to the streets of Valencia to shake out our legs. Within moments, it becomes abundantly clear to me that Venezuelan stoplights are purely decorative. Cars come and go at their own pace, drivers barely taking note of the pretty red and green lights above them. After a few minutes more, Guiseppina and I discover we have cycled ourselves onto the Venezuelan interstate. She seems unfazed. Doesn't even turn her head when a tractor trailer burps out a lingering trail of black exhaust. She tells me this is how she trains at home in Mexico City. I try to imagine training on I-10 between Tucson and Phoenix, but my mind takes the first exit. As we cycle ourselves down the shoulder of the freeway, it turns out our biggest obstacles are not cars and semis but the stray dogs and grape vendors that line the highway. It also turns out that, in following my Olympic dream, I have either become very brave or very stupid.

The night before the first race, WonderMinion goes to the race meeting as my manager. She picks up my bib number, finds out where the start line is, and lets me know that the race will be a ten-lap circuit totaling fifty-two kilometers. The national teams competing are Venezuela, Brazil, Colombia, Mexico, Dominican Republic, Trinidad and Tobago, and St. Kitts and Nevis. Trinidad and Tobago, Amanda explains, is the reason I'm at this race. The race allows teams of four to enter, and Trinidad and Tobago only had three women on their roster, so the race directors added me to their team. While I still represent St. Kitts and Nevis, I will take to the start line as a guest rider for the Trinidad and Tobago team. Because my new St. Kitts and Nevis cycling kit (uniform) is still graciously being made by Louis of Champion System back in China, I wear my Sport Beans kit, which the race directors have kindly okayed despite the numerous sponsor logos that are illegal to wear in some international races.

"Kathryn," Amanda says, "the top eight riders across the finish line will receive UCI points, and there will be three different sprint bonuses, which will award the first three riders with extra UCI points."

Okay. The good news is that this course has two large hills and I'm a climber. The bad news is that there will be three sprints and I am not a sprinter. Also not in my favor: I don't really have a team. The Trinidad and Tobago cyclists are not working for me (nor should they be expected to), as my Champion System teammates did in Chongming. For the individual nations with too few riders, it's each woman for herself. I will have to be my own team: sprint, climb, chase, lead, try.

At the start line, I put myself in front. Not only for aggressive measures, but to be able to see clearly. The roads of the Venezuela course are the worst I've seen, featuring moon-crater-size potholes, chip seal pavement (layers of asphalt and aggregate), and one nasty manhole cover that is not only raised but pointed into a sharp cone. While the thing clearly belongs in the Tower of London torture museum, it seems happy in its new home at the base of our steep hill, just before a tight corner, around the bend from my Olympic dreams. And even if I weren't worried about the Manhole Cover from Hell, I would be sufficiently panicked by Paquito the Ice Cream Vendor, who's snuck into our closed race course to sell *helado* from the belly of his giant, smiling, plastic pengiuncycle.

In the moments leading up to the start of the race, my mind is blank and I am thankful for it. Strange countries, unfamiliar roads, unknown competition, unreserved riders, and the possibility of life-threatening crashes—these distractions my adrenaline pushes out of the way, just in time. As the starter raises his gun, I notice that nearly 99 percent of the women in the peloton cross themselves with a Hail Mary. I'm hoping she'll look out for me by association.

Right off the gun, the pack jumps into a sprint. Then slows. Then sprints again. We jostle for position, testing to see who among us are the instigators, the aggressors, the followers, the seasoned, and the inexperienced. It is still so hard for me to tell, especially among these women I've never seen or raced with before. I stay in the front, keeping steady among shoulder bumps and shouts in foreign languages. On the sprint laps, I'm shocked to find I have the strength to come in fourth, which is great personally but terrible mentally, seeing as only the top three get points. I'm still vying for one of the top eight spots at the finish. I know I have the strength for that. But on the eighth lap of the ten-lap race, a nasty, unavoidable pothole not only snaps my carbon fiber water bottle cage but drops my chain from its ring. This is a disaster! Dropping a chain is the cycling equivalent of a car dropping its transmission. Sometimes quickly pedaling and shifting can jiggle the chain back into place, but this is not one of those times. I dismount as quickly as possible and re-attach the chain to its ring. An overly friendly spectator jumps out of the crowd on the sidelines to give me a jump start up the hill by placing his hand on my ass and pushing. I've never been this happy to have a strange hand on my ass. Still, the incident leaves me thirty-two seconds behind the pack. Despite the fact that I speak only a little Spanish, I discover that I am strangely fluent when it comes to expletives.

To come this far, halfway across the world, only to have a pothole ruin the day? Unfathomable. For two laps, I chase the pack on my own, giving everything I have in my body and mind and throat blood.

"Thirty seconds down!" WonderMinion yells from the sidelines. *It's no use*, I think. Still, try.

Two kilometers later, I pass Amanda again. "Twenty-five seconds down!"

Another lap. "Nineteen down!"

Yet another. "Eleven!"

One to go. I hardly need to remind myself that Olympic points go only to the top eight finishers.

On the start of the last lap, I catch back onto the peloton. Shattered, exhausted, I dig as hard as I can at the finish line and cross it in thirteenth place.

Two seconds behind the winner.

I try to think of something to make me feel better about the closeness of the finish. Luge comes to mind. At least in cycling two seconds is almost winning, whereas in luge two seconds pretty much necessitates retirement.

Afterward, Amanda and I return to the hotel to rest up for tomorrow's race, only to discover that the next day's event is not in the same city.

"They're busing us to Guanare," Amanda explains.

"How far's that?"

"Four hours. We leave at 9 P.M. You race at 8 A.M."

"WHAT? They're taking us four hours away in the middle of the night to do a short, twenty-mile race? Are you kidding me?!"

"I think it has to do with the sponsor."

"Who's the sponsor?"

"Jesus."

"WonderMinion, I'm really not in the mood for—"

"Seriously. The race is called Race for the Life of Jesus. It's sponsored by a church. A church in a town four hours away."

I'm pretty sure Jesus doesn't want his athletes cramped in a bus for four hours between races, but I have little say in the matter. All I know is that I'm tired, I'm in a strange place, and I'm now on a bus for four hours in the middle of the night with a blaring Marc Anthony techno mix on repeat, a driver going twenty miles over the speed limit, and an overzealous air-conditioner that is close to cryogenically preserving us all. In this environment, my mind goes to interesting places.

I love this job, I love this opportunity, I love this quest. I'm not really loving Venezuelan buses, but I love being in the moment. And what a moment I am in, trying to get myself to the Olympics. Despite how much I love it all, sometimes this quest is harder than I expected. Physically and mentally, I knew this journey would be difficult. We're talking about the Olympics, after all. Duh. I welcome the pain, the perseverance, the pushing of physical and mental boundaries. None of that bothers me. But then there is the emotional side. The side that you think you've got under control until it shows up mid-bus ride at 1:36 A.M. in a foreign country when you're tired and hungry and lonely and every familiar comfort seems very, very far away. I'm on the second of five weeks away from home and I can barely see a day into what my future holds and I'm subsisting on everything from empanadas to yak livers. Never in my life, except maybe the first year of it, has there been so much change.

The bus ride is not made any easier by the fact that after two years, my boyfriend Steve and I have parted ways. Over the past few months, it's seemed inevitable. We didn't see eye to eye on some pretty key issues, such as taking the distance out of a distance relationship. Underlying it all was a larger, elephant-in-the-living-room factor. Resentment. Steve had grown tired of working long hours in a finance career, and it wasn't easy for him to watch his girlfriend travel around the world on a bicycle. "No big deal," he rationalized, "there's resentment in every relationship." Perhaps there is. But not in my relationships. Ugh. Resentment is nothing but the residue of envy, passive aggression, miscommunication, lack of initiative, and broken Happy buttons. I find it pretty hard to love and resent simultaneously, but more than that, resentment seems so ... *unnecessary*. Why resent what someone is or does when you can go out and be or do something, too? Despite knowing that parting ways was the right thing to do, I was still sad and moody about the breakup. A little confused, too, seeing as a broken engagement followed by another unsuccessful relationship was not exactly the dating pattern I was shooting for. A big, emotional What If asked, *What if it's always going to be this way?*

What if you stop whining about boys and go kick some ass on a bike? another part of me replied. Didn't even know I had that part! Quests, man. Turns out that some points worth getting have nothing to do with Olympic qualification.

The second day of Venezuelan racing goes similar to the first. Today is a thirty-eight-kilometer, a six-lap course with three sprint bonuses. We are racing For the Life of Jesus, but due to the rain, potholes, and sharp corners of the roads, I am unable to scan the crowds to see if He's watching. I take seventeenth place in a pack finish, a mere one second behind the leader, but win none of the bonuses. Ah, cycling—thankless and rewarding. Again, I have this feeling of being simultaneously proud and disappointed in my results. I came here for points, didn't get any, and have to put that behind me immediately. There are nine more races to go. Or so I think.

At the finish line, Guiseppina, my let's-go-cycling-on-the-interstate friend from Mexico, says, "See you in Uruguay!"

"What?" I say, summoning WonderMinion to translate. As it turns out, the Pan American Cycling Championships are set to take place in Uruguay in six days. As a national team member of St. Kitts and Nevis—a nation that is part of North, Central, and South America, even if it is technically floating around in the Caribbean—I am eligible for the race.

"I never saw it on the UCI calendar," I say. I read that thing cover to cover, every week, for the past six months. What Pan Am Games?

Amanda translates Guiseppina's response—that the race wasn't on the women's calendar, it was listed on the men's, but women are still eligible to go. Ah, of course. This calendar was apparently written by the same people who came up with the one-size-fits-every-gender idea for dressing female athletes. Guiseppina goes on to say that the race in Uruguay will offer double the Olympic points as the China and Venezuela races. Well, then. Let's go to Uruguay.

After a seven-hour bus ride from Guanare to Caracas, Amanda and I get to the airport at 3 A.M. While I know I'll physically recover in time for the Pan American Games in Uruguay next week, right now I'm shattered to the core. After buying our tickets for the eight-hour flight to Montevideo, Amanda and I take turns napping on the terminal benches. When we arrive, I'll have four days of rest before the twenty-kilometer time trial and 100-kilometer road race. I'm equal parts ecstatic and exhausted. Not to mention thrilled that I'm no longer traveling solo. As I watch WonderMinion snore softly in the Caracas airport, I'm reminded that nothing worthwhile in life can ever be achieved alone.

March forth.

Three weeks and thirteen races to go.

WATER BREAK

HOW TO LOVE A FEMALE ATHLETE

For a female athlete, personal relationships can be a bit of a challenge. In my experience, sometimes the traits that initially attract a man are the very ones that he has the hardest time handling. "Wow! She's driven, motivated, athletic, competitive, health conscious, and doesn't wear a lot of makeup!" sometimes turns into "Ugh, she sets that damn alarm for 5 A.M. every day, even if it's raining, always has to run a half-step ahead of me, leaves the dirty smoothie blender in the sink, and she kind of tastes like sunscreen." These things are aggravating, but in my mind they need not kill a relationship.

It has dawned on me that perhaps spirited, independent female athletes have a tough time finding the right match because they don't communicate exactly what they need. Which is, mostly, just a little resentment-free encouragement. Most supportive males, in return, will not be displeased with the outcome of such encouragement. I've written a poem to help us all just get along.

How to Love a Female Athlete

When we're sweaty and covered in
    grime, tell us we're hot.
When we're clean and smell nice, tell us we're hot.
We spend a lot of time in gym clothes, so if we take
    the time to put on clothing without Lycra or
    elastic or chamois, notice. And tell us we're hot.
If we prance around the house bellowing, "Check it
    out, I put on *makeup* today!" tell us we're hot.
If we experience a moment of weakness and stare
    at the mirror wondering if our muscles look
    too bulky, tell us we're crazy. And hot.

When we're lying on the couch in a state of
    disheveled athleticoma, tell us we're hot.
When we train together, tell us we're hot.
When we beat you in a race, tell us we're
    hot. Or at least mumble it.
When we win, when we lose, and when we absolutely
    tank, tell us we're hot, hotter, and hottest because
    effort is the hottest-est damn thing out there.
When we question ourselves, tell us not to.
When we doubt our ability, tell us you don't.
When we wonder if we can do it, tell us we will.
Tell us you're proud, tell us you believe, tell us
    you're amazed.
When we break down, just hug us and let us whimper
    for a while and let us wipe our nose on your shirt.
    Don't tell us we're hot, we won't believe you on
    this one. But you can think it if you want to.
Say these things to a female athlete, and we will
    love you.
Say these things and mean them, and we will give you
    lots of sex.

19

IT ONLY FEELS LIKE
YOU'RE DYING

May 2007

The last time I was in Uruguay, I was wearing sequins and fishnets and a face caked with makeup. I also had blonde hair. It was 1998 and at the time I was a professional figure skater on tour in South America, completely unaware that bicycles would have anything to do with my future. Now, exactly one decade and nine days later, I find myself back in Uruguay wearing a helmet and duct tape and a face caked with sunscreen. About the duct tape …

Amanda the WonderMinion and I arrive in Uruguay's capital city, Montevideo, for the Pan American Cycling Championships which, until three days ago, I had no idea existed. Every country in North, Central, and South America (and any nations floating in the oceans in between) is eligible to send its national team to the Pan American

Champs. So here I am, the lone St. Kitts and Nevisian, proudly representing my new nation and answering the question, "Where exactly is
St. Kitts and Nevis?" a minimum of ten times a day. After our eight-hour
red-eye flight from Venezuela (Uruguay is tucked just under Brazil and
to the right of Argentina), I immediately collapse into my hotel room
bed while WonderMinion heads to the race meeting. Acting as my
manager, Amanda will make sure all is well with my registration, see
that my uniform is race legal, and that I am in compliance with all UCI
rules and regulations. Turns out not all is perfect. Gee. Now there's big
a surprise.

A few hours later, Amanda bursts into the hotel room throwing a
heap of red and black Lycra at me.

"Try this on. Quick," she orders. She is slightly out of breath. I unfold
what appears to be a time trial skinsuit, cycling's aerodynamic equivalent
of a body stocking. Only this one is about three sizes too big.

"But I already have a skinsuit," I tell her.

"No, you don't. I took your Sport Beans suit to the race officials and
they said it has too many sponsor logos on it. It isn't UCI legal for the
Pan Am Games."

"No, silly. The *new* St. Kitts and Nevis skinsuit from Champion
System is coming by mail, remember?"

"No it isn't. Just got an e-mail. There wasn't enough time to ship it
from China."

"Where did you get this one?" I ask her, looking at the saggy
spandex.

"Just hurry."

I try on the red-and-black men's medium skinsuit. It fits perfectly …
over my street clothes.

"Good enough," Amanda decrees. "Now give it back."

WonderMinion grabs it, bolts out the door, into the car of a strange
man from the race meeting, and heads back to the race officials on the
other side of the city. For the past two hours, it turns out Wonder-
Minion has been flying around Montevideo in search of a bike store.
Finally tracking one down, she explained my uniform situation to the
shop owner, Javier Gomez. He did not carry skinsuits. But Javier had

his own personal one he would lend me. Said it was good luck, even. That he won the time trial world championships with it back in 1999. Amazing. One dream, so many people helping. The head honchos of UCI okay my new race suit with one condition: that I duct tape over the brand name of the clothing manufacturer—an emblem of a giant letter Z—emblazoned Zorro-like on the chest, back, and legs of the suit.

"I have to race wearing duct tape and men's clothes?" I whine to Amanda before she takes off.

"Dude, I just saved your ass from riding naked," Amanda says, ripping silver strips of tape with her teeth. WonderMinion 1, Kathryn 0.

At the start of the 20-kilometer time trial, I look around at my Pan American competitors. Teams from all over North, South, and Central America are warming up on rollers and trainers. Team managers, mechanics, coaches, doctors, massage therapists, and assistants gather around the cyclists like NASCAR pit crews. Sleek aero helmets are donned, disc wheels are mounted on $10,000 bikes while mechanics check every nut, bolt, and measurement and coaches mentally prep their athletes. I, however, didn't have enough hands/luggage space to bring a stationary trainer with me. Because of storage space issues, I wasn't permitted to bring my time trial bike to China, so it isn't with me in South America, either. One of my composite teams told me I'd be outfitted with a new aero helmet, so I left my old one at home. That didn't come through.

So here I am among the world's elite with a too-big skinsuit, a wind-catching helmet, well-worn wheels, and a less-than-aerodynamic road bike with left-right clip-on aerobars that WonderMinion accidentally put on the wrong sides. The good news is I could care less. I am here, and it's been a hell of a fight to get to this point. I may not have the best equipment or a team of people to take care of my athletic needs, but I've got two working wheels, two able legs, one willing mind, and a WonderMinion with more heart and soul than any team of cycling professionals. *I am here.* There are Olympic points to be chased. I'd ride a tricycle if I had to. With duct tape streamers.

Rolling down the start ramp of the Pan Am Champs time trial, I feel good. Strong. Stronger than usual. In fact, I feel really, really super duper. Off I go. The Spanish-speaking race official announces my name and country into his bullhorn, "Keeatrin Berteeeen de St. Kittens and Novice." For the next half hour, I battle into the wind, hungry for a top-five finish. I know I can do it. I pedal with every ounce of strength I have. A piece of duct tape comes loose from my skinsuit and ensnares my braid, taping it securely to my back. At least my hair is now aerodynamic. The normal pain of a time trial comes flooding in—blood tasting and muscle screaming—and today's mental mantra is a Floyd Landis quote I keep in the back of my head: "It only feels like you're dying. You don't actually die." Before his Tour de France testosterone/doping issues, Landis was best known as one of Lance Armstrong's teammates and the recipient of one of Lance's best lines about race tactics: "Ride like you stole something, Floyd." I think about the one thing I've been trying to steal for the past eighteen months—time. It is running out.

When I cross the line in thirty minutes and one second, I am ecstatic. While all courses and conditions are different, this race result is five minutes better than my time trial finish at the U.S. nationals ten months ago. I dispatch Amanda to grab the final results from the officials. She returns with a piece of paper and a blank expression.

"I double-checked," she says. "They're correct."

I look down the results to find my name in fourteenth place. Out of fifteen riders. The time is correct, 30:01. Despite hellacious winds and non-aero everything, this is my fastest 20-kilometer time trial result to date. But the winner put up a twenty-seven-minute finish. And twelve others crossed the line between us.

The disappointment overwhelms me. I can handle it when I drop my chain on a pothole or snap a water bottle cage on nasty pavement. I can handle getting elbowed by giant Chinese cyclists or bumped by aggressive Brazilians or narrowly missing sprint bonuses or nearly crashing out on a dangerous corner or finishing two seconds behind the winner but without winning any points. I can handle those things.

But I'm having a hard time with the fact that I went as hard and as fast as I could. And I went five minutes faster than I did in July. And I *still* finished second to last! I'm trying so hard to stay positive and optimistic and think good thoughts. For example, today I was 2:45 behind the two American cyclists who beat me by more than four minutes last July. Or that I was competing against the national champions of a multitude of countries spanning two different continents. I try to think thoughts like this, but it simply hurts like hell when you're confronted with the truth that your best just isn't good enough.

In my lifelong athletic experience there is only one way to deal with a crappy race result, a poor-me attitude, and the daunting prospect of another race less than twenty-four hours away.

It's called beef.

Amanda and I find a Uruguayan grill and refuel my depleted body with a giant steak, heaping potatoes, leafy salad, and a boatload of tasty little dulce-de-leche-filled bakery cookies. Everything looks a little brighter with a belly full of fat, protein, and carbs. Bright enough to remember that I've got ten days of racing to go before the Olympic points cut-off date. Maybe my best wasn't good enough in today's time trial. I've got twelve tomorrows left in this quest. Twelve days to keep fighting. Twelve chances to win points.

Make that eleven. While the next day's Pan American Champs 100-kilometer road race was a strong effort, a giant pack finish of sixty or so riders was not enough to gain me any points. Despite every effort to position myself in the lead, the frenzy of a sprint finish sees every wheel gunning for the nanoseconds separating first and twelfth places. To fall short by mere milliseconds is something all cyclists accept. I can see so much progress in my cycling. I ride in the front, despite having no teammates to help protect me from attacks, breaks, sprints, and wind. I hold a steady line. I don't give way to others who try to bump me from my spot. These are good lessons. Lessons that come naturally to most of the women I'm racing against. But I've only been in this sport for fifteen months, so for a thirty-two-year-old rookie, nothing comes easy.

Make that thirty-three. The day after the road race, May 11, I celebrate my thirty-third birthday. How does a cyclist celebrate her birthday while on an international tour for Olympic points? Sleeping. Better still, dreaming. Curled up in front of the hotel television in Uruguay, my favorite movie, *Invincible*, comes on Uruguay's version of HBO. With Spanish subtitles, I watch (for the millionth time) the story of Vince Papale, the thirty-year-old bartender/substitute teacher who, against all odds and never having played more than high school football, earned a spot on the Philadelphia Eagles in 1975, for whom he kicked some serious ass, made game-winning plays, and earned three trips to the Super Bowl. This man is my athletic hero, and I don't even particularly like football. But his story spoke to me, so I got in touch with him earlier in the year and told him about my Olympic quest. Awesome guy that he is, Vince answered back. We had dinner when he visited Arizona a few months ago.

"Kathryn, keep grinding, don't let anything hold you back," he told me. He talked about his amazing life, his football experiences, and humored me when I asked him to tell me all about Mark Wahlberg (twice). I love this man. Vince, that is. Well, Mark too. But that's a different kind of love. Strangely, I went to see *Invincible* in the theater the night my first ESPN column was posted in 2006, so it's a nice omen to find it on TV on my birthday in the middle of my own Olympic walk-on attempt. Later that night, I actually dream that I am playing quarterback for my high school football team and that a scout for the Olympic Football Committee is in the stands. I am immediately recruited to represent the first St. Kitts and Nevis Olympic gridiron team. Vince is the coach. Marky Mark is my very supportive boyfriend who can't stop telling me how hot I am. When I wake up, Mark and Vince aren't in Uruguay with me, but luckily WonderMinion is. She's already packing up my bike and getting our bags together. "Ready for El Salvador?" she asks.

When flying across continents, it is vital to have a travel partner who understands you. Or at least tolerates you. WonderMinion does both. Amanda is now used to my odd custom of continually updating her on my hydration status. When I announce with glee that I've peed four times during the twelve-hour flight from Uruguay to El Salvador and that my urine is the correct color for optimal performance (pale yellow, meaning well-hydrated), WonderMinion congratulates me with a fist-bump of approval. "Nice, Bertine! Gonna race fast tomorrow!" While I am barely able to move my exhausted, post-race body beyond the Bermuda triangle of athleticoma (bed, bathroom, and television) from day to day, Amanda pilots the details of my Olympic dreams. In a ten-day, twelve-stage event, WonderMinion will become my bike mechanic, gear carrier, get-outta-bed-Bertine-er, water bottle feeder, calf-cramp healer, hunter of Chamois Butt'r, Internet connection pilferer, AK-47 deflector, and Pizza Hut dialer. The last role will, in the near future, literally save my life.

Many people don't know this, but the Central American country of El Salvador has another name: Hades. We arrive at the San Salvador airport at 11 P.M. and the temperature reads ninety degrees. I understand immediately I am in for a sweat-soaked painfest unlike anything I have ever known, as I contemplate ten days of nearly hundred-kilometer races, often up volcanoes. We are also in for something of a cultural shock. For the race (Vuelta a El Salvador), we are officially housed at the equivalent of El Salvador's Olympic Training Center—(the Albergue Indes Sports Hotel)—but we are not permitted off the compound without armed guards. While the country is geographically beautiful and the people are kind and welcoming, the political strife and poverty have wreaked social havoc. For example, due to a shooting in the neighborhood, we are not allowed to do a warmup ride the day before our race. In fact, AK-47-toting guards will accompany us to the start lines of all our races. You know, just in case.

Fortunately, the arrival of the prerace adrenaline fairies provides much-needed protection from reality. *Here I go on a superfast bike ride! Look at all the pretty weapons! Nothing bad can happen to me! I wanna be an Olympian! La la la la la!*

As with my races in China and Venezuela, to race the Vuelta Ciclista Femenina a El Salvador I needed to be on a sanctioned UCI composite team of four to six riders. The race director groups me with five other cyclists, all of who are trying to chase down Olympic points. Joelle Numainville from Canada, Anita Valen from Norway, myself, and three young local El Salvadoran girls make up Team GSB, short for Le Grand Saint Bernard Swiss-Resort Hotel Domaine du Chene. Awesome. I'm a big St. Bernard in white spandex. Each member of Team GSB is given one race kit (jersey and bib shorts) for a ten-day, twelve-stage event. This means nightly sink-laundering and two lovely days where we'll have to be in wet, dirty clothes because we will race a morning *and* afternoon event. By the end of the two weeks in El Salvador, my kit will be holey, stinky, and gray from pollution. While we are all friendly with one another, there will be no team tactics or camaraderie among Team GSB. While other professional and national teams have women assigned to designated roles (sprinter, leader, domestique, etc.), we will be each woman for herself. I am used to this by now.

What I am not used to, however, is the idea that the reigning world champion, Marianne Vos, and her team of studettes (DSB Bank) are here in El Salvador. So is Giant Pro Cycling, the Chinese team of eight-foot-tall women. (How do you say "Get out of my way!" in Chinese, again? *Gun chu!*) Also racing will be the national teams of Spain, Ukraine, Mexico, Venezuela, Colombia, Cuba, Costa Rica, Brazil, and a few random composite teams like Team GSB. Months ago, Coach Gord and I decided that racing in El Salvador—as opposed to going to some of the races simultaneously being held in Europe—might give me a better shot for points. After all, how many cyclists would venture all the way to Central America to chase Olympic points? Answer: a lot. In the final qualification stages of an Olympic year, everyone comes out of the woodwork looking for points. And they're all fast and strong. In El Salvador, we have a start list of eighty riders on the first day. Points will go only eight places deep. While my chances are slim, winning one stage on one day would get me nearly all the points I'd need to put me in the top one hundred in the world rankings. Of course, with the best team in the world racing here, such a task could be nearly impossible. Luckily, "nearly" is good friends with my favorite word, "doable." Odds don't mean anything. A chance is a chance is a chance.

Chances are, however, that detailing every stage of a ten-day, twelve-stage cycling race will leave most readers blind, bored, or both. A snapshot of the beginning, middle, and end is the best way to go, so ...

The first day of racing is the Grand Prix Santa Ana, a ninety-six-kilometer adventure in the mighty hills of El Salvador. After four weeks of mostly flat-course races in China, Venezuela, and Uruguay, where the sprinters dominated the points and ranks, I am feeling a bit dejected with my results. Putting myself on the line day after day, giving my all but coming up short again and again—this beats up a brain and body. I wonder if I have it in me anymore. I wonder if I belong here, among the best, with no teammates and so little international experience. Then something changes. I stop wondering. I don't have time to wonder. When I see the profile of the El Salvador race courses—rife with hills—I feel a strange sense of calm. Hills are my homeboys. All of a sudden I have teammates of the topographical kind.

And so, fifteen kilometers into the first race, there comes a large, long hill. And a break of nearly thirty girls, including world champion Marianne Vos of the Netherlands. And lo, I am in this break! Off we go. I keep up with every surge and sprint and attack. Better still, I initiate some of them! When the pace backs off with twenty kilometers left to go, a voice inside me says, *There is no way I am slowing down, there is no way I am going to let a sprinter win this race. A climber will win this race, and I'm going to make sure of it.* So I go. With no teammates to help me, the other women sit in and wait for me to get tired. But I don't get tired—not yet. A rider from Spain comes up to me and takes her hand off her handlebars and puts it across my waist like a mother protecting her child in the front seat of a car, saying, "Stop. Slow down."

A string of expletives flies out of my mouth, though I'm not sure which language I use. I shake her free and keep going. When the finish line rolls around, there is (of course) a sprint for it, but only the climbers are left in the pack. I do not win. Marianne Vos wins. I come in twentieth place. But this is the highest level race on the UCI calendar. Qualifying points for this stage go twenty places deep. I have points! Three of them! Disbelieving, Amanda and I double-check with the head official. WonderMinion asks in Spanish and English. "Points go twenty places deep, correct?" "*Sí, sí!*" the official answers. I cry gushy girly tears.

Points? I was never even supposed to be here. I was never supposed to get this far in this quest. Three whole points for coming in twentieth is what the UCI rulebook says. Sure, I'll need about forty more to get me into the top one hundred ranked female cyclists in the world, but with a win offering twenty to forty points, each day really is an

Olympic chance. And now I have three whole points! It may not be enough to get me to the Olympics just yet, but hot damn, it sure did open the door. Today was a very good day.

That night, I wash my one race kit in the sink, soaping the chamois and scrubbing out the sweat and stench and bacteria as best I can. The humidity is such that nothing dries quickly, and the only way to ensure a dry kit for the next day is to wash it immediately after each race, roll it in a towel for a while, then tie it to the little lights under the ceiling fan and watch it dance and sway in the artificial wind all night. Usually it is dry by morning. But not always.

A few days later, I wake up with a saddle sore the size of Pluto growing where the sun don't shine. The heat, humidity, sweat, and ill-fitting chamois (the race kits are male-specific, not female) have joined forces to occupy the left trench where my thigh, butt, and you-know-what meet. Also attempting to inhabit this area is the bike saddle itself. This war will rage for the next nine days and the result is an angry, volcanic welt of grape-size nastiness that hurts so bad I have to waddle when I'm off the bike and wobble when I'm on it. Without ice or antiseptics, I try to operate on it with a needle, but the mass is too new and too solid. The only thing that comes out is a very loud scream. No position on the bike is comfortable and relief comes only when I take a very deep breath and lean all my weight directly on the sore until it goes numb. Or, on the third day, explodes. The open-wound chafing I experienced during track cycling was nothing compared to this despicable atrocity, this welt of pus and doom.

But brace yourself, because here is the really sick part: I like my saddle sore. Not so much the sore itself, but the barometer of pain it represents. For two weeks of physical anguish, that merciless lump asks me the same question: *Is that all you got, Bertine?* Two years ago, the answer might have been yes. *Yes, thank you, saddle sore, that is all I have.* But in the last two weeks of my Olympic dream, I can look that pain in the eye—and believe me, it actually has an eye—and answer no. *Hell no. Let me show you exactly what I've got, you pathetic excuse for a cyst! I'll show you pain. I'm going to kick your sorry ass—even if, technically, you are my ass. You're going down, sore. Gun chu!*

As if trash-talking my saddle sore isn't doing enough damage to my mental state, cycling up El Boqueron—one of El Salvador's active volcanoes—pushes me to the actual brink of sanity. The funny thing about cycling up a volcano with a 19 percent gradient is that at the base, you hope to God it doesn't blow. About twenty minutes later, you start hoping it will. To gain a perspective on how steep 19 percent is, pick out a wall in your house and try to climb up it. While the road up El Boqueron is "only" thirteen kilometers long, it's situated at the end of our eighty-three-kilometer race. Exhausted, dehydrated, and depleted of all things mental and physical, my immediate reaction to the ridiculous steepness is to laugh at its absurdity. I laugh at my bike computer, which indicates I am traveling three kilometers per hour. I laugh at the fact that I can barely grip the handlebars because the humidity and sweat have saturated my gloves to the point of uselessness. I laugh at the spool of ruby-colored Gatorade-infused drool dangling from my mouth, unable to spare the energy to wipe it away. I laugh at WonderMinion, who attempts to hand me a water bottle on the steepest pitch, but I can't steady my bike enough to grab it, so she pours it on my head. I watch two women ahead of me tip over onto the pavement because they could not turn their pedals quick enough to remain upright. And I laugh at them, knowing I am probably next. I laugh at the enormous dead horse lying in the bike lane, because there is no way that can be real. Right? Wrong. Okay, not so funny.

Humor returns on the last kilometer of the climb, where local villagers sell handmade furniture along the road. What kind of furniture? Beds and chairs. I am at the top of a volcano, about to die from exhaustion, and all around me are beds and chairs that I am not allowed to sit in. My saddle sore finds that one particularly amusing.

As if the climbing in El Salvador isn't enough, the descents are just as deadly. We are not on a closed course, so oncoming traffic is a threat. Being part of a pack of eighty women screaming downhill at over forty miles per hour through switchback roads is an interesting thing. I call on the adrenaline fairies once more to calm me, they whisper their special blend of motivational denial, and before I know it I'm telling myself things like, *I've got a helmet, I can take a bus head on! Yellow lines are so decorative! What's a little love tap from a rearview mirror?* When you're at the brink, you'll tell yourself whatever it takes to keep going. The road surfaces are often choppy patchworks of chip seal and well, no seal. The only thing worse than the conical manhole covers I encountered in Venezuela is the absence of manhole covers in El Salvador. On many roads, wide, gaping, uncovered sewer openings that may or may not be portals to hells are something we all try to avoid cycling into.

On one stage I get a flat twice on potholes, destroying two strong, expensive tubular tires. According to protocol, riders needing mechanical assistance move to the side of the road to wait for the team car to pull alongside and provide the necessary service. In my case, the team car for GSB is number fourteen in today's caravan of fifteen teams. By the time it reaches me, I can only watch as the peloton moves farther and farther away. A less than quick wheel change leaves me at a further disadvantage. I am alone, and I have to time trial my way back to the peloton with no help from my team car. Our driver, Miguel, fearing a penalty, will not allow me to ride in his draft for even a second. He speeds off.

I begin my solo time trial to rejoin the peloton, but some attacks are under way and the pace has quickened. I catch onto a group that has fallen back from the main pack, but no one organizes to chase. I keep trying, riding alone, but at the finish line I find I am four minutes behind the winner. Frustrated, it is all I can do to calm down, cool off, and replenish with some electrolyte gels and jelly beans. Flats happen. They cause gaps and losses and wreak havoc on riders who need to make up time because of them. It is all part of cycling. You have to let it go. You have to forget about points and Olympics and everything else and just focus on finishing the stage. *Tomorrow,* you tell yourself, *tomorrow will be better.* Providing your bicycle and you make it to tomorrow.

On the way back from the stage, Miguel drives the GSB team car *muy rapidamente* over the bumpy highways of El Salvador. There's a loud popping noise from the roof of the truck, where the bikes are racked, and I glance out my window to see my Trek Madone dangling next to me. I let go something between a scream and a howl and yell at Miguel to pull over *ahora!* As he veers to the shoulder, the team mechanic, Peechy, sitting next to me attempts to quell my panic by offering me a cookie. From his pocket. Unwrapped.

Are you crazy? My bike is about to fall off the car onto an interstate in the middle of Hades and you're offering me a cook— is that a chocolate cream center? *Yeah, okay. Gracias.* Amazingly, my bike, which had come loose after the not-so-secure skewer popped its bolt, has suffered only a paint scratch or two. I'm all set for tomorrow's race, feeling tired but hopeful, and enjoying a slightly linty sugar buzz. Maybe today wasn't the best stage, but no matter. A pack finish in today's stage isn't so bad and hey, I still have points!

Actually, I don't. At dinner that evening, Amanda discovers that the race official who confirmed my points for twentieth place was wrong. That race only gave points up to twelve places, not twenty. "But," he offers as a consolation, "You did win prize money."

"Oh, how much?"

"Twenty dollars, U.S. currency!"

"Excellent. How many points will that buy?"

Perhaps if I laugh at this, too, no one will truly know how close I am to jumping into El Boqueron. But it could be much worse. At least I still have the ability to race the last five stages. Not everyone will. The effects of today's volcanic efforts have taken their toll on all of us. At dinner in the dining hall, two athletes faint into their food. Another is taken to the hospital with severe cramping. Another tore her groin from the intensity of the 19 percent gradient. Ten women will drop out of the race by next morning. Points or no points, I am still going strong.

Or so I think. No points, giant saddle sores, six weeks of traveling between China, Hong Kong, Venezuela, Uruguay, and El Salvador, and now three days racing left ... I drag my body to bed only to wake up a few hours later with fever sweats. My body, seven pounds lighter than ten days ago, has had all it can handle of the low-fat chicken and rice dishes the dining hall provides at every meal. But without a way to travel to the local stores and restaurants, there aren't a lot of options. However, WonderMinion discovers that Pizza Hut delivers. I am likely the only person in El Salvador for whom the globalization of fast food is actually going to prolong life. I order an extra large Meat Lover's pizza, two orders of breadsticks, two salads, and a liter of soda, then hand the phone to WonderMinion so she can place her order. When the pizza arrives, I can instantly feel the meaty grease oozing life back into me. But I'm still so depleted from all the races that, while the pizza is helpful, it isn't a miracle worker. I have a fever, and pepperoni can't cure everything.

The heat and humidity make it nearly impossible to stay hydrated, and without a personal medical team there is little chance for IV fluid replacement. I drink all I can and force-feed as much pizza as possible, but volcano days and sweat-ridden nights have left me completely drained. For the first time in two years, I entertain the notion of quitting. Not because I want to, but because my body is insisting that something is wrong. I'm sick. Three women on Team GSB have already dropped out. Happens all the time in cycling, I've been told. Most cyclists know their limits, and when they're done they're done. Experienced cyclists have a good handle on the difference between stopping and quitting. They seem to understand that *stopping* revolves around physical issues and *quitting* comes down to mental fortitude. I fully agree. It makes total sense. I should stop. I have a fever, too much weight loss, and my organs feel like they're in a heated game of musical chairs. Stopping is smart. At 6 A.M., Amanda wakes me up. "Can you get up?" she asks.

"I don't know."

"If you can't race, it's okay," she says calmly. "You've done your best." She tells me the cyclists' bus will leave at 8 A.M., and she'll have my bike ready just in case. If I quit—or stop—on any given day, the rules of racing do not permit a rider to start the next day. I will have a DNF (did not finish) next to my name and be out of contention for points, for Olympics, for the race itself. For two hours, I roll around in sweat and tears and What Ifs. *Yes you can, Body!* says my mind. *Mind, you're a raging idiot,* says my body. At 7:55 A.M., I roll out of bed, put on my still damp chamois and pollution-stained-gray-tinged-armpit-reeking jersey, and trudge onto the bus, moaning incoherently and looking like an extra from *Dawn of the Living Dead*. I slink down next to WonderMinion, who offers me a silent fist bump. I can live with quitting.

I can live with stopping. But I simply cannot grasp not starting.

Every day, there is a chance for points, a chance to put myself into the top hundred cyclists in the world. I will have to win, though—be the first one across the line. Not second or twenty-second or thirty-second by a millimeter, but first. I remind myself that a win can come down to chance as well as talent, that all I need to do is "Pull a Bradbury." In 2002 at the Salt Lake City Olympics, Australian speedskater Steven Bradbury was in last place when he came around the final turn for his short track speed skating event. Just as it looked like there was no chance for him to medal, the first- through fourth-place skaters—including the heavily favored Apolo Anton Ohno—crashed in a mass pile-up. Bradbury dodged the wreckage, sailing past them to win Australia's first Olympic gold medal at a Winter Games. Some belittled Bradbury's win and dismissed it as luck, overlooking the fact that he had earned his way into the finals and deserved to be there. Bradbury's triumph is a reminder of the truth of Olympic glory: You don't have to be the best of all time, just the best on that day.

For twenty races in six weeks on three continents, I arrived at each start line with the same thought: *Just today.* Of course, every other woman thought the same thing in her own way. Every day there was a fight for the finish line. Today I am lucky just to finish. I make it to the end of the stage without getting time cut. Without getting sucked down to hell by an uncovered manhole. My fever breaks, but my dream does not.

The final two stages of the Vuelta a El Salvador are difficult, but physically I recover enough to stay with the peloton. Both days, however, find me finishing thirty-eighth out of the fifty-five women remaining from our original field of eighty. And just like that, it's over. The Vuelta a El Salvador ends and I don't have, nor can I earn, the forty-five points it would take to put me in the top one hundred ranked cyclists in the world. It is May 22 and the cutoff date for points is May 31. There are no more races for me, no more composite teams to ride for, no more Olympic chances. I won't be an Olympian in 2008. And that is that.

Amanda and I leave El Salvador the next day. We take a shuttle to the airport, paid for with the twenty dollars I won in the first stage of racing. I look out the bus window, watching the trees and hills and volcanoes and vendors, completely unaware of the strength and stamina and experience and courage that my body is bringing home as souvenirs. It will be a while before I unpack those items.

20

THE TROPICANA FOLDER OF INNER PEACE

June 2007

For two years, I have been keeping a folder with me while I traveled to races and events. It is white, with a Tropicana logo that says in block lettering, "OJ is more than OK." I don't know where it came from, but it now contains twenty-four months' worth of hotel receipts, business cards, pages torn from brochures, and the occasional discount coupon for a sandwich shop in a town I'll likely never visit again. Shortly after getting back from China and South America, I attempted to sort through it and throw out most of the contents. But I found that I couldn't.

This tattered white folder of what I thought were hotel receipts and rental car agreements really contains the reminders of my effort and achievement. What I thought was clutter now seems priceless: a printout for an Ironman entry, a postcard from a marathon swim event, a download on track cycling technique and another entitled *How to Play Team Handball,* an order confirmation for ancestry.com, invoices for Jimmy's and Gord's coaching fees, the 2007 National Cycling Race Calendar, the 2008 UCI Race Calendar, a web page bookmark on Beijing culture, scrawled notes of frequent flyer numbers, national team federation numbers, international calling codes, an unidentifiable confirmation marked MX5G3RT0012, directions to the Olympic Training Center in Colorado Springs, directions from the Olympic Training Center in Lake Placid, a note pad marked Oualie Beach Hotel of Nevis, stickers for Xoom Juice Smoothies, flyers for Sport Beans, TriSports.com promotions, the business card of my Trek sponsor, physical therapy bills, race entry receipts, a local Arizona race prize money envelope that serendipitously still has the five-dollar bill in it, a list of extremely important emergency phone numbers written on a Post-it with Homer Simpson consuming multicolored donuts with an underscored note reminding me to call, in the following order, dad, plumber, and Poland. Plus an abundance of random quotes and important thoughts that are in my handwriting but not my memory.

I look at this collection of yellowed customer copies and fraying local coupons and digital e-mail reminders and I understand now that these are the receipts of living. Who knew? Colby Pearce did. The track cycling coach in Colorado Springs was the first to listen to my Olympic dream and utter the world "doable" while looking me in the eye. I believed him. Doable. Not *maybe*, not *possibly*, not *perhaps*. Those words leave a lot to chance. Doable, with its amazing ability to promise nothing and everything all at once, still left me in charge. I hung onto that word fiercely, to its calm positivity, its quiet hope, and its spunky little go-getter syllables—the *do* and the *able*. This is a good word, doable. Made even better by the fact that there is no don'table. Shortly after my track cycling experience, Colby left his position as the women's development coach and immersed himself once again in the sport from which he retired. At thirty-six, it seems he isn't quite done with doable.

Ironically, it's in this clutter that I see my journey in a clearer light. I see that I truly achieved the one thing I set out to: find the boundaries of doable and render it didable. In sorting through the refuse of my journey, I found myself overwhelmed with a sublime feeling of inner peace.

It is hard to pinpoint the emotion that comes with the ending of my quest. The best I can come up with is this: fulfilled emptiness. I have emptied myself physically and emotionally into my goal. Not just for the past six weeks and four continents, but for two years and nine sports. And that kind of emptiness is more fulfilling than anything I've ever known. Some people go through their entire lives without experiencing the rush, joy, fear, and bottomless emotion of living in the moment. For two years, ESPN gave me the chance to live in the moment—all 63,113,852 of them, if you define moments as seconds. How can I possibly be disappointed about that? I am not upset. I am not sad. I am not angry. I do not have the impulse to kick or throw anything. I did not make the Olympics ... and honestly, I think that's awesome.

My quest began because some magazine editors wondered about the state of the Olympics and whether or not the games upheld the highest standards of athleticism. I already knew the answer heading into my mission, seeing as I'd been trying to get to the Olympics my whole athletic life. I just didn't know the extent of the effort and excellence involved. Now I do. The Olympics are no joke. The games are stronger than ever. I was a professional athlete going into this project and I'm twice as strong now—head, heart, and body—than when I started, so I know that the athletes who went to Beijing deserved to be going, and those who did not qualify can hold their heads high, knowing they competed against the very best. I did everything in my power to get to Beijing, given my resources, time, and talent. While some will say I failed, I would rather look at my Olympic journey from Thomas Edison's perspective: "I did not fail. I successfully found ten thousand ways that did not work."

I would now say that no one—myself included—can be expected to make an Olympic team with less than two years of experience. Maybe twenty years ago there were a few "fringe" sports that had so few competitors that it was possible to qualify with so little training. Today, there is not one sport on the Olympic roster that is easy (trust me, I've tried them all) or under-subscribed. It is still a common mis-conception—judging from the collection of e-mails I receive—that any country can send any athlete they want to the Olympics. In reality, making a national team no longer ensures an athlete a berth in the Olympics in any sport, just as my hard-won dual citizenship of St. Kitts and Nevis didn't automatically qualify me for the games. And with 161 nations and more than seven hundred female riders registered with the Union Cycliste International, there is no way to get to the Olympics without experience, hard work, dedication, qualifying points, and what Coach Gord summarized as "paying your dues."

Chatting with twenty-one-year-old Marianne Vos in the El Salvador airport, I asked the reigning world champ when she started racing. "When I was five," she answered. Those are some well-paid dues. She has one year of experience for every month of my cycling career. At five, she spent her Saturdays beginning to learn the intricacies of racing a bicycle. At five, my biggest concern on a Saturday was figuring out whether Smurfette was the sister or the girlfriend of all the other Smurfs. Sixteen years later, Vos has a world title while I'm still unsure about Smurfette.

So what now?

Well, since long before ESPN was ever in the picture, I've wanted to be an Olympian. So, What If I continue to get stronger, faster, better? What If my love of sport grows even more? What If a pro cycling team signs me, and if not, What If I keep racing alone? What If I continue to race for St. Kitts and Nevis and make a run for the Olympic Games in London 2012? I'm not ruling that out. I love cycling. Love conquers all. Even saddle sores.

So here I am, an above-average athlete who attempted greatness. I don't have an Olympic medal. But I do have a torn folder filled with clippings and chicken scratchings that tells me I tried, reminds me I showed up, confirms I marched forth, and gives me this bizarre sense of inner peace. Strange are the medals life gives out, and how sometimes a pile of crumpled paper can be as good as gold.

WATER BREAK

THE PRICE TAG OF AN OLYMPIC DREAM

Trying to be an Olympian is as financially depleting as it is physically exhausting. The price tag of my Olympic dream, which included two years of training, racing, and travel, came to $67,665. Here's the breakdown:

Airfare: $22,560

Bike box travel fees: $2,464

Hotel: $15,772

Food while traveling: $3,511

Rental cars and cabs: $3,959

Coaching: $4,450

Race entry fees: $1,734

Physical/massage therapy: $1,939

Equipment repairs, maintenance: $6,736

Miscellaneous (visas, passports, country visitor taxes, caffeine): $4,540

ESPN graciously covered these expenses for me. But my consumer mentality, shaped by so many lean years, made it impossible for me to indulge. Even if ESPN was willing to put me up at a nice hotel or cover a swanky meal, it wasn't in my nature to seek out such luxuries. Not many single, working-class Olympic hopefuls (myself included) can afford such perks, so I stuck as closely as possible to the budget I would have had if ESPN weren't in the picture. I first looked for homestay options, asking race directors if free, in-home host accommodations were available for athletes. If not, I stayed at Econo Lodges and Motel 6s. All hail the glorious trend of free hotel breakfasts! I flew economy class, middle-seat style. I earned 175,000 United Airlines frequent flyer miles, 28,000 on American, and 57,000 on Continental. I became familiar with the three rental cars in National/Alamo's economy-size fleet that best accommodated my beastly bike box: the Pontiac

Vibe, Dodge Caliber, and Chrysler PT Cruiser. Bike maintenance and repairs can be incredibly expensive, but the total above is extremely low because my sponsors at TriSports.com, Trek, and Fair Wheel Bikes all extended extremely helpful discounts. In addition to my own expenses, ESPN shelled out about $30,000 more to have my journey photographed and filmed.

Indeed, the best things in life are free: attempting, striving, doing, living. Reality, however, carries a price tag. I received a monthly paycheck from ESPN for the articles posted on E-Ticket, as well as an advance for this book. Without either of these sources of income, it would have been impossible to make it as far as I did without incurring serious personal debt. Flying to Nevis to meet the premier, jetting off to a UCI points race in Shanghai, swimming seven miles across an Australian bay—the ingredients of a two-year What If? are anything but inexpensive. There is no way I could have done this on my own.

In fact, I was not alone for one minute of my quest. ESPN. com gets over ten million hits a day. As my articles were posted, ESPN put up conversation links where readers could share their comments about my quest. Most were encouraging. Some weren't. There was a spike in angst-ridden posts when I became a dual citizen of St. Kitts and Nevis, as some U.S. "patriots" believed representing another country was simply outrageous. terrible, unpatriotic. The only effect my critics had on me was positive; they simply added more fuel to my desire to succeed. Besides, the way I see it, a true patriot of our nation is not someone who believes "America first" or "America only" but rather "America and ..." In other words, what can we do (individually and as a country) to help this world grow, thrive, and achieve?

St. Kitts and Nevis is giving me an ongoing opportunity to answer that question. I'm just a girl on a bike. But maybe that is enough to make a small change in the world. We'll see. I am just getting started. But I already know that one e-mail can make a difference. Returning home from Nevis to Tucson, I circulated a single e-mail through my Arizona cycling community. I asked my fellow riders if they had any used equipment I could send down to Nevis so the kids there don't have to ride (the few bikes they have) in flip-flops and torn jeans. I hoped a few of my cycling buddies would respond. After three weeks, I received:

84 cycling shoes and pedals

112 cycling kits (outfits)

17 helmets

64 pounds of components and parts

4 full bicycles

8 sets of wheels

10 wetsuits for triathletes

When it was all boxed up, the weight of generosity totaled nearly one thousand pounds. Friends and strangers and entire cycling teams, both amateur and professional, gave to my new country. TriSports.com donated most of the international shipping costs. Winston and Greg were able to hold the first national championships ever in St. Kitts and Nevis, getting dozens of kids hooked on cycling. For some people, patriotism has definitive boundaries. Good thing humanism doesn't.

EPILOGUE

TURN YOUR BRAIN
OFF AND SUFFER

The week after I returned from El Salvador, I headed off to yet another race. I left my bike at home, though. This time I get to be the WonderMinion—for my father. At seventy-two, he is racing in the ITU Triathlon World Age Group Championships, held in Vancouver, British Columbia. The weekend was rainy and windy and race day was less than ideal. So much so that the officials eliminated the swim and made the race a run-bike-run event. But before they canceled the swim, they postponed it to see if the weather would clear. A great migration of wetsuit-wearing septuagenarians waddled into the local coffee shops along Stanley Park, waiting an hour or so to see if they would be allowed to swim.

In my father's seventy-to-seventy-four-year-old age group were twenty-nine competitors. As he shuffled by on each lap of the looping run course, he joked with me as I took pictures. "This is my sprint lap!" he called, never increasing his pace. "I must have passed everyone!" he quipped as the run course became less and less populated. He was joking, but in fact, I think he's right on. Dad, you have no idea how far out in front you really are. He finished twenty-fifth, but as far as I'm concerned, he's an Olympian.

A few months later, some other Olympians took the stage. In August 2008, the Beijing Games began, For two weeks, I glued myself to the broadcast coverage. Only I didn't exactly watch the events; I *felt* them. More so than ever before. Friends and readers asked me if it would be hard to watch the games, bittersweet perhaps. But while watching China, it was the scenery of London in 2012 that unfolded in my mind. As did a whole new set of What Ifs.

Simultaneously, the immediacy of the Beijing Olympics was not lost on me. I savored every moment, and felt personally connected to so many of the sports. I watched open water swimming and felt the fatigue *and* the jellyfish. I gaped at the magnificent pentathletes, and air-dodged their swords and felt the heft of the pistol in my shoulder. Margaux Isaksen, sixteen, who showed me the ropes during my modern pentathlon tryout, competed brilliantly while Sheila Taormina's history-making presence simply gave me the chills. At thirty-seven, Sheila represented the USA in pentathlon ... after already competing in the 2000 and 2004 games in swimming and triathlon. No one has ever competed in the Olympics in three different sports. And at thirty-seven? This woman should be on a Wheaties box for the rest of Wheaties' existence.

As for the other sports, just looking at track cycling made my thighs burn, while race walking made my hips wince, and lightweight rowing made my palms bleed and appetite skyrocket. I marveled at Michael Phelps, gawked at prepubescent Chinese gymnasts, endured more hours of beach volleyball than there are grains of sand on earth. When women's cycling came on I paced my living room the entire broadcast, my heart rate approaching the athletes'. I saw the women

I'd raced with in Asia and South America. There was Mexico's Guiseppina Grassi, my roommate in Venezuela. Norway's Anita Valen, my composite teammate in El Salvador. There were the three Brazilians I'd bumped shoulders with in Uruguay and the towering Chinese women who dominated my race in Shanghai. The South African girls I sat with in the Chongming dining hall, the U.S. women I tried to emulate at the Pan Am Championships. I identified them not by helmet color and national jersey, but by their body posture and pedal stroke. I saw Kristin Armstrong, Amber Neben, and Christine Thorburn of the USA ride valiantly—and was encouraged that all three women are older than I. When Kristin obliterated her competition and won the gold medal in the time trial event, I jumped up and down on my couch. Then promptly fell off my couch when Jeannie Longo of France finished fifth. Jeannie is forty-nine years old.

Only one thought continued to cycle though my mind as I watched the games, the same thought I'd had since the day my 2008 Olympic quest ended: *I still want this. I'll try for 2012. Now that I know what I'm doing, imagine what could happen in four years.*

I also glued myself to the track and field coverage, hoping to catch a glimpse of the four St. Kitts and Nevis Olympians—Virgil Hodge, Mertizer Williams, Tiandra Ponteen, and the 2003 100-meter world champion, Kim Collins—take to the 100-, 200-, and 400-meter events. I also thought about the people I encountered during my quest who were not in China: Colby Pearce, the women of team handball, and every hopeful athlete who dared to try, try again.

One condition of all quests is that the quester must come away having learned something. Two years ago, I started my Olympic journey with only three tools to carve my path: desire, enthusiasm, and Google. There is nothing in the world this trilogy cannot achieve. While the last delivers possibility, the first two—desire and enthusiasm—*create* possibility. Such is the ultimate lesson of questing, that anything is possible, failure is a myth, and there is much truth and beauty in the proverb, "From small acorns do big oak trees grow." And when in doubt, march forth.

During the Olympics, I spoke frequently with Winston Crooke, the head of the St. Kitts and Nevis cycling federation, about my plan to visit Nevis in the winter of 2008-09 to help build a development program in cycling. This gave Winston another idea, and toward the end of the Olympic Games, he called me with an exciting opportunity.

"Kathryn, our country can send one female rider to the world championships in Italy in September. What do you think?" Translation: Hey Kathryn, do you want to go race against all the girls who just competed in the Olympics, plus the three to five next best riders of each nation?

"YEEEAAAAHHHH, baby!! Wooooohooooo!!" Translation: Yes, Winston. I would very much like to go to the world championships, thank you.

I started to get the feeling that maybe some quests never really end.

Gearing up for worlds meant very little rest time after my Olympic attempt, as I stayed in shape by racing both national events and local time trials in the United States from July through September 2008. I placed quite well at a few races in Massachusetts (Fitchburg and Tour of Hilltowns) and won the team time trial state championship in Arizona with three wonderful women—Sarah Swanson, Corinna Pietruszynski, and none other than the WonderMinion herself, Amanda Chavez. After returning from our South American adventures, WonderMinion took a real job that does not involve slinging my bike box around the southern hemisphere; she became a contactor for the U.S. government, doing background checks on prospective government employees. Unable to take time off from her new job to accompany me to the worlds, I knew there was only one other person who could handle the task of becoming WonderMinion II: Coach Gord.

On September 20, 2008, Gord and I landed in Milan, a twelve-hour flight from Tucson, and drove an hour north to the town of Varese, just a few miles from the Swiss border, where we met Winston at the hotel. Some countries brought as many as fourteen cyclists and an entourage of coaches, managers, mechanics, and massage therapists. The St. Kitts and Nevis team consisted only of Gord, Winston, and me. Still, in two years of race travel, it was just about the biggest team I'd ever been on.

Signs and posters for the UCI World Road Cycling Championships were everywhere, even the back of the little luggage wheelie carts in the airport. Shop windows were filled with vintage bicycle displays to show community support. I started to understand this was a very big deal: two races in Italy (the 24-kilometer time trial event and the 138-kilometer road race event), and three fields—pro men, pro women, and an elite group of junior men under twenty-three years of age. Gord and I spent a few days training on the race course, which was hard, hilly, fast, and filled with descents that could maim a momentarily distracted cyclist. There were two rather monstrous climbs that could be deadly, depending on the peloton's pace. Yet none of it intimidated me, for missing were the things that do: potholes, sewer grates, stray dogs, and ice cream vendors who have snuck onto the closed course. *I have arrived*, I think.

"All worlds courses are like this," Gord attested. A three-time Canadian Olympian and Tour de France competitor—and once named North America's Greatest Sprinter—Gord had been to the world championships twice.

"How'd they go?" I inquire.

"Didn't finish either one. Hardest races I've ever done."

Time to change the subject. "Hey look, gelato!"

The day before the time trial, Gord headed to the race meeting and procured the start list. I spent the day with my feet up, mumbling "*contre du montre ... contre du montre ...*" which is French[11] for "time trial" and lots of fun to say. There were be forty-three women in the event, with no more than two women per country represented. This meant that my competitors were likely each nation's time trial champion and runner up. The top ten countries from last year's world championship standings went last, and the remaining start order was determined by each country's overall ranking. Unranked, unknown, unreserved countries go earlier. While it doesn't really matter when a rider goes off, seeing as we're racing against the clock and not each other, it is much more fun to go later in the order. Knowing there are women up ahead gives a cyclist something to shoot for, to focus on hunting down and passing.

"You're going off first," Gord told me.

"First?!"

---

11 French is the official language of the UCI.

"Yep. Think of it this way: It'll be good camera time for St. Kitts and Nevis."

Awesome. A TV camera capturing my first-time-at-worlds nerves! Yay! Yet somewhere deep inside, I really did think it was awesome. I was at the world championships, representing a country that is finally going to get on the charts of international racing. Not to mention, I was getting the most valuable experience yet—racing against the Olympians, learning how it's done. With ninety-second intervals between each rider, there was a huge bonus to going first; if no one passed me, then I would get to be the world champion for at least a few seconds. Okay, first it was. Maybe starting first was an omen.

Warming up on the stationary trainer before the race (using a spare wheel we borrowed from U.S. national champion, Olympian, and Tour de France cyclist Dave Zabriskie), I asked Gord if he thought I should go with the long sleeve or short sleeve skinsuit.

"Which is more aerodynamic?"

"Let me see your arms," Gord said.

I hold out my forearms.

"You're not too hairy. Short sleeves are fine."

While it is always nice to be reminded I'm not a Yeti, I noticed most other women were donning the full sleeves, so I followed suit. I felt fast and sleek and ready in my Saran Wrap-ish, St. Kitts and Nevis flag-colored skinsuit. Gord borrowed a radio from the friendly Canadian team and slipped it into the neck of my suit, then smushed the earpiece into my ear and taped it in place.

"We'll be behind you in the team car and you'll be able to hear me the whole way," Gord explained.

"Where's the receiver that allows me to talk to you?"

"I don't need to hear you. Plus, you won't be able to talk at maximum effort."

"Roger that."

Winston walked me to the start line, carrying my bike. He was wearing his St. Kitts and Nevis jersey and looking proud, which made me feel pretty darn happy. Winston took my arm and said, "St. Kitts and Nevis has never been to a cycling world championship before,

Kathryn. We're here because of you."

"No Winston," I assured him, "we're here because of *you*." He gave the big booming Winston laugh and I stepped up to the start ramp. I heard my earpiece cackle into action. Gord's voice reverberated off my eardrum.

"Okay, you've done the work. You know the course. As soon as the clock starts, turn your brain off and suffer."

Despite the fact that I usually suffer much more when my brain is on, I nodded. And hit the off switch.

"Go get 'em," he said.

Go I did. Get 'em? Not so much. While the experience of racing through the northern Italian countryside, lined with fans and supporters and TV cameras, was intensely unforgettable, my race itself was rather, well, forgettable. During the entire time trial, my legs lacked my usual punch and power. Gord barked encouragement in the form of helpful reminders such as "pedal," "breathe," and "go go go," which were frighteningly easy to forget in the midst of physical suffering. Despite turning out good watts and power, I felt clunky and slow. I knew enough about cycling now to accept that some days are on, some days are off, and some linger in the vast purgatory of athletic effort known as "blah." I could speculate about the reasons for all eternity—not enough racing, too much racing, twenty straight months without an off-season, forty-two national champions as my competitors—or I could accept the day for what it was. Not my best, but not my worst.

Since no one passed me, I was able to be world champion for about thirty glorious seconds. I finished the race 5:20 behind winner Amber Neben of the USA and 4:52 behind Olympic gold medal winner Kristin Armstrong. I finished in forty-first place out of forty-three women. If I can knock off one minute per year, I'll be all set for London 2012. Alas, forty-first doesn't come with a medal but it gave out one prize I really needed: experience. That, and countless photos of my rear end as taken from the team car behind me. What more could a girl want?

Later that night a British commentator named Emma Jones Davies stopped me in the lobby of the hotel. She recognized me as the cyclist from St. Kitts and Nevis and told me that while I stood on the start ramp of the time trial, she and her colleague had no information on me as a cyclist. No statistics, no prior world championship results, no history to comment on. "So we talked about your lovely skinsuit; the reds and greens and stars. You were very color-coordinated, so that helped us out." Emma asked how the time trial went. "I prepared well, but didn't quite have it today," I said. Gord quickly pulled me aside.

"Kathryn, don't tell anyone you *prepared* well for this race," Gord whispered. "Tell them you *trained* well."

"What the heck's the difference?"

"Saying you've 'prepared well' is a cycling euphemism for doping."

"No way!"

"Way."

"Great. So I just told a television commentator that I was doping?"

"Seeing as you came in forty-first, I think you're safe from being labeled a doper."

Oh. Well then. I guess losing has some advantages after all. But hear this, you big, dumb, blood dopers out there: I'm reclaiming "prepared well" for all the clean-competing, hardworking, bonafide athletes right now. I *did* prepare well, I *do* prepare well, and I *will* prepare well. Maybe I didn't win worlds, but at least I ride clean, hard, and with literary correctness.

Two days after the time trial, the worlds road race offered me another opportunity to compete against the best in the world. I was called to the start line last, behind 139 riders who represented ranked countries. Without any ranking, three lone riders from St. Kitts and Nevis, Slovakia, and Estonia rolled up to the back of the pack. No cyclist was allowed to move up or jockey for position until the gun went off. I was stuck far from the front, where a) it was safer; b) there was less yo-yo effect in the speed/pace; c) you could see the road in front of you; d) it was easier to avoid crashes and pile-ups; and e) you didn't feel like a loser. My plan was to move up through the pack on the first hill, less than three hundred meters away from the start line. Regrettably, the 139 riders ahead of me didn't give a hooey about my plan and it got shot to pieces within three minutes. When the gun went off, the USA team (nicely situated at the front of the line) had their own plan—to cripple me. Or so it felt. They didn't actually know me, so I tried not to take it personally as they beat the daylights out of my legs and lungs.

With eight laps of a grueling, hill-infested sixteen-kilometer course (138 kilometers total), most cyclists were expecting the race to start out moderately conservative, with maybe some speedy attacks to surface after a few miles. Nope. Not today. Instead, the Americans apparently decided that their only shot at the podium involved kickin' it from the get-go with everyone else following close behind. The American cyclists sprinted, and about twenty seconds later the back of the pack rolled through the start line. Immediately, my speedometer jumped to twenty-seven miles per hour. *What a ridiculous starting pace! It'll calm down,* I thought. And that was the last thought I remember having for the next four hours.

It took less than four minutes into the race for the first crash to occur. Blammo! A Swiss rider fell over and took out a wave of cyclists, domino style, as we headed up hill. The crash created so much congestion that we back-of-the-packers had to stop and unclip from our pedals, which is the equivalent of putting a pin into a balloon. All momentum was lost … except for the women ahead of the crash. Off they went. Bye bye! Then, two minutes later on a tough left-hand downhill corner, another rider bit it. We in the back logjammed again, while another unscathed group ahead of the crash frolicked off, unimpeded.

We remnants of the peloton were not strong enough in number to hold off the big groups that escaped the pileups. Over the course of four hours, we could conceivably be lapped, which would disqualify us with instant DNF status—did not finish. I am highly allergic to DNF. Luckily, I found two other cyclists with the same allergy, a Venezuelan and an Irish, and we banded together to keep the main peloton away for as long as possible. But a group of three didn't have the aerodynamic advantages of a group of fifty to sixty. Still, we tried. It was all we could do. Our other choice was to drop out voluntarily, which nearly 50 of 139 women—national champions and Olympic medalists included—chose to do. Dropping out is common in bike racing, but it wasn't an option for me. Not after all St. Kitts and Nevis had done for me, not after the opportunities ESPN had given me. If I got lapped, I got lapped, but there would be no voluntary DNF. I would only go out KNS—kicking 'n' screaming.

On the fifth lap of eight, a UCI official drove by and told our group of three to quit. "The peloton will catch you," the woman said. "Quit now."

Never, in all my sporting life, have I had an official urge me to quit midrace, no matter how high the odds seemed. The Irish and Venezuelan and I decided not to hear the officials. We agreed to keep going and drop out only if we were lapped. If we could make it to the start of the eighth lap before getting caught, we'd be okay. Up ahead, the UCI officials told a small group of five cyclists (to whom we were catching up) to do the same thing—quit—and they obliged.

Up the hills and through the town of Varese, European cycling fans were out in full force. For nearly seventy-five miles, the Italians screamed their favorite chant: *"Dai, dai, dai"* which means "Go, go, go" but is unfortunately pronounced "Die, die, die" and was therefore no help, help, help to me. On the seventh lap, physics, strength, and experience conspired against us. The peloton caught the three of us, and we watched the leaders whoosh by. Exhausted, dejected, and in slight disbelief that all our hard work and effort hadn't produced the Disney movie ending I saw so clearly in my oxygen-deprived brain, I dismounted and got off the race course. The Irish disappeared into the crowd, but the Venezuelan and I made our way back to the race venue along the sidewalks of Varese. My first world championship was over and I had learned three things: I was lucky to be there, I would know what to expect next year, and if I ever again had to take the start line as the last rider I would consult illusionist Criss Angel as to how best to teleport myself to the front.

When the final results were posted, I found comfort in the fact that there were fifty DNF riders—many of them Olympic medalists and national champions. I was stunned to learn that, according to international cycling policy, the five riders who obeyed the "Quit now" command on the fifth lap had been awarded prorated finish times, whereas my stalwart group of three had been punished for our persistence by being given DNFs. Injustice like that really ruffles my feathers.

When I asked Gord if I should protest, he agreed with my sentiments, but warned that officials could ultimately blackball or red flag my future in cycling.

"Choose your battles carefully," Gord advised, and I decided to put this one on the back burner. It would do me more good to focus on what I could change—my own performance and my training plans for 2009.

🚲　🚲　🚲

Back in Tucson, I took a few weeks to rest, during which I planned my upcoming trip to Nevis. I also tried to find an international or U.S.-based pro team to cycle for in 2009. It was not looking good. Many women's teams in North America had recently folded, thanks to the faltering economy's effect on so many sponsors of pro cycling teams. The precious little media exposure given women's cycling didn't help. It was sad to watch a good, healthy, and empowering sport struggle like this. While I would continue to represent St. Kitts and Nevis on the international scene, I would probably have to go it alone in 2009. I had four more years until London 2012, but in the meantime I had a new quest: to help put women's cycling on mainstream sports media's map—and to build the St. Kitts and Nevis cycling federation.

I soon got back on the bike for winter training. One morning at 7 A.M., in the remote, serene Saguaro National Park on the east side of town, I took my time trial bike onto the empty road to do an interval workout. There were no cars. There were no other cyclists. Other than me, the only thing moving was a three-inch-long desert lizard that skittered off into a patch of prickly pear cactus as I approached. The speed limit was five miles an hour, and I slowly rolled through the only stop sign in the park. Within seconds, lights were flashing and I was pulled over by a park ranger who lectured me that bikes have to stop, too, even if there isn't a car for miles around.

"I'm citing you for failure to stop," he said.

I got the impression this officer was in no mood for my soliloquy on failure. Yet as he wrote my ticket, he also attempted to make small talk.

"What do you do for a living?" he asked.

"I make a living by failing to stop."

BIBLIOGRAPHY

Connor, Floyd, *The Olympics' Most Wanted: The Top 10 Book of Gold Medal Gaffes, Improbable Triumphs and Other Oddities*. Dulles, Virginia: Brassey's, 2001.

Krabbé, Tim, *The Rider*. Translated by Sam Garrett. New York: Bloomsbury USA, 2003.

Reese, Anne, and Irini Vallera-Rickerson, *Athletries: The Untold History of Ancient Greek Women Athletes*. Costa Mesa, California: Nightowl, 2002.

Salvage, Jeff, *Race Walk Like a Champion*, 2nd edition. Medford, New Jersey: Walking Promotions, 2007.

RESOURCES

About St. Kitts and Nevis: www.gov.kn

Canyon Ranch Peak Performance programs and testing: www.canyon ranchtucson.com/signature_programs/peak_performance/

Carmichael Training Systems: www.trainright.com

Ironman: www.ironmanlive.com

National Triathlon Training Camp: www.nttcracing.com

The Bloody Big Swim: www.thebloodybigswim.com or bruce@bloody bigswim.com

The Nevis Cycle and Triathlon Club: www.neviscycleclub.com

U.S. Open Water Swimming: www.usopenwaterswimming.org

U.S. Rowing: www.usrowing.org

U.S. Team Handball Women's National Team: www.usateamhandball women.com

USA Cycling, track cycling, road cycling, mountain biking, and velodrome locations: www.usacycling.org

USA Luge: www.usaluge.org or jonl@usaluge.org

USA Pentathlon: www.usapentathlon.org

USA Track and Field race walking: www.usatf.org/groups/RaceWalking/ or dunnphilip@yahoo.com

USA Triathlon: www.usatriathlon.org

TAKE ACTION

What you can do to encourage, educate, and grow athletics in our country:

• Sponsor an athlete (especially in a sport you've never heard of).

• Talk about these sports—positively.

• Try one. Most sports offer entry level programs for all ages. Encourage kids to get into sports. Don't forget the fringe sports.

• Specifically, encourage girls to try sports. Encourage boys to think that's cool.

• Write to your local newspapers and ask them to include more articles on women's sports.

• Write to Microsoft Word and ask them to include the following words that are not currently recognized by spellcheck: triathlete, pentathlete, velodrome, saddlesore, luge, spellcheck.

ACKNOWLEDGEMENTS

If even one of these people or corporations did not exist, then likely neither would this book. My great thanks to the following people, who played a vital role in this quest/book:

Editor and champion R.D. Rosen, John Papanek, Kevin Jackson, Jay Lovinger, Sean Hintz, Steve Wulf, Chris Raymond, Sandy DeShong, Annika Ruscoe, Dawn Tremblay, David Halpern, Ian King, Kathy Robbins, Aaron Goodman, Patrick Borelli, John Glenn, Beth Adelman, Andrew Kozak, Nippy Feldhake, Jimmy Riccitello, Gord Fraser, Dr. Sal Tirrito and XOOD, Seton and Debbie Claggett, TriSports.com and employees, Ralph Phillips, Bruce Stauffer, Fair Wheel Bikes and employees, Gold's Gym of Tucson, my local YMCA, Melika Clothing, Jake Rubelt, Justin Peschka, and Athlete Octane, Mark Wendley and NTTC, Stephanie Scott and the Jelly Belly Candy Company, Trek Bicycles, Barrett Ladd, Geoff Clark, Scott Daubert, USA Team Handball, USA Modern Pentathlon, USA Cycling, USA Luge, the USOC, the UCI, AZ Cycling, Colby Pearce, Jon Lundin, Duncan Kennedy, Bruce Dixon, Andy Lee, Vince Peters, Erin Taylor, Ray Sharp, Philip Dunn, Canyon Ranch, The Shootout, my parents, and the one, the only WonderMinion, Amanda Chavez.

Also to Kathrine Switzer, who broke barriers for all women in sport—first in the Boston Marathon in 1967, then by lobbying the women's marathon to Olympic eligibility in 1984. It is because of women like Kathrine Switzer that today's female athletes have the opportunity to attempt an Olympic dream in a male-dominated sport.

Finally, with love, hugs, and the utmost gratitude to the people of St. Kitts and Nevis, including Winston Crooke, Greg Phillip, Wendy Brear, Reggie Douglas, James Weekes, Honorable Premier Joseph Parry, Prime Minister Dr. Denzil Douglas, and the SKN Olympic Committee. I will march forth for you, always.

ABOUT THE AUTHOR

KATHRYN BERTINE is the author of *All the Sundays Yet to Come: A Skater's Journey,* and her work has appeared in *ESPN The Magazine,* the *Los Angeles Times, Details,* and *Triathlete,* at ESPN.com, and in the anthology *Fathers & Daughters & Sports.* She lives in Tucson, Arizona, and St. Kitts and Nevis.

www.kathrynbertine.com